# THE END OF DEMOCRACY?

# THE END OF DEMOCRACY?

The Celebrated *First Things* Debate
with Arguments Pro and Con

and

## "The Anatomy of a Controversy"

by Richard John Neuhaus

*Edited by Mitchell S. Muncy*

SPENCE PUBLISHING COMPANY • DALLAS
1997

Published in the United States by
Spence Publishing Company
501 Elm Street, Suite 450
Dallas, Texas 75202

The end of democracy? : the celebrated First Things debate, with
    arguments pro and con and, The anatomy of a controversy, by
    Richard John Neuhaus / edited by Mitchell S. Muncy
        p. cm.
    Includes bibliographical references (p. ).
    ISBN 1-890626-03-1 (hardcover). — 1-890626-04-x (pbk.)
    1. Political questions and judicial power—United States.
    2. Conservatism—United States. 3. Christianity and Politics—
    United States. 4. Jews—United States—Politics and government.
    5. United States—Social policy.        I. Muncy, Mitchell S.
    (Mitchell Shannon), 1968-  .  II. Neuhaus, Richard John.
    Anatomy of a controversy. 1997.
    KF5130.A75E53 1997                                      97-22959
    340'.115—dc21

Printed in the United States of America

# CONTENTS

# PREFACE

THIS PREFACE CAN BE BRIEF. It all began with a symposium in the November 1996 issue of *First Things*, "The End of Democracy? The Judicial Usurpation of Politics." The question mark in the title was missed by many critics, and indeed was omitted in some published comments on the symposium. The present book contains the original symposium and a representative selection from the storm of controversy it provoked. At the end, in an extended essay, "The Anatomy of a Controversy," I offer my own evaluation of what has happened, is happening, and is likely to happen as this discussion continues. While mine is the last word in this book, it is certainly not the last word in the great debate that has now begun in earnest.

As the editors said in that November issue, discussion about "judicial activism" and "the imperial judiciary" is hardly new. Such discussion has been a staple in our public discourse for some decades, usually under the auspices of thinkers who are viewed as conservatives. Why then did the symposium spark such intense debate? The simple answer and, I believe, the accurate answer is that we took the Supreme Court up on the challenge that it has issued in a number of decisions, including several remarkable decisions of the 1996 term. We did not raise the question of the "legitimacy" of the judicial regime by which we are governed. The Court itself did. A majority of the Court has pronounced the doctrine that the legitimacy of the Court, and indeed the survival of the rule of law, depends upon the American people's submitting to its edicts.

That doctrine is astonishing enough, but some of us were also astonished that public commentators, on the left and the right, seemed not to be astonished by it. The radical character of the Court's jurisprudence—and the Supreme Court sets the pace for the entire judiciary in both federal and state government— went almost entirely unremarked. The position the Court has taken forces us to think about something much more profound than conventional concerns about judicial activism, for this is, as the subtitle of the symposium suggests, the judicial usurpation of politics. That is to say, we are witnessing the displacement of a constitutional order in which the people, through the institutions of representative democracy, are thought to have the capacity and the right to govern themselves. It is true that the symposium addressed radical questions—questions that go to the roots of what the Founders called an experiment in ordered liberty—but we did so only because the judiciary has so egregiously and explicitly challenged the constituting truths of our polity.

The current debate is about the American constitutional order and the procedural rules by which law is made. Beyond the procedural, it is also a substantive debate about the connection between laws and higher law—whether the latter be understood as rationally determined moral truth, natural law, or as the Declaration of Independence proposes, "the laws of nature and of nature's God." Whether we have addressed these questions in a responsible manner or with a recklessness reminiscent of the revolutionary madnesses of the 1960s (as some critics charge) is for the reader to judge.

The symposium was planned at a meeting of the editorial boards of *First Things* in May 1996. That meeting included some of the authors in the original symposium, as well as a number of people who have figured prominently in the subsequent debate. These are, in my judgment, very prudent people. Prudent not in the sense of timid but in that they are judicious and shrewd in their appreciation of practical affairs. Most of them are of an age that they have been through the radicalisms of several decades ago, either as participants or opponents, and all of them understand the sobering implications of the questions to be addressed. We discussed thoroughly the danger that our arguments might be confused with radicalisms past, and resolved that, with that danger in mind, they must be made with most particular care. We resolved, too, that we would not be intimidated, either by the Court or by those who might choose to misunderstand our intention.

We knew that the stakes were very high. The Court had seen to that by raising the question of its legitimacy—and by giving ample reason to question its legitimacy. We did not expect the intensity of negative reaction, especially on the part of friends, although I admit that my editorial colleague James Nuechterlein was more prescient on this score than was I. One can sympathize, as I do, with those who were so shaped by the experience of the 1960s that they believe that ideas and arguments that were grossly abused then have been permanently discredited. One can sympathize but still disagree. We learn from the past, but our consciences, our minds, and our public discourse cannot be held hostage to the past. The appropriate response to the abuse of important ideas is the careful use of such ideas. When Americans stop arguing about legitimacy, about just government derived from the consent of the governed, and about the relationship between laws and higher law, this country will have turned out to be something very different from what the Founders intended.

The reader is cautioned that there is polemic and acrimony in the pages that follow. But there is also, and much more importantly, a serious exploration of what needs to be understood and what needs to be done if, as we devoutly hope, we are not to be faced by the very real prospect of the end of democracy.

*Richard John Neuhaus*

# Acknowledgements

THERE ARE MANY to whom I owe thanks for assistance in preparing this volume for publication. *Primus inter pares* is Father Richard John Neuhaus, who granted permission to reprint the essays from the November 1996 and January 1997 symposia in *First Things* and undertook the difficult task of summarizing and analyzing the controversy. I also appreciate Father Neuhaus's willingness to work with a newcomer to the field of publishing. Mrs. Mary Z. Hittinger did yeoman's work in compiling the bibliography. Whatever original contribution this volume makes to the discussion at hand is due almost entirely to their efforts.

The editors of *First Things*, in particular associate editor J. Bottum, assisted in the preparation of the manuscript and the compiling of the bibliography. The following individuals graciously granted permission to reprint their copyrighted essays from the February 1997 issue of *Commentary* magazine: Peter L. Berger, Walter Berns, Gertrude Himmelfarb, William Kristol, Norman Podhoretz, Irwin Stelzer, and George Weigel.

In addition, I gratefully acknowledge permission to reprint the following essays in this volume:

"First Things First" by Tom Bethell, *The American Spectator*, January 1997, pp. 18–19: © 1997 by The American Spectator, 2020 North 14th Street, Suite 750, Arlington, Virginia 22201. Reprinted with permission.

"First Things Last" by Samuel Francis, *Chronicles*, March 1997, pp. 32–34: © 1997 by The Rockford Institute, 934 North Main Street, Rockford, Illinois 61103. Reprinted with permission.

"From the Camp of the Incendiaries" by Hadley Arkes, *Crisis*, February 1997, pp. 14–15: Reprinted by permission of The Morley Institute, publisher of *Crisis*, Washington, D.C. To subscribe, call 1-800-852-9962, or visit crisismagazine.com.

"Neocons, Theocons and the Cycles of History" by John J. Reilly, *Culture Wars*, February 1997, pp. 12–13, 31: © 1997 by Ultramontane Associates, Inc., 206 Marquette Avenue, South Bend, Indiana 46617. Reprinted with permission.

"First Things First," *National Review*, November 11, 1996, pp. 16, 18: © 1996 by NATIONAL REVIEW, Inc., 215 Lexington Avenue, New York, New York 10016. Reprinted with permission.

"The War of the Roses," *National Review*, December 31, 1996, pp. 10, 12: © 1996 by NATIONAL REVIEW, Inc. Reprinted with permission.

"Con Job" by Ramesh Ponnuru, *National Review*, January 27, 1997, pp. 36–39: © 1997 by NATIONAL REVIEW, Inc. Reprinted with permission.

"Neocon v. Theocon" by Jacob Heilbrunn, *The New Republic*, December 30, 1996, pp. 20–24: Reprinted by permission of The New Republic; © 1996 by The New Republic, Inc.

"The Right's Anti-American Temptation" by David Brooks, *The Weekly Standard*, November 11, 1996, pp. 23–26: Reprinted with permission.

The pieces in Parts I and II have not been edited, although I have not retained the divisions of the text in the original publications. In their original form, most of the pieces in Part III contained an account of the November 1996 symposium, and I have edited to alleviate this repetition. Although it is true that a reader receives an author's interpretation even in the rehearsal of facts, it was my judgment that it was unnecessary to treat readers of this volume to half a dozen such rehearsals in addition to the symposium itself.

Lastly, I should state for the record that any errors or flaws in this volume should be attributed to its editor rather than its distinguished contributors or those who so generously assisted in its publication.

*Mitchell S. Muncy*

# PART I

# THE END OF
# DEMOCRACY?

# INTRODUCTION

*The Editors of* FIRST THINGS

RTICLES ON "JUDICIAL ARROGANCE" and the "judicial usurpation of power" are not new. The following symposium addresses those questions, often in fresh ways, but also moves beyond them. The symposium is, in part, extension of the argument set forth in our May 1996 editorial, "The Ninth Circuit's Fatal Overreach." The Federal District Court's decision favoring doctor-assisted suicide, we said, could be fatal not only to many people who are old, sick, or disabled, but also to popular support for our present system of government.

This symposium addresses many similarly troubling judicial actions that add up to an entrenched pattern of government by judges that is nothing less than the usurpation of politics. The question here explored, in full awareness of its far-reaching consequences, is whether we have reached or are reaching the point where conscientious citizens can no longer give moral assent to the existing regime.

Americans are not accustomed to speaking of a regime. Regimes are what other nations have. The American tradition abhors the notion of the rulers and the ruled. We do not live *under* a government, never mind under a regime; we *are* the government. The traditions of democratic self-governance are powerful in our civics textbooks and popular consciousness. This symposium asks whether we may be deceiving ourselves and, if we are, what are the implications of that self-deception. By the word *regime* we mean the actual, existing system of government. The question that is the title of this symposium is in no way hyperbolic. The subject before us is the end of democracy.

Since the defeat of communism, some have spoken of the end of history. By that they mean, *inter alia*, that the great controversies about the best form of government are over: there is no alternative to democracy. Perhaps that, too, is wishful thinking and self-deception. Perhaps the United States, for so long the primary bearer of the democratic idea, has itself betrayed that idea and become something else. If so, the chief evidence of that betrayal is the judicial usurpation of politics.

Politics, Aristotle teaches, is free persons deliberating the question, How ought we to order our life together? Democratic politics means that "the people" deliberate and decide that question. In the American constitutional order the people do that through debate, elections, and representative political institutions. But is that true today? Has it been true for, say, the last fifty years? Is it not in fact the judiciary that deliberates and answers the really important questions entailed in the question, How ought we to order our life together? Repeatedly, questions that are properly political are legalized, and even speciously constitutionalized. This symposium is an urgent call for the repoliticizing of the American regime. Some of the authors fear the call may come too late.

The emergence of democratic theory and practice has a long and complicated history, and one can cite many crucial turning points. One is the 1604 declaration of Parliament to James I:

"The voice of the people, in the things of their knowledge, is as the voice of God." We hold that only the voice of God is to be treated as the voice of God, but with respect to political sovereignty that declaration is a keystone of democratic government. Washington, Madison, Adams, Franklin, Jefferson, and the other Founders were adamant about the competence—meaning both the authority and capacity—of the people to govern themselves. They had no illusions that the people would always decide rightly, but they did not invest the power to decide in a ruling elite. The democracy they devised was a republican system of limited government, with checks and balances, including judicial review, and representative means for the expression of the voice of the people. But always the principle was clear: legitimate government is government by the consent of the governed. The founders called this order an experiment, and it is in the nature of experiments that they can fail.

The questions addressed have venerable precedent. The American experiment intended to remedy the abuses of an earlier regime. The Declaration of Independence was not addressed to "light and transient causes" or occasional "evils [that] are sufferable." Rather, it says: "But when a long train of abuses and usurpations, pursuing invariably the same Object evinces a design to reduce them under absolute Despotism, it is their right, it is their duty, to throw off such Government and to provide new Guards for their future security." The following essays are certain about the "long train of abuses and usurpations," and about the prospect—some might say the present reality—of despotism. Like our authors, we are much less certain about what can or should be done about it.

The proposition examined in the following essays is this: The government of the United States of America no longer governs by the consent of the governed. With respect to the American people, the judiciary has in effect declared that the most important questions about how we ought to order our life together are outside the purview of "things of their knowledge."

Not that judges necessarily claim greater knowledge; they simply claim, and exercise, the power to decide. The citizens of this democratic republic are deemed to lack the competence for self-government. The Supreme Court itself—notably in the *Casey* decision of 1992—has raised the alarm about the legitimacy of law in the present regime. Its proposed solution is that citizens should defer to the decisions of the Court. Our authors do not consent to that solution. The twelfth Chief Justice of the Supreme Court, Harlan Fiske Stone (1872-1946), expressed his anxiety: "While unconstitutional exercise of power by the executive or legislative branches of the Government is subject to judicial restraint, the only check upon our own exercise of power is our own sense of restraint." The courts have not, and perhaps cannot, restrain themselves, and it may be that in the present regime no other effective restraints are available. If so, we are witnessing the end of democracy.

As important as democracy is, the symposium addresses another question still more sobering. Law, as it is presently made by the judiciary, has declared its independence from morality. Indeed, as explained below, morality—especially traditional morality, and most especially morality associated with religion—has been declared legally suspect and a threat to the public order. Among the most elementary principles of Western Civilization is the truth that laws which violate the moral law are null and void and must in conscience be disobeyed. In the past and at present, this principle has been invoked, on both the right and the left, by those who are frequently viewed as extremists. It was, however, the principle invoked by the founders of this nation. It was the principle invoked by the antislavery movement and, more recently, by Martin Luther King, Jr. It is the principle invoked today by, among many others, Pope John Paul II.

In this connection, Professor Robert George of Princeton explores the significance of the encyclical *Evangelium Vitae* ("The Gospel of Life"). Addressing laws made also by our courts, the Pope declares, "Laws and decrees enacted in contravention of the moral order, and hence of the divine will, can have no binding force in conscience. . . . Indeed such laws undermine the very nature of authority and result in shameful abuse." We would only add to Professor George's brilliant analysis that the footnotes to that section of *Evangelium Vitae* refer to Pius XI's 1937 encyclical *Mit Brennender Sorge* ("With Burning Concern") and other papal statements condemning the crimes of Nazi Germany. America is not and, please God, will never become Nazi Germany, but it is only blind hubris that denies it can happen here and, in peculiarly American ways, may be happening here.

We are prepared for the charge that publishing this symposium is irresponsibly provocative and even alarmist. Again, it is the Supreme Court that has raised the question of the legitimacy of its law, and we do not believe the Pope is an alarmist. We expect there will be others who, even if they agree with the analysis of the present system, will respond, So what? Unmoved by the prospect of the end of democracy, and skeptical about the existence of a moral law, they might say that the system still "works" to the satisfaction of the great majority and, niceties about moral legitimacy aside, we will muddle through so long as that continues to be the case. That, we believe, is a recklessly myopic response to our present circumstance.

Some of our authors examine possible responses to laws that cannot be obeyed by conscientious citizens—ranging from non-compliance to resistance to civil disobedience to morally justified revolution. The purpose of the symposium is not to advocate these or other steps; it is an attempt to understand where the existing system may be leading us. But we need not confine ourselves to speculating about what might happen in the future. What is happening now is more than disturbing enough. What is happening now is a growing alienation of millions of Americans from a government they do not recognize as theirs; what is happening now is an erosion of moral adherence to this political system.

What are the consequences when many millions of children are told and come to believe that the government that rules them is morally illegitimate? Many of us have not been listening to what is frequently being said by persons of influence and moral authority. Many examples might be cited. Supreme Court Justice Antonin Scalia in a recent lecture: "A Christian should not support a government that suppresses the faith or one that sanctions the taking of an innocent human life." The Archbishop of Denver in a pastoral letter on recent court rulings: "The direction of the modern state is against the dignity of human life. These decisions harbinger a dramatic intensifying of the conflict between the Catholic Church and governing civil authorities."

Professor Russell Hittinger observes that the present system "has made what used to be the most loyal citizens—religious believers—enemies of the common good whenever their convictions touch upon public things." The American people are incorrigibly, however confusedly, religious. Tocqueville said religion is "the first political institution" of American democracy because it was through religion that Americans are schooled in morality, the rule of law, and the habits of public duty. What happens to the rule of law when law is divorced from, indeed pitted against, the first political institution?

"God and country" is a motto that has in the past come easily, some would say too easily, to almost all Americans. What are the cultural and political consequences when many more Americans, perhaps even a majority, come to the conclusion that the question is "God *or* country"? What happens not in "normal times," when maybe America can muddle along, but in a time of great economic crisis, or in a time of war when the youth of another generation are asked to risk their lives for their country? We do not know what would happen then, and we hope never to find out.

What is happening now is the displacement of a constitutional order by a regime that does not have, will not obtain, and cannot command the consent of the people. If enough people do not care or do not know, that can be construed as a kind of negative consent, but it is not what the American people were taught to call government by the consent of the governed. We hope that more people know and more people care than is commonly supposed, and that it is not too late for effective recourse to whatever remedies may be available. It is in the service of that hope that we publish this symposium.

# Our Judicial Oligarchy

*Robert H. Bork*

THIS LAST TERM of the Supreme Court brought home to us with fresh clarity what it means to be ruled by an oligarchy. The most important moral, political, and cultural decisions affecting our lives are steadily being removed from democratic control. Only Justices Antonin Scalia and Clarence Thomas attempt to give the Constitution the meaning it had for those who adopted it. A majority of the court routinely enacts its own preference as the command of our basic document.

Most members of the Court seem to be gnostics, firmly believing they have access to wisdom denied the rest of us. "What secret knowledge, one must wonder, is breathed into lawyers when they become Justices of this Court?" Scalia has asked. "Day by day, case by case, [the Court] is busy designing a Constitution for a country I do not recognize."

This last term was unusually rich in examples. The Court moved a long way toward making homosexual conduct a constitutional right, adopted the radical feminist view that men and women are essentially identical, continued to view the First Amendment as a protection of self-gratification rather than of the free articulation of ideas, and overturned two hundred years of history to hold that political patronage is unconstitutional.

A few cities in Colorado, reflecting the political influence of homosexuals, had in recent years enacted ordinances prohibiting discrimination on grounds of sexual orientation. Even private persons who believe strongly that homosexual conduct is immoral or prohibited by religion were forbidden to act on those beliefs. A person with a room to rent, for example, could not turn away a homosexual couple. In a statewide referendum Coloradans adopted a constitutional provision, Amendment 2, which pre-cluded local governments from adopting such provisions. The Court, in an indecipherable opinion (*Romer v. Evans*), held that this denial of special status to homosexuals violated the equal protection clause of the Fourteenth Amendment. The theory, apparently, was that homosexuals were impermissibly burdened if they had to secure special protection, equivalent to that afforded racial minorities, at the state rather than the local level. The law could be explained, the Court said, only by animosity toward homosexuals. The opinion closed with the preposterous assertion that "Amendment 2 classifies homosexuals not to further a proper legislative end but to make them unequal to everyone else."

To the contrary, any constitutional provision does what Amendment 2 did—it removes from some groups the capacity to alter the law except at the state or federal level. If one took the majority's assertions seriously, as Scalia's dissent noted, state con-stitutional provisions prohibiting polygamy would violate the equal protection principle. The State of Utah, for example, was admitted to the Union only on condition that its constitution's prohibition of polygamy could not be revoked without the consent of the United States—thus requiring polygamists to persuade the entire nation and not simply the voters of Utah.

Matters are even worse than that, however. Under what appears to be the majority's rationale, it is difficult to see how any federal or state statute could be constitutional. Persons adversely affected by any national or state law are by definition unable to get relief at the local level. If homosexuals in Colorado were unfairly burdened by Amendment 2, then we are all unfairly burdened by the very existence of federal and state law.

The majority did not even mention the ten-year-old decision in *Bowers v. Hardwick*, which had held, in keeping with long-standing constitutional understanding, that a state may make homosexual conduct a criminal offense. Since the Court has now held that the denial of special status to homosexuals is unconstitutional, *Bowers* must be taken to have been silently overruled.

*Romer* is a prime instance of "constitutional law" made by sentiment having nothing to do with the Constitution. What can explain the Court majority's decision? Only the newly faddish approval of homosexual conduct among the elite classes from which the justices come and to which most of them respond. We are on our way to the approval of homosexual conduct, despite the moral objections of most Americans, because the Supreme Court views such moral disapproval as nothing more than redneck bigotry.

The cultural elite have more fads than one, however. Radical feminism overrode the Constitution in *United States v. Virginia,* which held, seven votes to one, that the equal protection clause required Virginia Military Institute to admit women. VMI had been an all-male military college for over 150 years and had co-existed peaceably with the said equal protection clause for 128 of those years. The historic understanding was that such single-sex schools were fully consistent with the Constitution. VMI provided "adversative methods" of training, which meant a program that was extremely rigorous mentally, physically, and emotionally. The admission of women will change the nature of the institution; women will not get what they supposedly sought: VMI training. Only sterile feminist logic could lead anyone to imagine that there are no inherent differences between men and women in these matters.

Once again, Justice Scalia (Justice Thomas took no part because his son attends The Citadel) destroyed the majority opinion:

> Much of the Court's opinion is devoted to deprecating the close-mindedness of our forbears with regard to women's education, and even with regard to the treatment of women in areas that have nothing to do with education. . . . The virtue of a democratic system with a First Amendment is that it readily enables the people, over time, to be persuaded that what they took for granted is not so, and to change their laws accordingly. That system is destroyed if the smug assurances of each age are removed from the democratic process and written into the Constitution. So to counterbalance the Court's criticism of our ancestors, let me say a word in their praise: they left us free to change. The same cannot be said of this most illiberal Court, which has embarked on a course of inscribing one after another of the current preferences of the society (and in some cases only the counter-majoritarian preferences of the society's law-trained elite) into our Basic Law.

Scalia understates how radical an antidemocratic course the Court has taken. The Justices are not inscribing current preferences of our society into the Constitution, for those preferences can be easily placed in statutes by legislatures. When the Court declares a statute unconstitutional it *overrides* current popular desires. The counter-majoritarian preferences are not simply those of a law-trained elite, but those of a wider cultural elite that includes journalists, academics, entertainers, and the like. If only a law-trained elite were involved, the Court could not do what it is doing.

Also during this past term, the Court majority struck down, on First Amendment grounds, a federal statute which required cable television operators who leased access to channels to others to segregate on a single channel "patently offensive" depictions of sexual activities or organs. The operator had to block that channel from viewer access and to unblock it only upon a subscriber's written request. The Court found this speech-restrictive, continuing its transformation of the First Amendment as a guarantee of the free exchange of ideas to a guarantee of individual self-gratification.

In a pair of cases, the Court found that normal patronage by government violated, of all things, the First Amendment. A company was removed from the list of available companies to perform towing services for a city, allegedly because the owner had supported the mayor's opponent in a reelection campaign. Another city terminated a trash hauler's at-will contract, allegedly because the hauler had been an outspoken critic of the Board of County Commissioners. Such practices are as old as the nation and are regulated by innumerable statutes, but the Court suddenly elevated patronage to the level of a First Amendment violation.

Not one of these five decisions bears any resemblance to the actual Constitution. There is no question of a mistake being made. The Justices know full well what they are doing, which means that Scalia and Thomas are right: a majority of justices have decided to rule us without any warrant in law. If there is an "actual" Constitution it can only be the set of principles those who made the Constitution law understood themselves to be ordaining.

The idea that the Constitution should be interpreted according to that original understanding has been made to seem an extreme position. That is convenient for those who want results democracy will not give them, but the truth is that violation of original understanding ought to be the extreme position. Would it be legitimate for a judge in the United Kingdom, which has no constitution comparable to ours, to strike down an act of Parliament on the ground he did not like it? Obviously not. But a U.S. judge who goes beyond the Constitution behaves like the hypothetical U.K. judge. Democratic theory requires that a judge set the majority's desires at naught only in accordance with a superior law—in our case, the written Constitution. A judge who departs from the Constitution, as the majority did in the five cases mentioned, is applying no law other than his will. Our country is being radically altered, step by step, by justices who are not following any law.

This is not entirely new. During the nineteenth century, the Court often made up its own Constitution, most notoriously in the 1857 decision in *Dred Scott v. Sandford*. Chief Justice Roger Taney's opinion for the Court found a constitutional right, good against the federal government, to own slaves. But it wasn't until this century, when the Court invented the theory that the Bill of Rights limited states as well as the federal government, that the opportunities for judicial government exploded. The First Amendment speech clause has been made a guarantor of moral chaos, while its religion clauses have been reshaped to banish religious symbolism from public life. The Court invented a right of privacy and used it to create a wholly specious right to abortion. The list of such incursions into the legitimate sphere of democratic control goes on and on.

Lower courts, state and federal, catch the fever. Hawaii's Supreme Court is about to make marriage between homosexuals a constitutional right. Connecticut's court has ruled that racial imbalance in public schools violates the state constitution even though the imbalance is a result of residential patterns and not the product of any government action. Two federal courts of appeals have invented a constitutional right to assisted suicide, and one court is apparently willing to extend the right to euthanasia. God knows what will come next.

On the evidence, we must conclude, I think, that this tendency of courts, including the Supreme Court, is the inevitable result of our written Constitution and the power of judicial review. Even in the depths of the Warren Court era some of us thought that the Court's performance, though profoundly illegitimate, could be brought within the range of the minimally acceptable by logical persuasion or the appointment of more responsible judges, or both. We now know that was an illusion. A Court majority is impervious to arguments about its proper behavior. It seems safe to say that, as our institutional arrangements now stand, the Court can never be made a legitimate element of a basically democratic polity.

Republican Presidents have used the nomination process in an effort to change the direction of the Court with almost zero results on the major issues. After twelve years of Presidents Reagan and Bush, each of whom made a determined effort to appoint Justices who would abide by the Constitution as originally understood, we seem farther than ever from a restrained Court. Between them, Reagan and Bush had five appointments. Only two try to relate their decisions to the Constitution as the men who wrote, proposed, and ratified it understood it. A majority of the Justices has become more arrogantly authoritarian than ever.

The illegitimacy of the Court's departures from the Constitution is underscored by the fact that no justice has ever attempted a justification of the practice. At most, opinions have offered, as if it solved something, the observation that the Court has never felt its power confined to the intended meaning of the Constitution. True enough, but a long habit of abuse of authority does not make the abuse legitimate. That is particularly so when the representative branches of government have no effective way of resisting the Court's depredations.

Viewing the carnage created by the Court, George Will referred to the Justices as "our robed masters." When the VMI decision came down, my wife said the justices were behaving like a "band of outlaws." Neither of those appellations is in the least bit extreme. The Justices are our masters in a way that no President, Congressman, governor, or other elected official is. They order our lives and we have no recourse, no means of resisting, no means of altering their ukases. They are indeed robed masters. But "band of outlaws"? An outlaw is a person who coerces others without warrant in law. That is precisely what a majority of the present Supreme Court does. That is, given the opportunity, what the Supreme Court has always done.

The astonishing thing is that anybody is surprised at this. Without realizing quite what they were doing, generations of

Americans have accorded all courts, and most especially the Supreme Court, unchecked power. We ought to have known what would inevitably happen. Lord Acton's famous aphorism about power corrupting turns out to be right: Given unchecked power, most human beings, even those in robes, will abuse that power.

Only a change in our institutional arrangements can halt the transformation of our society and culture by judges. Decisions of courts might be made subject to modification or reversal by majority vote of the Senate and the House of Representatives. Alternatively, courts might be deprived of the power of constitutional review. Either of those solutions would require a constitutional amendment. Perhaps an elected official will one day simply refuse to comply with a Supreme Court decision.

That suggestion will be regarded as shocking, but it should not be. To the objection that a rejection of a court's authority would be civil disobedience, the answer is that a Supreme Court that issues orders without authority engages in an equally dangerous form of civil disobedience. The Taney Court that decided *Dred Scott* might well have decided, if the issue had been presented to it, that the South had a constitutional right to secede. Would Lincoln have been wrong to defy the Court's order and continue the Civil War? Some members of the Supreme Court were edging towards judging the constitutionality of the war in Vietnam. Surely, we do not want the Court to control every major decision and leave only the minutiae for democratic government.

The truth, however, is that I must end on a pessimistic note. The Court will not be reformed by persuasion or by changes in its membership. But the public appears supine, willing to watch democracy slip away. Can public apathy ratify what the Court is doing? Not in our constitutional tradition, it can't. If a real constitutional right of one person is being violated with the unanimous approval of the rest of the United States, we have always held that the right must be vindicated regardless. Under our Constitution, each of us has a right to representative government and no amount or length of majority inertia can legitimate what the Court is doing to that right.

# A Crisis of Legitimacy

## Russell Hittinger

I N *PLANNED PARENTHOOD V. CASEY* (1992), the Supreme Court made abortion the benchmark of its own
legitimacy, and indeed the token of the American political
covenant. To those who cannot agree with the proposition that
individuals have a moral or constitutional right to kill the unborn,
or that such a right defines the trans-generational covenant of
the American political order, the Court urged acceptance out of
respect for the rule of law. "If the Court's legitimacy should be
undermined," the Court declared, "then so would the country be
in its very ability to see itself through its constitutional ideals."

If the Court does not claim to act merely in its own name,
but for the common good and the rule of law, how then should
citizens regard the effort to link abortion with the legitimacy of
the Court itself and thus, it would seem, with the legitimacy of
our current political regime? We could put this in a different way
by asking whether the Court—in laying down rules without
authority to do so and then asking for obedience in the name of

the common good—has acted *ultra vires,* beyond its constitutionally assigned powers. If so, its commands are not legitimate. The rule of law prohibits reallocation of shares of authority without the consent of the governed. Since the political common good depends on no branch of government taking more than its share of authority, obedience should not be given to an act that violates the foundation of the rule of law.

So put, we have only stated a principle. Does it apply to the actions of this Court? It seems to me that the situation is ambiguous and admits no clear answer. There is no doubt but we live today under an altered constitutional regime, where the rules are no longer supplied by a written document but by federal courts defining the powers of government ad hoc, through their own case law. This profound change from our previous order of government is often hidden by political and judicial rhetoric that gives honor to and even cites the written Constitution; yet, in contemporary theory and in practice, the document is really an authoritative occasion for, rather than a norm of, judicial interpretation. The changes have been further obscured by the fact that the new regime was not ratified by amendment or constitutional convention.

But this profound and confusing change does not necessarily make the new constitutional order illegitimate—at least not in the sense we are exploring here. It is plausible to argue that this new regime evolved over time with the tacit consent of the governed. Operationally speaking, every sector of government has acquiesced in the Court's understanding of its own powers and the powers of rival authorities. Though the elected representatives of the people may complain about particular judicial rulings and try to influence those rulings through judicial appointments and party platforms, none challenge the authority of the ruling principle itself. Our elected representatives do not merely comply with, but obey, the Court's understanding of the constitutional order, and they have tendered obedience for fifty years.

Thus, when the Court in *Casey* asks that its case law be given the obedience due to the Constitution, and when it insists that, above all, it must remain loyal to its own recently established precedents, it makes a reasonable request within the context of the new constitutional regime. In this new regime, judicial interpretation rules the text, according to the Court's perception of the common good and the changing needs of the polity. It can be pointed out that this is a reckless kind of polity—allowing the Court to define the nature and scope of political power on an ad hoc basis, without benefit of the debates of a legislative assembly or a constitutional convention, and without the contest of facts typical of an ordinary trial court. One would be very surprised indeed were it not to engender great injustices. For all of that, however, the Court does not necessarily act *ultra vires*.

But the issue of legitimacy can be examined from another point of view. Citizens can have a duty not to obey a law if it seriously injures the common good. And were such laws propounded as essential features of the constitutional order itself—which is to say, propounded as laws governing the making of any other laws—then we could reasonably ask about the legitimacy of that regime. Bearing in mind that we are speaking not of isolated statutes, but of authoritative renderings of the fundamental law, such laws would be laws (1) that deny protection to the weak and the vulnerable, especially in matters of life and death, and (2) that systematically remove the legal and political ability of the people to redress the situation. A polity that creates and upholds such laws is unworthy of loyalty.

The first thing to realize about our new regime is that the abortion right is not a unique or isolated feature of contemporary jurisprudence. The Court's own case law shows that in order to maintain the abortion right at the level of fundamental law, many other sectors of the states' legal order, at both statutory and common law, need to be altered: family law, marriage law, laws regulating the medical profession, and, as we now see with the recent circuit court decisions, criminal laws prohibiting private use of lethal force. The principle of *Casey* cannot leave the other institutions of the polity unaffected. Moreover, the Court's own case law shows that it is impossible to disempower political opponents of abortion without going on to disempower them politically on other issues as well. What is one's place in a political regime that regards abortion as defining of the constitutional covenant, that expands the principle to other institutions of both private and public law, and that politically disempowers opponents?

Three decisions reached by federal courts this past spring reveal a pattern of fact that will allow us to take a broader view of the situation. These decisions exemplify both the inherently expansive nature of the new regime's abortion jurisprudence as well as its disempowerment of political opponents.

By statewide referendum in 1991, voters in the state of Washington had reaffirmed the provision of the criminal code that outlawed persons in its jurisdiction from "knowingly causing or aiding other persons in ending their lives." On March 6, 1996, the Ninth Circuit Court of Appeals ruled in *Compassion in Dying v. Washington* that the state of Washington is constitutionally powerless to prohibit physicians (its own licensees) from using lethal force to assist suicides. Seizing upon the infamous dictum of the abortion decision in *Casey*—"At the heart of liberty is the right to define one's own concept of existence, of meaning, of the universe, and of the mystery of human life"—Judge Stephen Reinhardt not only posited a "right to die," but also deemed the state's legislative motive cruel: "Not only is the state's interest in preventing such individuals from hastening their deaths of comparatively little weight, but its insistence on frustrating their wishes seems cruel indeed."

Meanwhile, in New York, the Second Circuit Court of Appeals ruled in *Quill v. Vacco* that while there is no "historic" right to die, the state of New York violates the equal protection clause of the Fourteenth Amendment with its prohibition of assisting suicide. By permitting patients to refuse treatment at the end of life, but not allowing physician-assisted suicide, the state unfairly treats similarly situated persons. The court brushed aside the distinction between letting die and killing. Although it was claimed in the press that the Second Circuit's opinion was more moderate because it did not posit a "right to die," both decisions reach the same result from the same principle.

Not surprisingly, in New York that principle was also the dictum in *Casey*. Judge Miner, writing for the majority in the Second Circuit, asked: "What concern prompts the state to interfere with a mentally competent patient's 'right to define [his] own concept of existence, of meaning, of the universe, and of the mystery of human life,' when the patient seeks to have drugs prescribed to end life during the final stages of a terminal illness?" Miner answers, "None." In other words, given two patients, each of whom can define the meaning of the universe, New York violates equal protection when it allows the one to "define" himself by having treatment withdrawn while it forbids the other to "define" himself by requesting that a physician assist his suicide.

The third decision concerned a 1992 statewide referendum in which the voters in Colorado adopted an amendment, known as Amendment 2, to their constitution prohibiting laws that make homosexual orientation, conduct, and relationships the bases of special entitlements to minority status, quota preferences, and claims to discrimination. On May 20, 1996, in *Romer v. Evans*, the Supreme Court ruled that the amendment is totally without a rational basis, and is "born of animosity toward the class of persons affected." The Court declined to say whether its decision silently overturns *Bowers v. Hardwick* (1986), which upheld the state of Georgia's anti-sodomy law. Yet if Colorado's amendment has no basis other than animosity toward homosexuals, it is difficult to understand what rational grounds might exist for anti-sodomy laws, or, for that matter, laws restricting marriage to man and woman.

These decisions have two things in common. First, they expand individual liberty against traditional morals legislation.

And second, they impugn the motives of legislators, which the Ninth Circuit found "cruel" and the Supreme Court found hateful. This is the pattern that we need to notice if we are to understand the legal and political mind of the new regime. This pattern did not begin, however, with the decisions of this past spring.

Earlier in the century the Court aggressively protected individual rights of contract against the democratic process in the states. But after World War II, the Court began to insert itself into what James Madison called the "internal" objects of state governments, particularly the culture-forming institutions, including education, religion, marriage, and government's domestic control over matters of life and death. Reasoning that the people do not wish these things to be left to the ordinary legislative process, the Court incrementally created individual rights as immunities from the political ordering of these "internal" objects.

The Court's religion jurisprudence was especially important, and indeed was a kind of seedbed for the new regime. In 1947, the Court ruled that the establishment clause must be applied against the states, and that no establishment means no "promotion" of religion. In 1948, John Courtney Murray called the new religion jurisprudence "rigid, ruthless, sweeping," and insisted that the Court's doctrine "cannot be approved by the civic conscience" (in an essay first printed in *First Things*, October 1992). Murray was correct about the sweeping nature of the new doctrine; over the course of twenty years, religion was removed, bit by bit, from the civic order of state polities. Murray, however, did not live to see the next step. In 1971, nonestablishment came to mean that legislation could have no religious "purposes," even when the immediate matter and effect of the legislation is secular. Justice O'Connor would later add that such secular purposes must even be "sincere."

Thus, the Court prohibited public events which had been practiced in every jurisdiction since the founding of the nation. Then, to sustain its reasoning in the face of new litigation, the Court found itself having to bring ever new objects under its scrutiny, such as moments of silence and abstinence education.

Indeed, Justice Kennedy recently has gone so far as to maintain that the belief that "there is an ethic and a morality which transcend human invention" is itself religious. Ultimately, the Court had to interrogate the subjective motivations of legislators in order to detect the presence or absence of religion.

In a separate line of jurisprudence, the Court moved on to issues of sex, marriage, and abortion. In hindsight, we see that the new lifestyle rights were inherently expansive. In *Griswold v. Connecticut* (1965), the new right of privacy was meant to protect marriage, and was justified by reference to the "traditions and conscience of the people." In *Eisenstadt* (1972), however, the privacy right was expanded to cover any reproductive decision made by individuals. In *Roe* (1973), it included elective abortion. In *Carey* (1977), it included the right of teenagers to have access to contraceptives. In *Casey*, it mushroomed into an all-purpose right to define the meaning of the universe. The circuit courts now insist that it includes the liberty to contract a physician to assist one's death. What began as a judicial effort to stretch the Constitution to make it better reflect the "traditions and conscience of the people" quickly became the opposite—it became a reason for constitutionally invaliding those very traditions as the ground for public policies and laws.

This line of jurisprudence, for a time, steered clear of the motivational analysis used in religion cases. To be sure, the issue of religious motivations would, from time to time, emerge in a concurring or dissenting opinion, when members of the Court would speculate that state governments have no authentic secular purpose for laws restricting sexual conduct.

These two lines of jurisprudence have begun to coalesce. Judge Reinhardt of the Ninth Circuit acknowledges that judicial acceptance of physician assisted suicide would cause "great distress" to people "with strong moral or religious convictions." The "or" is interesting, especially in the light of Justice Kennedy's virtual equation of religion with any ethics thought to "transcend human invention." Reinhardt warns, "They are not free, however, to force their views, their religious convictions, or their philosophies on all the other members of a democratic society, and to compel those whose values differ with theirs to die painful, protracted, and agonizing deaths." Laws prohibiting physician-assisted suicide, he concludes, do "injury" to some citizens for no other reason than "to satisfy the moral or religious precepts of a portion of the population." On this view, legislation informed by religion or by traditional morality expresses a malicious desire by some citizens to apply power against other citizens.

In this light, we can begin to understand the Court's decision in the case of Colorado's Amendment 2. Although in *Romer v. Evans* Justice Kennedy does not venture an opinion about the religious nature of animus against homosexuals, his decision depends heavily upon the attribution of motives. "Laws of the kind now before us," he writes, "raise the inevitable inference that the disadvantage imposed is born of animosity toward the class of persons affected." "If the constitutional conception of 'equal protection of the laws' means anything," he continues, "it must at the very least mean that a bare . . . desire to harm a politically unpopular group cannot constitute a legitimate governmental interest." In other words, individual liberty is defined not merely by the kind of act or decision that one is free to engage, but by immunity from a certain kind of motive or purpose on the part of the legislator.

This analysis of animus has been linked to equal protection before. In *Bray v. Alexandria Women's Clinic* (1993), the Court examined whether anti-abortion demonstrators could be held liable—under the Ku Klux Klan act of 1871 (amended in 1985)—of conspiring to deprive women of the equal protection of the laws by depriving women seeking abortions of their right to interstate travel. The *Bray* case is unlike *Romer* in dealing with private citizens' animus against a class. The two can be seen together, however, insofar as the definition of discriminatory purpose holds for both public or private agents. Discriminatory purpose, as defined in *Bray*, implies that the agent selects or reaffirms a particular course of action in part "because of" and not merely "in spite of" its adverse effects upon an identifiable group.

In *Bray*, it was proposed that women qualify as precisely such an "identifiable group." Justice O'Connor reasoned that the law must reach "conspiracies whose motivation is directly related to characteristics unique" to women. These characteristics are defined as "their ability to become pregnant and by their ability to terminate their pregnancies." For his part, Justice Stevens wrote, "When such an animus defends itself as opposition to conduct that a given class engages in exclusively or predominantly, we can readily unmask it as the intent to discriminate against the class itself."

The proposition that pro-life demonstrators are liable for such discrimination was defeated in *Bray* by a single vote—Justice White was still on the bench. For our purpose, however, it is important to note the strong analogy to what the Court now accuses Coloradans of doing in adopting Amendment 2. When Justice Kennedy asserts that there is no rational basis for the amendment, and that the "inevitable inference" is that the action is "born of animosity toward the class of persons affected," he is saying, in judicial terms of art, that the amendment was adopted "because of " and not merely "in spite of " its adverse effects upon an identifiable group. It is true, of course, that women have a federal right to have abortions, while homosexuals do not (as yet) have a federal right to perform acts of sodomy. But the animus analysis reaches the same result, for a class is allegedly picked out and bullied in violation of the equal protection clause; whether the class is entitled to special judicial protection doesn't matter if the legislators or voters can be ascertained to have a suspect motive.

In sum, the political ability of the people to address legislatively common concerns in the terms of traditional morality must pass through a gauntlet of judge-made law in this new regime. If not disqualified on grounds of religion, legislation and other forms of public business may be disqualified on grounds of insufficiently "secular" motivation. And if not knocked down for that reason, they may be disqualified for failure to comport with what Gerard Bradley has called the "mega-right" of self-mystery definition posited in *Casey* (a right that now moves by analogy into physician-assisted suicide). And if not disqualified because of that, then it may be disqualified on grounds of motive to do injury, to discriminate, or to deny to persons equal protection of the laws.

These disqualifiers have been used alone and in concert to place public expressions of traditional morality outside the new political order. In fact, the Court may not need to invent a constitutionally protected right to die or to commit sodomy. Its current repertoire of nullification tests and devices is already sufficient to knock down prohibitory legislation on religious and equal protection grounds.

While it allows individuals to be self-governing, the federal judiciary's new constitutional order radically undercuts their ability to be self-governing in the political sense of the term. It excludes from the political process the objects of mutual deliberation that make political order desirable, indeed even possible. Desirable, because the culture-forming institutions of society cannot be sustained without common effort; there would be no need for politics were there not some important goods that require the deliberation, direction, and authority of the community. Possible, because once private individuals are allowed rights to use lethal force for vindicating justice in their own cause (as in abortion or euthanasia), it is difficult to see how even the most rudimentary foundations of the older political society—those that reserve the use of lethal force to public authority—still remain.

The new constitutional regime is a very bad regime. It withdraws protection from the weak and vulnerable, allowing the strong to define the status and rights of the weak; it privatizes matters which, in any legitimate political order, must be public in nature; it sets innumerable roadblocks to the rectification of the problem through mutual deliberation of citizens in legislative assemblies; and it has made what used to be its most loyal citizens—religious believers—enemies of the common good whenever their convictions touch upon public things. In 1994, the Court not only allowed the Racketeer Influenced and Corrupt Organizations (RICO) statutes to be applied against anti-abortion demonstrators, putting them in the same category with mobsters, but also allowed to stand a Florida law restricting the speech of pro-life, but not pro-choice, demonstrators in the vicinity of abortion clinics.

Unless the new constitutional order is profoundly reformed, citizens of rightly formed conscience will find themselves in a crisis. Insofar as private citizens have given tacit consent to the new regime, and thus allowed it to speak in their name, they face an unavoidable moral crisis. But the crisis falls even more immediately and heavily upon public officials, for the new regime orders them to do what they ought not to do, and not to do what they ought to do. They are ordered not to regard the unborn as having moral rights, and not to take those steps otherwise available to their offices to protect and remedy the injustices against that class of persons. Soon, the same will be true with respect to the dying and infirm. Moreover, legislative, executive, and judicial officers in the states are ordered by the Court to prevent the application of laws and policies of citizens on no other ground than the citizens' moral or religious motivations.

It is late in the day, and our options have dwindled. Either right-minded citizens will have to disobey orders or perhaps relinquish offices of public authority, or the new constitutional rulers will have to be challenged and reformed. The first option leads inevitably either to withdrawal from politics or to civil disobedience. Since there is still a window of opportunity with regard to the second option, it would seem to be the responsible course. In order to adopt it, we must take three steps.

First, the people through their elected officials must withdraw whatever tacit consent has been given to the new constitutional order. Because the new regime was not erected by any ordinary process of amendment, referendum, or ratification, in principle the people still may alter it through their elected representatives. Perhaps the U.S. Congress will be able to invoke its powers under section five of the Fourteenth Amendment; perhaps Congress can use its powers under Article III to alter the Court's appellate jurisdiction. How this might be done must urgently be studied by those having experience and expertise in the actual institutions of government.

Second, issues like abortion, euthanasia, and gay marriage should not be treated as isolated from the broader constitutional crisis. Those who would try to play within the game imposed by the Court, in the hope of incrementally improving the situation issue-by-issue, actually deepen rather than mitigate the authority of the new order. Indeed, it tends to confirm the suspicion that citizens who hold conservative opinions about morals and religion lurch from issue to issue, trying to use the public order merely to win a point, if not to punish those who believe otherwise. Particular issues therefore need to be advanced for the purpose of prompting a constitutional crisis; and prompting the constitutional crisis is the responsible thing to do.

Third, of all the features of the new regime, the one that must be tackled first is the Court's motivational analysis, which first emerged in connection with religion, but which now spreads to other matters of legislation informed by substantive moral purposes. In effect, the Court makes it impossible to have anything other than a procedural common good as a motive or purpose for political activity. There is a real possibility that the moral and religious motivations of some citizens will become not only actionable at public law, through constitutional suits challenging legislation informed by such motives, but also actionable at private law. Unless the elected representatives of the people can compel the Court to refrain from invalidating political activity merely on the basis of the citizens' moral or religious motivation, the task of reform is blocked. Should that continue, the option remaining to right reason is the one traditionally used against despotic rule: civil disobedience.

# A Culture Corrupted

*Hadley Arkes*

WE WERE TAPING, early in May, a program for public television dealing with "same-sex marriage." Opposite me was a professor of law, openly gay, who had just written a book in favor of gay marriage. The question before us was whether the states would be obliged to honor the marriage of homosexual couples if the courts in Hawaii delivered to the country that unsolicited gift. After all, the states bore a residual authority to object, on moral grounds, to certain kinds of marriage—as in the case, for example, of incestuous unions. But with the same claims to residual authority, some states in the past had objected on moral grounds to interracial marriages. That ground of objection had been removed from the states as soon as the courts became clear that policies of that kind were in conflict with the deeper principles of the Constitution. The question then was whether the Supreme Court was about to do the same thing in relation to gay marriage with the decision, then pending, in *Romer v. Evans*. The case was not about gay marriage, but it could undercut the authority of a state to withhold any privilege or franchise from people on account of their homosexuality. When the question was posed, the professor reacted with a blank stare. Of *Romer* and its implications—and its connection to gay marriage—he professed to know nothing.

No more than a fortnight after the decision was handed down in *Romer v. Evans,* the same professor was in print, in *The New Republic,* not only aware of the connection, but quite emphatic now in his opinion: *Romer v. Evans* would in fact call into question the authority of a state in refusing to honor gay marriages. And indeed, as he suggested, it would call into question the power of the Congress to act now, with the Defense of Marriage Act, in seeking merely to preserve, for the states, their freedom to refuse.

That *Romer* should have any bearing of this kind on the law of marriage is still barely understood even by people who make their living by following public affairs. That the decision could have vast, unsettling effects on our law—that it could be used as a powerful lever in changing the professions, the universities, and the cast of our private lives—is well beyond the imagining of a public that does not spend its days absorbed in the life of the courts. And of course the media have taken care to shelter the public from any account in these matters that may be too precise or jolting for the public to hear.

There should be, by now, nothing startling in this pattern, for it has marked the ways of our courts and our politics over the past thirty years. The judges form a virtual concert to advance the interests of gay rights and other parts of the liberal agenda, and those who would resist these initiatives, even with the most modest measures, are branded as the aggressors and the zealots. Whether the issue has been abortion, or euthanasia, or "gay rights," the courts have taken steps that were noticeable even at the time as novel and portentous. But these moves seemed to have struck no chord, no moral or religious nerve, running through the broad public. All of which must make us wonder whether we are indeed in post-Christian or post-religious America. But if these events have not set off alarms, it is even less likely that people would be sensitive to that subtler shift of power that runs to the root of the American regime itself: In one issue after another touching the moral ground of our common life, the power to legislate has been withdrawn from the people themselves, or the "consent of the governed," and transferred by the judges to their own hands. And on this point, there has been no example more striking than the recent run of cases on "gay rights."

In November 1992, the voters of Colorado, in a referendum, foreclosed to legislatures at all levels the authority to treat gays and lesbians on the same plane as groups that have suffered discrimination based on race, religion, and gender. In effect, the amendment to their constitution (Amendment 2) would have removed from legislatures the authority to pass statutes that barred discriminations based on "sexual orientation." Those statutes provided a club for the law in meting out public humiliations for people who hold moral and religious objections to homosexuality. In one telling case, the wife of a shopowner in Boulder, Colorado had given a pamphlet on homosexuality to a gay employee. For that offense, she was charged under a local ordinance on gay rights, and compelled to enter a program of compulsory counseling.

We will hear, no doubt, many different accounts of Amendment 2 in Colorado, but I would offer this construction: The Amendment merely sought to preserve for people, in their private settings, the freedom to honor their own moral understandings on the matter of homosexuality. The Amendment licensed no criminal prosecutions directed at gays or lesbians, and it withdrew from homosexuals no protections of the law. Still, the Court overturned this move by the people of Colorado, acting in their sovereign capacity, to shape their fundamental law. Ten years earlier, in *Bowers v. Hardwick,* the Court had upheld the power of a state to make sodomy a crime; but now, as Justice Scalia pointed out, the Court was willing to strike down a law merely for "disfavoring homosexual conduct." And in the sweep of its judgment, the Court produced a decision that could be read by activists among the judges to encompass this principle: that it would now be immanently suspect on constitutional grounds to plant, anywhere in the laws, a policy that casts an adverse judgment on homosexuality, or accords to homosexuality a lesser standing or legitimacy than the sexuality "imprinted in our natures." Armed with this decision, judges throughout the country would be able to tie up, or overturn, any statute in a state that refused to recognize gay marriage.

During the hearings on the Defense of Marriage Act, Representative Pat Schroeder declared that the issue of gay marriage involved simply our willingness to honor, with equal respect, the love we encounter in all couples. And yet, as others were quick to point out, no one doubts the love of men for men, or women for women, just as no one doubts that there may be abiding relations of love between brothers and sisters, or grandparents and grandchildren. But those loves cannot be diminished as loves because they are not attended by penetration or expressed in marriage. Marriage is not needed to mark the presence of love, but a marriage marks something matchless in a framework for the begetting and nurturance of children. It means that a child enters the world in a framework of lawfulness, with parents who are committed to her care and nurturance for the same reason that they are committed to each other.

But that is to say there is a connection, long understood, between marriage and what may be called the "natural teleology of the body"—the inescapable fact that only two people, not three, only a man and a woman, can beget a child. As Michael Uhlmann has remarked, it becomes impossible finally to talk about marriage without using that "N-word," nature, and without talking about the sexuality imprinted in our "gendered" existence: "Male and female created He them." There is a purpose plainly marked in the fact that we are born man and woman, and it was once understood that this purpose found its expression in marriage as a blending of nature and law. If marriage were entirely a matter of law, then the positive law could prescribe virtually anything as a marriage: Brothers then might marry sisters—or brothers; they might even marry their household pets. Or, they might marry more than one person. If marriage is detached from that "natural teleology of the body," on what ground of principle could the law rule out the people who profess that their own love is not confined to a coupling of two, but woven together in a larger ensemble of three or four?

When this question was posed in the hearings on the Defense of Marriage Act, it produced, among the defenders of gay marriage, a show of bafflement. Yet, the people who were inclined to dismiss the matter of polygamy were treating with a certain nonchalance something that deserved to be treated with far more caution and sobriety. For many years, there have been centers of polygamy in southern Utah and northern Arizona that have proven intractable. Some telling commentary was offered by Paul Van Dam, the Attorney General of Utah, in 1990:

> Every law enforcement officer in Utah knows there are tens of thousands of polygamists in the area, and they are clearly violating the law. Yet if we prosecute these men and women, we know [from experience] that we will produce an incredible social disruption. Thousands of children must be cared for emotionally and otherwise, and that's a terribly expensive proposition.
>
> In addition, if you go after polygamists for illegal cohabitation, can you limit such a policy to polygamists, or do you pursue every couple in this state that is living together without benefit of a licensed marriage?

In other words, the authorities are already aware that the principled grounds of their restrictions have been compromised by the changes in the climate of opinion that have swept away the moral inhibitions on couples living together outside of marriage. One state legislator could remark, with offhandedness, that polygamy just doesn't happen to be a big issue back in Iowa. But it seemed to elude this earnest man that polygamy does not happen to be an issue in his state precisely because the law, for many years, has cast up serious barriers against the practice. And if those legal barriers started coming down, do we really think that our species would be incapable of manifesting once again an interest in that arrangement?

For my own part, I would credit the avowals made by gay spokesmen like Barney Frank and Andrew Sullivan that they do not have the remotest interest in promoting polygamy, or in weakening the laws that sustain families. But their argument runs beyond their intentions. The arguments for gay marriage must in fact put into place the premises that make it untenable for the law to hold back from the acceptance of polygamy. And one thing may be attributed to the gay activists quite accurately and fairly: they have the most profound interest, rooted in the logic of their doctrine, in discrediting the notion that marriage finds its defining ground in nature. For that reason, we can count on the fact that there will be someone, somewhere, ready to press this issue by raising a challenge in the court and testing the limits even further.

In a widely noticed essay in 1991 the lawyer-activist Nan Hunter argued, with an unsettling directness, that "the impact of [gay and lesbian marriage] will be to dismantle the legal structure of gender in every marriage." For this arrangement, she said, has "the potential to expose and denaturalize the historical construction of gender at the heart of marriage." For several years, Ms. Hunter was the director of the AIDS Project and the Lesbian and Gay Rights Project for the American Civil Liberties Union. With these credentials, and these published sentiments, she was eminently suited to her appointment, in 1993, as the "deputy general counsel/legal counsel" in the Department of Health and Human Services under the Clinton Administration. She is, in other words, one of the most highly placed lawyers within the government likely to be consulted for an official judgment on matters relating to "the family." And she is in a position, of course, to stoke the engines of litigation.

For what drives the litigation for gay rights is the need to have the gay life recognized and confirmed in principle in every setting in which the issue may arise. Gay activists seem to understand that their interests will not be secured as long as there persists in the public a residual moral sense that there is something about homosexuality that is not quite right. Hence, the need to seek more and more occasions for inducing the public first to tolerate, and then, in small steps, to endorse or approve. And now, with *Romer v. Evans*, the Court has handed the activists a powerful new device for advancing the movement ever further.

The reach of this device becomes ever clearer when we recall that the Court was not faced , in *Romer*, with an attempt to stir up prosecutions or withdraw the protections of the law from gays and lesbians. Colorado had already repealed its laws on sodomy. With Amendment 2, the people of Colorado had decided simply to withhold endorsement or favoritism: The coercions of the law would not be used to punish those people who bore moral objections to homosexuality. And yet, this perspective, reflected in the law, was characterized by the Court now as an "animus," a form of blind prejudice that could not justify itself in the name of any rational purpose. As Scalia noted, his colleagues were now "disparaging as bigotry adherence to traditional attitudes," rooted in religious teaching. In a stroke then—and without the need to marshal any reasons—the Court could pronounce the traditional moral teaching of Judaism and Christianity as empty, irrational, unjustified.

Justice Scalia has found his own, distinct touch as a jurist in offering the concrete example that illuminates the jural landscape; and in this case, he marked out with a chilling precision the path that leads out from *Romer*. Scalia noted that the Association of American Law Schools requires its members to extract, from the firms interviewing their students, an "assurance of the employer's willingness" to hire homosexuals. If an interviewer harbors traditional moral views on homosexuality, his firm could be in violation of the rule established by the Association of Law Schools. We can expect, of course, that rules of this kind will quickly make their way into the bar associations, as well as other groups of professionals. Will there not be an incentive then for the law firms to gauge whether any senior partners—or even young associates—hold views that may put the firm at odds with these regulations? And the incentives will not emanate simply from the conventions of the law schools. After all, the Supreme Court itself has now declared that a moral objection to homosexuality is indefensible, a distillation of an unreasoned prejudice. If a young, gay associate is denied standing as a partner, could it not be claimed that the climate in the firm was poisoned at the outset, that it was set in a discriminatory cast by the presence of senior partners who bore moral reservations about homosexuality?

And what can be said in this respect for law firms could be said even more forcefully about colleges and universities. Given the litigious experience these days in the academy, we can virtually count on the fact that such grievances will be filed. What if a member of an academic department has simply done what I have done—given public testimony, or published a moral judgment on gay marriage? Might that not supply prima facie grounds for a grievance later in a case involving the tenure of a young professor who was gay or lesbian? Would it not be argued that the situation was at least biased, or tilted, at the outset by the presence of that member of the faculty? Can we expect, then, certain pressures to separate those members of the faculty from decisions on tenure and hiring? And might it finally be best to remove the problem at the root simply by avoiding the hiring of people who bear these religious and moral sentiments, which the Supreme Court has now declared to be prejudicial? In sum, the Court has fashioned, in *Romer v. Evans,* a powerful new instrument for blocking from the academy and the professions people who are "overly serious" about their religion—which is to say, people who take seriously the traditional moral teachings of Christianity and Judaism.

Through a series of small steps there is produced, over time, a dramatic change. And now we find ourselves at the threshold of a situation in which a serious Catholic, in a law firm, can be seen as a source of liability and may need to be quarantined. But the oddity is produced by the same trend of affairs that stamps the Christian Coalition, or the religious in politics, as aggressors. The question goes strangely unasked as to what it was that "politicized" these groups in the first place and brought them into politics. During the controversy over gay marriage, the surveys showed about 70 percent of the public opposed to that novelty. But the same surveys would reveal portions of the public, comparably large, recoiling from the very people who are inclined to force a public discussion of the issue. There may be atavistic moral reflexes, drawn from a Christian past, but they seem readily matched these days by the reflexes of a newer sensibility that is wary of anyone who seems "judgmental." Gay marriage may seem wrong, but in the new scale of things there seems something harsh or tacky about the people who would argue about the matter in public. And so the political matrix: The judges advance the interests of gay rights at every turn, and those who resist them are labeled as the fanatics.

With the same dynamic, the "Christian Right" is tagged with the responsibility for unsettling our national politics by injecting the issues of abortion and school prayer. A former adviser to George Bush asks, earnestly, "Can't we just agree to get this issue [of abortion] out of national politics?" And he was evidently taken aback when I said, "Yes, we might make that deal—if by the 'national' government you also mean the courts." For what was it, after all, that made abortion into a national issue? It was nothing other than the move of the federal courts to create a new "constitutional" right to abortion, and, in the name of that right, to sweep away all of the laws in the separate states that treated abortion as wrong. The federal courts have shifted the power to themselves as branches of the federal government and politicized the issue at a new level of significance. Yet the people who would resist them are the ones who are condemned for bringing these divisive issues into our politics.

But this sense of the matter has taken hold precisely because the media and the public have absorbed the understanding put forth by the courts of the rights and wrongs of these matters. If there is something retrograde, something suspect, about making "discriminations" between forms of "sexuality," then serious Christians and Jews instantly qualify as bigots. And the laws that forbid all manner of discrimination seem to emanate from a disinterested public "ethic," suitably cleansed of any sectarian shading. The real question for us then is, How did we arrive at the state of affairs in which this sense of the world has been absorbed by a vast public in this country, which persists nevertheless in describing itself mainly as Christian and overwhelmingly as "religious"? On the question of euthanasia, the judges have quickly moved from the implausible to the unthinkable, inventing new rationales for ending the lives of people who were quite plainly alive and not dying at a decorous speed. On this matter, as on gay rights, there should have been more than enough to set off alarms for those whose sensitivities had been shaped by religious traditions.

We find ourselves asking, then, in a blend of wonderment and outrage: What would it take in this country—what would have to happen?—before serious Christians and Jews would recognize, at once, that a critical line has been crossed? It is one thing to say, as the courts already have, that the moral precepts of Christianity and Judaism may not supply the premises of the law in a secular state. It is quite another to say that people who take those precepts seriously may be enduring targets of litigation and legal sanction if they have the temerity to voice those precepts as their own and make them the ground of their acts even in their private settings.

Perhaps Rousseau, with an edge of madness, had it right: that all of this simply came along with the ethic of modernity, as it was spread through the diffusion of the sciences and the arts. "We have all become doctors, and we have ceased being Christians." Whatever the cause, it should be plain now that something in the religious sensibility has been deadened. My friend Russell Hittinger argues, with increasing persuasiveness, that the courts are making the political regime unlivable for serious Christians and Jews. To sound that alarm is to offer the call to political alertness. But the alarm cannot register, it cannot be felt, among people who have not been affected yet by the sense, as Christians and Jews, that there is anything taking place that is especially worth noticing.

# KINGDOMS IN CONFLICT

*Charles W. Colson*

I N AMERICA TODAY, we have very nearly reached the completion of a long process I can only describe as the systematic usurpation of ultimate political power by the American judiciary—a usurpation that compels evangelical Christians and, indeed, all believers to ask sobering questions about the moral legitimacy of the current political order and our allegiance to it. This is an inquiry undertaken reluctantly and, I hope, with due caution, for the stakes are very high. Among the questions we must address is whether millions of Americans are still part of the "We the People" from which democratic authority is presumably derived.

A little more than two hundred years into the American experiment, cultural conservatives stand convicted of unspeakable crimes in the eyes of most of America's media commentators. The opponents of abortion on demand, in particular, have felt the whip. Some columnists charge them with fostering a climate of hatred responsible for the Oklahoma City bombing and the

Michigan militia. One claimed that "the main form of political terrorism in the United States is perpetuated by right wing opponents of abortion," while another added that "most anti-abortion activists" are "religious fanatics who want to impose their version of God's word on the rest of us."

The Congress seems for the most part to agree with the media, if passage of the Freedom of Access to Clinics' Entrance Act—the act that narrowed the First Amendment rights of abortion protesters as an entire class of citizens—is any indication. And the Supreme Court appears to agree as well. In *Planned Parenthood v. Casey*, which enshrined the right of abortion as a specifically protected Fourteenth Amendment liberty, the majority lectured pro-lifers for continuing to contest the abortion issue. They were, in Justice Scalia's words, to "be taught a lesson"—a lesson the Court forcefully applied in *Madsen v. Women's Health Center, Inc.*, which created, around abortion clinics, a zone in which pro-choice advocates were free to demonstrate but even peaceful abortion protesters were subject to arrest.

Hostility against pro-lifers seems now to have spilled over into a distrust of any group of citizens seeking to connect public policy with a transcendent moral order. Writing the decision for the Ninth Circuit Court of Appeals in *Compassion in Dying v. Washington*, which overturned a state ban on euthanasia, Judge Reinhardt slammed the door on people "with strong moral or religious convictions," as he put it. "They are not free," he wrote, "to force their views, their religious convictions, or their philosophies on all the other members of a democratic society."

That Circuit Court decision has been appealed, but the Supreme Court itself has expressed similar sentiments. In overturning Colorado's prohibition of local civil rights statutes based on sexual preference, the Court in *Romer v. Evans* effectively branded a bigot any citizen who considers homosexuality immoral. Writing for the majority, Justice Kennedy declared, "Laws of the kind before us raise the inevitable inference that the disadvantage imposed is born of animosity toward the class of persons affected."

Without any supporting testimony or findings of fact, Justice Kennedy managed to divine that the sponsors of the referendum and the voters who ratified it must have been motivated solely by bias.

Kennedy's decision, now the law of the land, forces us to ask a series of critically important questions: Are citizens—whether Protestants, Catholics, Jews, or Mormons—who seek to apply transcendent moral values to public life welcome in political, legal, and cultural debates? Are citizens free to "impose" such values by referendum or legislative means in their respective states, or are their efforts inherently unconstitutional Does religion (equated by Justice Kennedy in an earlier case with the belief that "an ethic and a morality which transcends human invention" exists) have *any* role to play in the law?

The answers to these questions have ominous implications for cultural conservatives. Writing in the *Baylor Law Review* before the *Romer* decision, David Smolin of Samford University Law School argues that the present Court—rejecting "religiously based" claims as inherently particularistic—is increasingly dismissing "traditional theists" as too absolutist to join in public debate in a pluralistic society. This dismissal of religion (coupled with what he considers the Court's abandonment of the rule of law) helps explain the "frustrated religious patriotism" that drives much conservative political action. With political prospects increasingly out of reach, Smolin predicts traditional theists with political interests will be forced to abandon their religious beliefs and accommodate themselves to an amoral, libertarian regime. The only alternative seems to be an abandonment of their political interests, becoming what the theologian Stanley Hauerwas has called "resident aliens" in America—no longer concerned about the fortunes or misfortunes of a flawed republic, no longer considering this land their country.

As events at the 1996 Republican National Convention in San Diego show, the putative alliance between the religious right and the Republican Party offers little solution; and the truth is that grave dangers exist regardless when the independence of a religious mission is married to a particular political party's agenda. But utter political despair, at least, may be premature. Believers may have been told that their convictions disqualify them from public debate, but the news is news they've heard before. During the parliamentary struggle to curtail the British slave trade in the late eighteenth century, Lord Melbourne sounded much like the U.S. Supreme Court today when he huffed on one occasion, "Things have come to a pretty pass when religion is allowed to invade public life." Yet Christian reformers pressed on, rolling back, one by one, features of the slave trade until it was abolished in 1807 and slavery itself in 1833.

Unfortunately for us, however, events in America may have reached the point where the only political action believers can take is some kind of direct, extrapolitical confrontation of the judicially controlled regime. Following the logic in *Romer*, the Supreme Court can in time strike down state statutes barring polygamy, sodomy, and incest. Under the *Romer* logic, I believe, it will easily find no compelling state interest in confining marriage to a man and a woman, when the fallout from the case in Hawaii's state courts reaches the federal level.

A court empowered to judge a statute's constitutionality by that court's own inference of the animus of the statute's sponsors is a court set free from any limitations on its power—its power, on the one hand, to strike down any law enacted with the political aid of believers, and its power, on the other hand, to move directly against churches that display a perceived animus in their teaching toward certain behavior. The free exercise clause of the First Amendment poses no obstacle to a judge with any creativity, and —given the demonstrated animus of the current judicial regime against believers—a showdown between church and state may be inevitable. This is *not* something for which Christians should hope. But it is something for which they need to prepare.

When considering the relation of church and state, we must remember first, of course, that in the thirteenth chapter of his letter to the Romans, Paul has written what must remain for Christians the classic admonition of obedience to the governing regime. Most scholars and pastors, however, recognize that this admonition needs to be balanced with other biblical passages that suggest individuals will at times face a very clear choice between God and Caesar. The Old Testament prophet Daniel, rather than violate God's law, was granted permission not to partake of the king's food—though, we must acknowledge, he took the minimum resistance necessary, even seeking a pagan official's approval of an alternative action. His friends Shadrach, Meshach, and Abednego went further, risking their lives rather than worship pagan idols. In the New Testament Book of Acts, Peter and John refused to stop preaching the gospel even as they recognized the state's right to punish them. The biblical evidence suggests that where a state either demands what God prohibits or prohibits what God demands, the believer is to obey God and graciously accept the state's imposed consequences.

Not all Christian thinkers have applied these principles in exactly the same way. John Calvin, for instance, held a somewhat narrow line, stressing the responsibility of citizens to fear and honor whatever ruler is placed over them, even "the most wicked tyrant," a Nebuchadnezzar or Belshazzar. Though he conceded that disobedience to the state under certain (biblically identified) circumstances was a Christian's responsibility—and allowed for lower magistrates to take issue with rulers on behalf of the people—Calvin remained confident that God providentially works His will in all sorts of people, good and bad.

Augustine and Thomas Aquinas, however, saw more circumstances than the Swiss Reformer where a Christian citizen may need to question or resist civil authority. Augustine's dictum remains the most famous formulation of the broader view of a Christian's relation to the state: "An unjust law is no law at all." Aquinas argued that God's delegation of authority to civil authorities was linked to the fostering of virtue. When a ruler meets that test, when his laws and actions are in accord with the *lex divina*, and when human law promotes the *tranquillitas ordonis*, then human law is just; but if it "runs counter in any way to the law in us by nature, it is no longer law but a breakdown of law." Martin Luther King Jr. cited both these thinkers in defense of civil disobedience in his *Letter from the Birmingham Jail* in 1963: "A just law is man-made code that squares with the moral law of God. Unjust law is a code that is out of harmony with the moral law." We must observe, however, that King did not call for general disobedience or resistance to the state; only the unjust law, he argued in an important qualification, can be disobeyed.

Among Protestant thinkers, the Scottish Reformer John Knox also saw more circumstances than Calvin under which civil powers might be disobeyed. He called on the nobility not simply to resist but to overthrow what he considered the tyranny of Catholic rule in Scotland. He also believed that the common people could revolt if the nobility failed in an effort to bring Reformation to Scotland. A century later, the Scottish Covenanter Samuel Rutherford penned his classic work *Lex Rex*, arguing that the written law stands above the king, and when the king strays, his actions are unjust and may be resisted, indeed must be resisted. Rutherford was the inspiration for the twentieth-century theologian Francis Schaeffer, who claimed in his *Christian Manifesto* that "at a certain point there is not only the right, but the duty, to disobey the state."

The Pauline passage in Romans recognizes two realms: Caesar's and God's. But Scripture in general, including Paul, recognizes that Caesar rules under God's authority, with delegated power to achieve certain ends: justice, domestic tranquillity, the restraint of evil. Christian thought throughout history has held that any government which perverts these ends is acting *ultra vires*, in violation of its delegated authority. Dietrich Bonhoeffer, the German Lutheran pastor who was martyred for resisting Hitler, gave what may be the clearest expression of the principle: "If government persistently and arbitrarily violates its assigned task, then the divine mandate lapses."

This may be a sort of "preaching to the choir," for it strikes me hardly anyone would deny that a government can become so corrupt that it is the positive duty of Christians to resist it. The real questions facing us are, rather, these: At what point does a government become sufficiently corrupt that Christians must actively resist it? and, Has the United States, under its current judicial regime, reached such a point?

Sometimes, to their shame, Christians have not roused themselves to resist evil government, and sometimes, to their credit, they have. In 1985, after President Marcos invalidated a freely held election in the Philippines, Christians began gathering in prayer groups. The Roman Catholic Jaime Cardinal Sin (who emerged as a dominant figure in the opposition to Marcos) publicly withdrew moral legitimation for a corrupt regime, holding the state morally accountable before God for its failings. Shortly thereafter, nuns left their convents, and lay Christians their homes, to flood the streets where they disarmed the tanks Marcos had ordered to maintain control.

Protestant churches have acted similarly. In 1934, representatives from eighteen provincial churches gathered in Barmen to create a "Confessing Synod" of the German Evangelical Church, declaring ecclesiastical independence from the Nazi regime. While the convocation was concerned more with saving the Church than the state, it indirectly questioned the moral legitimacy of the government and gave impetus to the German resistance movement. A more obscure but nonetheless interesting case is the Reformed Presbyterian Church of North America, a small denomination with roots in western Pennsylvania. Declaring early in American history that the Constitution was "godless" because it failed to acknowledge the authority of Jesus Christ, the church up until a generation ago practiced "political dissent," not allowing members to vote, hold public office, or take oaths of allegiance to the flag or the Constitution.

The uniqueness of the American experiment provides an opportunity for a Christian critique of the legitimacy of the current regime. When the republic was founded, the biblical tradition and the Enlightenment—two distinct and often antagonistic understandings of the world—seemed to find a patch of common ground. God's authority was acknowledged ("All men are endowed by their Creator with certain inalienable rights"), but sovereignty was vested not in God but in the people who consented to be so governed. The subsequent experiment in "ordered liberty" was achieved because, while some saw their liberty secured by God and others by their status as human beings alone, all agreed to be bound together for the sake of that liberty.

To use a political term of the time, a "social contract" that included biblical believers and Enlightenment rationalists was the basis of the founding of the United States. Whether Christians ought to have agreed to that contract is an interesting historical and theological question, but not really of much significance in our present circumstances—for agree to it Christians did. Our pressing question is rather whether the successor parties—today's governed populace and their judicial governors—still recognize the essence of the contract. If one party no longer does, that party has breached what lawyers call a "condition precedent": the essential promise by which the other party's agreement was secured.

If the terms of our contract have in fact been broken, Christian citizens may be compelled to force the government to return to its original understanding—as even Enlightenment rationalists have acknowledged. John Locke, a principal Enlightenment force behind the theory of a social contract, advocated the right of citizens' resistance to enforce the terms of the contract. The writings of Thomas Jefferson, who spoke openly of the necessity of revolution, could also be called upon for support.

It seems to me, however, that only the Church in some corporate capacity, not the individual Christian, has the authority to answer the question of our allegiance to the present regime. While the fragmentation of American churches poses obstacles to the kind of ecclesiastical consensus reached in Germany in the

1930s or the Philippines in the 1980s, some kind of convocation of theologically orthodox bodies could presumably join to consider the duty of Christians under the present order. (The statement "Evangelicals and Catholics Together," published in *First Things* in May 1994, demonstrates that joint efforts are possible.) While such a convocation could not claim to speak with total authority as the Church, it could give voice to a consensus of opinion among Christians in America.

Only the Church collectively can decide at what point a government becomes sufficiently corrupt that a believer must resist it. But, with fear and trembling, I have begun to believe that, however Christians in America gather to reach their consensus, we are fast approaching this point. Most orthodox Christians are likely to find it impossible to support a political regime under which the judiciary—without any legislative license—sanctions abortion, euthanasia, and homosexual marriage. Few believers are likely to pledge their allegiance to a government under which the courts—in the name of "constitutional rights" they themselves have sole authority to read into the Constitution—can systematically close off any form of political opposition by declaring it to betray the "inevitable inference" of animus.

And if, after prayerful deliberation, Christians corporately determine that our present government has violated its God-given mandate, what then? After the pattern of the confessing German church, the Church would first have to separate herself and declare her independence, disavowing any moral legitimacy indirectly or unofficially provided for the state in the past. Through her teaching and preaching office, the Church would need to expose the nature of the state's rebellion against God—in effect, bringing the state under the transcendent judgment of God. Though clergy and ecclesiastical officers must refrain from partisan political activity, as I have cautioned elsewhere, condemning the taking of innocent lives is not partisan, whether through protesting abortion clinics or (as the British clergy did in World War II) denouncing a government for bombing civilian targets.

Churches and religious organizations in this country have already, in limited circumstances, asserted their independence at some cost. In the 1980s, when New York barred discrimination against the hiring of practicing homosexuals by private agencies with city contracts, the Salvation Army, Agudath Israel, and the Catholic archdiocese simply refused city funds; in the case of the archdiocese, that meant losing $72 million in funding.

But what if all these actions fail to deter the state? Churches must then consider a higher level of resistance. In the campaign against slavery in the nineteenth century, Protestant churches used internal discipline and external pressure. The revivalist Charles Finney refused communion to slaveholders. Others organized the Underground Railroad and rescued fugitive slaves from prison. Many ministers broke the law, and some were imprisoned.

But would even active disobedience be effective against our current judicial state? When peaceable means and limited civil disobedience fail—at least according to the Protestant theologians Knox and Rutherford—revolution can be justified from a Christian viewpoint. While Knox called for the overthrow of a ruler in the interest of the Reformation, Rutherford advocated revolt in any instance when a king or ruler acted contrary to the written law. Apparently, many Christians in colonial times agreed with Rutherford. After dumping tea in the Boston harbor, one Boston pastor, Jonathan Mayhew, argued that for a people to "arise unanimously and resist their prince, even to dethrone him, is not criminal but a reasonable way of vindicating their liberties and just rights."

Of course, the same standards Augustine used to evaluate the justice of a war apply to the justice of a revolution: no other alternative is feasible; the advantages outweigh the suffering caused; and the evil employed in the revolution prevents far greater evil. The churches would have to be convinced that our present government had become totally opposed to God's purposes and that there was no other solution to prevent massive evil. And this point, I believe, we have not yet reached.

Prudence requires greater understanding than most Christians presently have about the threat that recent and pending court decisions pose. In *Compassion in Dying v. Washington*, Ninth Circuit Judge Reinhardt literally dared the Supreme Court to reverse *Bowers v. Hardwick* (the 5 to 4 decision in 1986 that upheld Georgia's statute against sodomy). Three of the five justices in the *Bowers* majority have been replaced, and the decision appears to be, as judge Reinhardt eagerly pointed out, at odds with the rationale behind the *Casey* decision. If *Bowers* falls, the Court may likely require states to recognize homosexual marriage. Christians therefore would be forced to live under a government whose actions violate the biblical ordering of social life and threaten the first institution ordained by God.

Reinhardt's decision in *Compassion in Dying v. Washington* itself prohibited states from preventing euthanasia—which, if upheld by the Supreme Court, means that the medical murder of the sick and elderly has become our government's national policy. Similarly, President Clinton's veto of the congressional bill banning the murder of babies when partially delivered is tantamount to affirmation of infanticide. It would be hard to imagine that a Christian in good conscience could swear to uphold the Constitution or laws of a nation that practices the horrendous offense against God of taking the defenseless lives of the weakest among us: babies, the elderly, and the sick.

The fervent and ceaseless prayer of every Christian should be that the discussion of resistance and revolution remains an academic exercise. We must continue for now to work relentlessly within the democratic process. Abhorring a confrontation, we should be engaged in a search for wisdom and a consensus to help us respond to the crisis of the time. Our discussions about the duty of Christians to the current American political order must be conducted with great care, in a manner that is formal rather than intuitive, deliberative rather than spontaneous, regulative rather than pragmatic. Calmness and seriousness of demeanor is necessary both to prevent the media dismissing us as fanatics and to prevent individuals from taking matters into their own hands.

And, after all, the Supreme Court may possibly keep faith with the original contract that brought Christians into the republic; seeing what it unleashed with *Roe* and institutionalized with *Casey*, it may yet rediscover the principle of judicial restraint. Politicians may be persuaded of their error in supposing economic positions more important than moral positions. Perhaps some of our most vitriolic critics in the media may discover that Christianity has been historically a far more powerful force for common good than the reverse. God is sovereign, after all, and He is in the miracle business. And if the polls are right, believing Protestants and Roman Catholics, generally socially conservative, represent a viable political majority in this country.

We dare not at present despair of America and advocate open rebellion. But we must—slowly, prayerfully, and with great deliberation and serious debate—prepare ourselves for what the future seems likely to bring under a regime in which the courts have usurped the democratic process by reckless exercise of naked power.

# THE TYRANT STATE

*Robert P. George*

AMERICA'S DEMOCRATIC EXPERIMENT has been remarkably successful. Constitutional democracy in the United States has survived a civil war, a great depression, and two world wars. Our nation has assimilated into the mainstream of American life generations of immigrants—many fleeing poverty and oppression in their native lands. We have made tremendous strides towards overcoming a tragic legacy of slavery and racial segregation. We have secured safer conditions for working people and a meaningful social safety net for the most disadvantaged among us. We have demonstrated that citizens of different religious faiths can live and work together in peace and mutual respect. America's economic prosperity has made our nation the envy of the world. Oppressed peoples around the globe look to our Declaration of Independence for inspiration and our Constitution as a model of free government. In the great ideological struggles of the twentieth century, American ideals of personal, political, and economic freedom have triumphed over fascist and communist tyranny. Two cheers for American democracy!

Why not three?

In his encyclical *Evangelium Vitae* (1995), Pope John Paul II reminds us that "fundamentally democracy is a 'system' and as such is a means and not an end. Its 'moral value' is not automatic, but depends on conformity to the moral law to which it, like every other form of human behavior, must be subject." This doctrine of the necessary conformity of civil law to moral truth long predates the rise of modern democracy. It is present in both Plato and Aristotle, and was given careful, systematic expression by St. Thomas Aquinas. It has been a central feature of the tradition of papal social teaching.

As applied to modern democracy, the idea is that the moral legitimacy of a law or public policy cannot be established merely by showing that it was put into place through the workings of democratic institutions. It is true, as the Pope affirms, that democracy is uniquely valuable because it embodies more fully than any alternative system the principle of the fundamental moral equality of citizens. For this reason, the Pope says that the "almost universal consensus with regard to the value of democracy . . . is to be considered a positive 'sign of the times,' as the Church's magisterium has frequently noted." Nevertheless, even a democratic regime may compromise its legitimacy and forfeit its right to the allegiance of its citizens.

This happens when the institutions of a democracy are manipulated so that "'right' ceases to be such, because it is no longer firmly founded on the inviolable dignity of the person. . . . In this way, democracy, contradicting its own principles, effectively moves towards a form of totalitarianism." In such an event, democratic institutions become mechanisms of injustice and oppression, thus defying the moral law to which they, like all human institutions and actions, are subject. As Pope John XXIII wrote in his encyclical *Pacem in Terris* (1963), "*Any* government which refused to recognize human rights, or acted in violation of them, would not only fail in its duty; its decrees would be wholly lacking in binding force."

These are no mere sectarian teachings. Belief that laws and the regimes that make and enforce them must be evaluated by reference to universal standards of justice is shared by people of different faiths and of no particular faith. It is the premise of any serious conception of human rights. And few people who are serious about human rights are naive enough to believe that democratic institutions can never be used to violate human rights. Indeed, a central justification for judicial review of legislation is to provide a check against the possibility that more democratically responsive institutions of government will disregard constitutional guarantees and tread upon people's fundamental rights.

One of the saddest lessons of American history, however, is that courts exercising the power to invalidate legislation as unconstitutional can themselves trample upon fundamental rights, and, indeed, can do so precisely in the name of protecting such rights. This happened, for example, when the Supreme Court of the United States, in a ruling that helped to precipitate the Civil War, held in *Dred Scott v. Sandford* that blacks were noncitizens— and, for all practical purposes, nonpersons—possessed of no rights that white people must respect. In our own time, the Supreme Court, in *Roe v. Wade,* struck down the abortion laws of all fifty states, effectively wiping out all legal protection of unborn human beings against being killed upon the request of their mothers. Most recently, federal courts of appeal for the Second and Ninth Circuits—the latter court relying explicitly on the abortion jurisprudence of *Roe* and its progeny—have invalidated laws prohibiting physician-assisted suicide in New York and California.

A familiar and important argument against the "judicial activism" on display in these cases is that such decisions constitute the judicial usurpation of legislative authority. This argument highlights the antidemocratic character of the decisions. It prescinds, however, from the substance of the moral questions involved—the rightness or wrongness of slavery or legalized abortion and euthanasia as a matter of public policy. Justice Antonin Scalia, perhaps the leading exponent of this criticism, emphasizes the purely procedural quality of the argument by declaring abortion, for example, to be a matter entirely outside the purview of constitutional law and, therefore, beyond the jurisdiction of courts.

In criticizing *Roe*, Scalia argues that the Constitution, properly interpreted, leaves the people of the states free to legislate against abortion. In a noteworthy address at the Gregorian Pontifical University in Rome, however, he recently declared that by the same token, "if the people want abortion, the state should permit abortion in a democracy." While the justice made clear his own preference for pro-life public policies, he argued that in itself democracy is neutral as between competing positions on issues such as abortion and euthanasia. "I do not know how you can argue on the basis of democratic theory," he said, "that the government has a moral obligation to do something that is opposed by the people." Responding to a questioner who raised the issue of the rights of minorities, Scalia declared that "the whole theory of democracy, my dear fellow, is that the majority rules; that is the whole theory of it. You protect minorities only because the majority determines that there are certain minority positions that deserve protection."

The Pope's argument in *Evangelium Vitae*, by contrast, highlights the sense in which the abandonment of the unborn to abortion and the infirm to euthanasia betrays the substantive principle of equal worth and dignity that is the moral linchpin of democracy. Any regime, including a democratic one, degenerates into what the Pope calls a "tyrant state" when its law exposes the weakest and most vulnerable members of the community—those most in need of the law's protection—to private lethal violence or other forms of oppression. The dark irony of American constitutional democracy is that our judges—whose special responsibility it is to preserve the core democratic principle of equality before the law—are the ones whose edicts have betrayed this principle. When considered in light of the substantive moral basis of democratic governance, *Roe v. Wade* and similar decisions stand out as "undemocratic" in a far more radical sense than the one justice Scalia has in mind.

If the moral law is anything like what Christians and Jews have long supposed it to be, then there are profoundly important respects in which the institutions of American democracy—particularly the courts—have made themselves its enemy. Mary Ann Glendon has observed that the abortion license manufactured in *Roe* and upheld in *Planned Parenthood v. Casey* is more sweeping than that of any other democratic nation on the face of the earth. "No other democracy," she remarks, "is so careless of the value of human life." Predictably, the legalization of abortion is paving the way to assisted suicide and euthanasia. The decisions of the Second and Ninth Circuit Courts will give the Supreme Court an opportunity to declare that the right "to define one's own concept of existence, of meaning, the universe, and the mystery of human life," to which it appealed in upholding the abortion license in *Casey*, includes the right to kill yourself, to a physician's assistance in killing yourself, and to someone else's "substituted judgment" that you should be killed when you are too infirm to decide for yourself.

What are serious Jews, Christians, and other pro-life citizens to say about such laws and the institutions that bring them into being? In *Evangelium Vitae*, John Paul II teaches that "laws which authorize and promote abortion and euthanasia are radically opposed not only to the good of the individual but also to the common good; as such they are completely lacking in juridical validity." The Pope is not here making a claim about the technical status of such laws within the legal systems of the countries that have them. He is, rather, concerned with their moral force, that is to say, their capacity objectively to bind the conscience of citizens. "A civil law authorizing abortion or euthanasia," he declares, "ceases by that very fact to be a true, morally binding law. . . . Abortion and euthanasia are crimes which no human law can claim to legitimize. There is no obligation in conscience to obey such laws; instead there is a grave and clear obligation *to oppose them by conscientious objection.*"

Plainly, the Pope's teaching is a firm rebuke to those who claim to be "personally opposed" to abortion and euthanasia but who act to advance these evils in the public sphere. "In the case of an intrinsically unjust law, such as a law permitting abortion or euthanasia," the Pope says, "it is . . . never licit to obey it, or to take part in a propaganda campaign in favor of such a law, or vote for it." But the Pope's call for disobedience and conscientious objection goes beyond even the condemnation of the craven "personally opposed, but pro-choice," position. His teaching is directed not merely to those who would join the ranks of Mario Cuomo, Bill Clinton, and Father Robert Drinan, but to all of us. We are, the Pope says, in the midst of a great conflict between "the culture of life" and "the culture of death": "We are all involved and we all share in it, with the inescapable responsibility of *choosing to be unconditionally pro-life.*"

When *Evangelium Vitae* was issued, the Pope's warning that ours is becoming a "culture of death" grabbed the headlines— and rightly so. An equally important aspect of his teaching, however, received less publicity. This was the Pope's call for all of us to "live the Gospel of Life." The Pope emphasizes again and again that this is a call to action. All of us must give witness to the sanctity of human life, not merely by personally refraining from abortion and euthanasia, but by working in various spheres— including the political sphere—to overcome these "crimes against life" and create a new "culture of life."

For some, this will mean making financial sacrifices to support the pro-life cause in its various dimensions. For others, it will mean volunteering to assist in the critical work of pro-life pregnancy centers and hospices. For still others, it will mean working in the educational, legal, and political realms to reverse the judicial decisions and legislative and executive acts that have ushered in the "culture of death." For all who believe in a God of love, justice, and mercy, it will mean constant prayer not only for the victims of the "culture of death," but also for those who are joined in the great struggle on their behalf, and, indeed, for those misguided souls who, by political action or by personal involvement in the killing of the unborn or infirm, have made themselves their oppressors.

To all who work in shaping public policy, the Pope directs a special plea to make a concern for the health of the family "the basis and driving force of all social policies." In this vein, he says, it is essential to resist "the trivialization of sexuality," which is "among the principal factors which has led to contempt for new life." Moreover, the Pope calls for greater support for adoption as a true pro-life alternative to abortion. Here, one is reminded of the profound witness of Mother Teresa at the National Prayer Breakfast in February of 1994: "Please do not kill the child. I want the child. Please give me the child. I am willing to accept any child who would be aborted." Those of us who would resist the culture of death must join our voices with hers. For us, and the society we must strive to create, there can be no such thing as an "unwanted" child.

Does the Pope not, however, call for even more? How are we to understand his teaching that resistance to the "culture of death" demands "disobedience" and even "conscientious objection" to unjust laws? Laws that authorize the killing of the unborn or infirm are permissive in form. They license and sometimes encourage private killing, but do not positively command it. (This is what enables supporters of abortion to describe themselves as "pro-choice." Of course, by this logic, so were supporters of antebellum laws that permitted slavery, yet required no one to own slaves or to demand return of fugitive slaves.) Therefore, disobedience and conscientious objection to such laws must, in most cases, be indirect. A good example is that of physicians in United States military hospitals abroad who announced their refusal to perform elective abortions when President Clinton issued an executive order lifting the ban on these abortions in such hospitals.

Another example is that of citizens of states which pay for abortions with public funds who refuse, as a matter of conscience, to remit to state government a portion of their taxes corresponding to the percentage of the state budget that goes to abortion funding. Yet another example is that of nonviolent protestors at abortion clinics who defy unjust restrictions of their freedom of speech in order to plead the case for the unborn to women contemplating abortion.

In upholding the abortion license in the *Casey* decision, a plurality opinion of Justices Souter, O'Connor, and Kennedy called upon pro-life Americans to stop their resistance to legalized abortion and accept "a common mandate rooted in the Constitution." For reasons the Pope makes clear, this is a proposi-tion that Catholics and other pro-life Americans cannot accept. The doctrine of the necessary conformity of civil law to moral truth imposes on conscientious citizens of a regime that authorizes the killing of the unborn and infirm a clear obligation of resistance. It is not merely that the claim of these justices to have found a pro-abortion "mandate" in the Constitution is manifestly ludicrous. The value of constitutional democracy lies ultimately in its capacity to serve and secure the common good, which demands, above all, the protection of fundamental human rights. If the Constitution really did abandon the vulnerable to private acts of lethal violence, and, indeed, positively disempowered citizens from working through the democratic process to correct these injustices, then it would utterly lack the capacity to bind the consciences of citizens. Our duty would not be to "accept a common mandate," but to resist.

Has the regime of American democracy forfeited its legitimacy? One way of avoiding an affirmative answer to this question is to observe that the judicial decisions at issue are gross misinterpretations of the Constitution. They are examples of what Justice Byron White, dissenting in *Roe v. Wade,* called the "exercise of raw judicial power." At the same time, however, these decisions have consistently been acquiesced in by the legislative and executive branches of government. Congress has not defied the Supreme Court, as it ultimately did in *Dred Scott*. And, although not every president has actively abetted the culture of death—as President Clinton did, for example, in issuing a series of pro-abortion executive orders and vetoing the congressional ban on partial-birth abortions—no recent president has worked steadily to ensure, by judicial appointments and other actions, that anti-life judicial decisions are reversed.

To say that the worst abuses of human rights have come from the least democratic branch of government—the judiciary—is true, but of increasingly questionable relevance to the crisis of democratic legitimacy brought on by judicial action in the cause of abortion and euthanasia. In practice, the American scheme of constitutional democracy invests the courts with ultimate authority to decide what the Constitution is to mean. Judicial action and appointments can, and sometimes do, become major issues in national elections. The refusal of the courts over more than twenty-three years to reverse *Roe v. Wade* must, then, be accounted a failure of American democracy.

The judicial movement toward euthanasia makes it plain that the hour is late. The "culture of death" is well-advanced in our nation. As the Pope says, "given such a grave situation, we need now more than ever to have the courage to look the truth in the eye and to *call things by their proper names*, without yielding to convenient compromises or to the temptation of self-deception." Let us, therefore, speak plainly: The courts, sometimes abetted by, and almost always acquiesced in, federal and state executives and legislators, have imposed upon the nation immoral policies that pro-life Americans cannot, in conscience, accept. Since the legitimacy of institutions of governance—be they democratic or otherwise—depends ultimately on their capacity and willingness to preserve and promote the common good by, above all, pro-tecting fundamental human rights, the failure of the institutions of American democracy to fulfill their responsibilities has created what is truly a crisis. People of good will—of whatever religious faith—who are prepared to consider seriously the Pope's teaching in *Evangelium Vitae* cannot now avoid asking themselves, soberly and unblinkingly, whether our regime is becoming the democratic "tyrant state" about which he warns.

# PART II

# QUESTIONS OF LEGITIMACY

## William J. Bennett

WHEN I READ STATEMENTS asking us to explore the question of "whether we have reached or are reaching the point where conscientious citizens can no longer give moral assent to the existing regime," I am reminded of my late 1960s graduate school days, when this sort of thing was all the rage – "the right to participate in decisions that affect our lives," "Amerika" with a *k*, the New Left, and all that.

There are important differences, of course—and among them are the well-argued and morally serious critiques that accompany the statements. When distinguished conservatives begin to ponder civil disobedience, and whether or not the United States has "betrayed" the democratic idea, and the prospects of American "despotism," it has—for this reader, at least—the effect of concentrating the mind. I strongly concur with some of the conclusions in the symposium, and I strongly disagree with some others.

Many important issues are raised in the symposium, two above all: the condition of the courts and the condition of the people. Most of the concerns expressed in the symposium were directed at the judicial usurpation of politics, and I understand why. If the Supreme Court and the Federal District Courts were acting in a responsible fashion, near-apocalyptic language would not make its way onto the pages of *First Things*.

But it has, for this reason: on many of the most important issues of our time, the courts are acting in remarkably inappropriate and injurious ways. In more and more recent cases, the Supreme Court is deconstructing the text of the Constitution and is often incoherent in its reasoning.

The Supreme Court is contributing to America's widespread social chaos—and not simply because of the acts that are sanctioned by the decisions. There is the matter of the "reasoning" that informs the decisions. Exhibit A is Justices Souter, Kennedy, and O'Connor's opinion in the *Casey* decision, in which they write that "[a]t the heart of liberty is the right to define one's own concept of existence, of meaning, of the universe, and of the mystery of human life." Here is an example of "values clarification" being written not into school textbooks, but into Supreme Court opinion. It is an open-ended validation of subjectivism; whatever and however one defines life is not only valid but constitutionally protected. If this relativism becomes the coin of the judicial realm, we are in for very bad times indeed— judicially, politically, morally. If these words are taken seriously, how can we legislate against doctor-assisted suicide? Or drug use? Or prostitution? Or virtually anything else, for that matter? The danger is the anarchy that could come from such officially sanctioned rulings. The best we can hope for is that this was Souter, Kennedy, and O'Connor's attempt at a "politics of meaning" speech disguised as a Court opinion, and that it is an aberration for them and for the Court. But that is a thin reed upon which to rest our hopes.

Let us stipulate, then, that the Supreme Court is doing considerable damage and that a corrective is needed. What about the other, and in many ways more problematic, issue, namely, the moral sensibilities of the broad public? Hadley Arkes points out that on issues ranging from abortion to euthanasia to "gay rights" the Court has taken steps which have struck no moral or religious nerve. What are we to make of this?

Among the possibilities: the majority of the people are basically ignorant of what the Court is doing, and if they knew they would be outraged; people are basically ignorant of much of what the Court is doing, and if they knew they would (by and large) agree with its decisions; the people know what the Court is doing and agree with many of its decisions; or the people know what the Court is up to and may disagree with those decisions but they are not exercised enough to right its or their fellow citizens' wrongs. It is worth noting that the first explanation is the only one from which we can draw much comfort.

Now I have little doubt that the Supreme Court is undermining democratic self-government. Should the Court rein itself in or, absent that, face being reined in? Yes, for both constitutional and moral reasons. *Can* the Court be reined in? Again, yes. But *will* the Court be reined in? My guess is that given the current state of affairs, the answer is probably no. And that is itself revealing.

There are legislative means at our disposal to correct the excesses of the Court (Judge Bork proposes subjecting decisions of courts to modification or reversal by a majority vote of the Senate and the House of Representatives, or depriving courts of the power of constitutional review). These reforms will happen if our legislative bodies choose to implement them. And that, in turn, will happen if the public cares enough to make the misconduct of the Supreme Court a national priority. Keep in mind that the elected representatives of this country are as responsive to the desires of the public as perhaps any legislative body ever; even if the Supreme Court undermines the popular will (as it so clearly did in the *Romer* decision), the citizens of America have several means of responsible recourse available to them. And that is just one of the many crucial differences that separate America from Nazi Germany, a regime invoked a number of times in the symposium. I take the demoralization of America quite seriously. But the analogy to Nazi Germany is both wrong and regrettable.

Yes, the "judicial usurpation" of politics has undermined the ability of the people to decide on matters of birth, marriage, and death. Yes, it is asking a lot of the public to exert the kind of sustained political pressure that is required if we are to properly check the abuses of the Court. But we are where we are. And we cannot ignore the fact that there are ways for the American people to regain their democratic prerogatives. If those ways are not utilized, then the problem is not simply with the Court; the problem is also with the citizenry itself. It seems to me that that is the heart of the matter: a culture of acedia has taken deep root in the soil of late twentieth-century America, which has led to acquiescence and passivity. Have we lost our capacity for justifiable outrage? Can we be roused to act against the spread of foul and wicked practices?

The Congress' failure to override President Clinton's veto of the "partial-birth abortion" legislation is illustrative. When it comes to the subject of abortion, I believe that there are a limited number of hard, wrenching cases. But here is an easy one: the presidential sanctioning of a procedure that is, for all intents and purposes, infanticide. What was most striking to me was the lack of virtually any public response. Now it is true that most people do not know about the partial-birth abortion procedure; that most people who do are opposed to that awful procedure; and that the pro-abortionists spread misinformation. Still, we cannot escape the fact that we had something of a national debate about infanticide – and infanticide prevailed (because of a popular President's veto); that very little was heard from those Americans who did follow the debate; that the Republican presidential and vice-presidential candidates, and many congressional candidates, said little or nothing about the issue during the 1996 campaign; and that Americans reelected as President, by a wide margin, the man who looked at infanticide and said yes to it.

Our task, then, is twofold: to make sure that the public knows what is going on in the courts, and to make the case for why people must care about it. We must be operational optimists and act on the assumption that they will care. We need to do a better job educating citizens about how the modern-day Supreme Court is improperly intruding into issues of birth, marriage, and death, and explaining which recourses are available to them. And yes, we have to do what we can to shake the public out of its servility, its complacency, its drift.

A final, crucial point: we are still America, not "Amerika." This premise ought to guide our future deliberations. Of course this nation has suffered tremendous moral regression during the last three decades. But the situation is not irreversible and our government is not illegitimate. My concern with declaring the American "regime" illegitimate is that it assumes that because of the actions of an out-of-control Court, America has become (or is about to become) a nation that is irredeemably antidemocratic, that we have exhausted all our options, that we are powerless to rein in the Court. That is simply not so. We have available to us the means. The question for our time is: do enough people have the will? I simply do not know the answer to that question—nor do I think enough has been done to inform citizens to be confident of the answer. We need to find out the answer to the question, and soon. Because one things is for sure, and on this I think we can all agree: the stakes are very high indeed and the hour is late.

*First Things*


## Peter L. Berger


T HE 1996 ELECTION did not reverse the conservative revolution of the 1994 election for the simple reason that there was no such revolution in the first place. I claim no great expertise in American politics, but it seems to me that both elections were primarily determined by fear. In 1994 many voters were scared that Hillary Clinton would push them, sooner or later, into some sort of Bolshevik health-care system; in 1996, they feared that Newt Gingrich would take away the health-care system they had. And, of course, there were other crisscrossing anxieties, none of which Bob Dole managed to allay.

Be that as it may, conservatives, of all people, should cringe at the word "revolution," no matter what adjective precedes it; and a "conservative revolution" is an oxymoron indeed. Rather, what can be observed over several elections and from other measures of American political life is a shift to the Right on a number of issues, notably on economic and welfare policies. This shift provides a chance for conservative politics. It is a sad commentary on the leadership of the Republican party that this chance has been consistently missed, at least since the end of the Reagan administration.

As for the alliance between "economic" and "social" or "values" conservatives, there were obvious tensions at work even in the heyday of that alliance, caused not least by class differences. On one side there were people who thought that being born-again was some sort of Hindu superstition, while people on the other side thought that Groton was a throat disease. As many observers have noted, the end of the cold war put further strain on the alliance. Nevertheless, given the continuing challenges from the Left, the alliance is still plausible.

The question is whether the "values" issues can be defined in such a way as to permit conservatives to expand into the middle ground of American politics. It seems to me that the answer to this will determine the future of conservatism.

The "radicalizing mood" referred to in the editors' statement is understandable in view of various disappointments, among which must certainly be included the role of the federal courts. If one is located in academia, as I am, the continuing domination of elite culture and some of its not-so-elite dependencies by various demented ideologies still sprouting from the decaying carcass of the late 1960s is enough to make one think of moving to another country (an impulse quickly enough checked as one goes over the list of possible destinations). But any radicalizing mood should be held at bay, especially by those who think of themselves as conservatives. Otherwise, the real opportunities for conservative politics will be lost for a long time, and conservatism will be relegated to a sectarian subculture.

Since there is no credible vehicle for conservative politics in America other than the Republican party, the failure of its leadership to articulate "values" positions that will appeal to larger numbers of voters is deplorable. (They have done much better, of course, on economic and welfare policies, with the bizarre result that President Clinton ran in 1996 by employing a rhetoric that, on those issues, could be well described as moderate Republican.) The reasons for this failure are not very mysterious. Most leading Republicans are economic conservatives, equally ill at ease with the Left-leaning culture (with which they are often afflicted in their own homes by their wives and children) and with their discomfiting allies on the "values" Right. As a result, they alternate between an avoidance of positions that might give ammunition to the Left and a patently awkward endorsement of positions of the "values" Right.

A particularly shameful example of appeasement of the Left was the failure of the Dole campaign to support the California Civil Rights Initiative, a failure that was as distasteful morally as it was politically dumb. On the other hand, the mouthing of evangelical religious sentiments and of vociferous anti-abortion rhetoric by upper-middle-class Republican politicians to whom both the sentiments and the rhetoric are clearly alien is unlikely to convince the groups thus being wooed. It takes the rare political skills of a Bill Clinton to be successfully insincere.

It is in this context that the episode involving *First Things* is more than a tempest in a teacup. I was one of those who resigned from the magazine's board over this matter and I address it here with reluctance, because I have great respect and affection for Father Richard John Neuhaus, whose sincerity is unquestionable and whose contributions to the conservative cause have been very great. But the questioning of the legitimacy of the American political system in the *First Things* symposium is a prime case of the counterproductive radicalizing mood mentioned earlier. If one decides that the system has become illegitimate, where does one go from there? Does one hole up with guns in the foothills of the Rockies? Engage in civil disobedience? Move abroad? Elect what Europeans call "inner emigration"?

Any of these options involves a withdrawal from meaningful politics. To consider such an option in the United States today strikes me as profoundly implausible as well as strangely parochial. If the American polity is illegitimate, where is legitimacy to be found? The allusions to Nazi Germany in this exercise are particularly offensive: are we back now to the "Amerika" language of the 1960s, this time in a Right translation?

A key concern of *First Things* is a usurpation of power by the courts, described most forcefully (and, to me, persuasively) by Robert Bork's contribution to that magazine's November symposium. But is this enough reason to cast doubt on the legitimacy of the system? The American separation of powers has always been a creaky affair. Time and again, the other two branches of government have usurped power in constitutionally dubious ways. Congress has tried to run foreign policy. Agencies of the executive branch have legislated by way of regulations.

It seems to me, however, that for most of the *First Things* contributors, and for the magazine's editors, the driving concern has been not so much the power the courts have improperly assumed but rather what they have done with this power. And at the center of this concern is the issue of abortion.

A simple thought–experiment will serve to illuminate the problem here. Imagine that abortion in the United States had achieved its present legal status through an act of Congress rather than a Supreme Court decision. Imagine further that the Supreme Court had then ruled this act to be unconstitutional. I doubt very much that most of the *First Things* contributors would have viewed the latter action as a serious usurpation of power, let alone a reason to question the legitimacy of the American polity.

In the same November issue of *First Things* a reader, Fred Ainslie, responded in a letter to an earlier review by Neuhaus of Daniel Jonah Goldhagen's book, *Hitler's Willing Executioners.* "Richard John Neuhaus suggests," this reader wrote, "that the

Holocaust is 'our only culturally available icon of absolute evil.' What about the monstrosity of abortion?" He then went on to describe abortion as "the number-one problem in America today." Neuhaus replied to this letter as follows: "Abortion is certainly the moral enormity that Mr. Ainslie suggests. Because, unfortunately, so many are blind to its reality, it is not the 'culturally available' icon of absolute evil that the Holocaust is. We must work and hope that this will change."

It is only with great difficulty that I can entertain the idea that abortion is an "icon of absolute evil" to be placed alongside the Holocaust. Indeed, that idea, even if taken as a theoretical exercise, strikes me as, precisely, a "moral enormity." Nevertheless, I must concede that to someone who sincerely believes that every abortion, no matter at what point it occurs in the development of a pregnancy, is an act of homicide, it must logically appear as absolutely evil and, given its frequency today, as America's number-one problem. It is also logical that, this being the case, one's position on abortion will become the most important litmus test of moral and political acceptability.

I myself do not hold this position on abortion (though, for good reasons, I am closer to a pro-life than to a pro-choice position, at least as these views are defined in America today). But, what is more germane to this discussion, most Americans do not hold such a position, either. Like me, they are somewhere in the middle. That being so, abortion as an "icon of absolute 'evil'" is thoroughly implausible, as is the aforementioned litmus test. (Incidentally, if abortion *is* taken as the key test of political legitimacy, the only democracy that, to my knowledge, would pass this test is the Republic of Ireland—though I understand that too is about to change. In any case, Ireland, undoubtedly a pleasant country, is hardly the last best hope of political legitimacy.)

The conservative mandate on the "values" issues is to spell out an authentically conservative position without falling into a radicalizing mood that proposes nonnegotiable absolutes. Such a position, I believe, could persuade a broad spectrum within the electorate. Most, but not all, of these issues belong in the political arena, and most can be dealt with by reversing the "long march through the institutions" which the Left began in the 1960s. Put differently, the conservative mandate is to build a politically viable social and cultural platform. I think I hear a reader's response to the preceding paragraph: put up or shut up! Fair enough. I hope to put up in the near future.

*Commentary*

## *Walter Berns*

YEARS AGO (how many, I do not remember) I was on a panel with the late Russell Kirk, the doyen of the paleoconservatives, and sitting behind him when, at the podium, he outlined his plan for a Christian commonwealth. Rather rudely, I must admit, I interrupted him by asking, in a voice audible throughout the room, "What are you going to do with us Jews?" The question obviously took him aback, first because he knew I was not Jewish, but most of all, I suspect, because it had never occurred to him to ask it, or to have to answer it. After a short pause, he mumbled something to the effect that, of course, he did not mean to exclude Jews or anyone else. Having raised the question, I felt obliged to point out that the Constitution provides a better answer: by separating church and state, I said, the Founders intended to provide (in the words of the Episcopal *Book of Common Prayer*) a haven "for all sorts and conditions of men," and the foundation of this haven—safe for the Jews and safe for the rest of us—was not Christianity, and certainly not the church of that prayer book, but liberty of conscience, a liberal principle whose provenance was John Locke's *Letter Concerning Toleration*.

Russell Kirk had become famous among paleoconservatives, in part, by arguing that John Locke had nothing to do with the

Constitution; in effect, Kirk denied its liberal foundation. As he saw it, the Constitution was the work of men inspired by the "conservative" Edmund Burke. This paleoconservative misunderstanding has now been carried one step further by Richard John Neuhaus, a former Lutheran minister and now a Catholic priest. As Neuhaus sees it, the Constitution is essentially a religious document, embodying the moral law, and specifically—as some of his fellow essayists in the November 1996 *First Things* make explicit—the natural law as espoused by Thomas Aquinas in the thirteenth century and enunciated in various papal encyclicals even today. From this religious perspective, and with the help of his colleagues, Neuhaus examines recent decisions of the courts, especially the abortion, assisted-suicide, and Colorado "gay-rights" decisions, and concludes that the "regime" has become "morally illegitimate," rather like Nazi Germany. From the same perspective, he then pronounces anathema on this regime, by which he means "the actual, existing system of [American] government." Finally, appealing to what he says is one of "the most elementary principles of Western civilization," he suggests that the time has come when "conscientious citizens" might properly engage in seditious activities "ranging from noncompliance to resistance to civil disobedience to morally justified revolution."

Of course, Neuhaus is right about the courts and the judges. Self-righteous zealots (not unlike Neuhaus in that respect), they have indeed usurped power that the Constitution assigns to other agencies of the government or to the states. Two years ago, for example, the Supreme Court ruled that a Colorado constitutional amendment, denying *special* rights to homosexuals, violated the federal Constitution because, when adopting it, the voters had acted out of "animus." Then, even since Neuhaus wrote, a federal district court judge suspended the implementation of the California Civil Rights Initiative (which had received the support of 54 percent of the people), arguing that the provision, by *prohibiting* discrimination on the basis of race or sex, could be held to deny blacks and women the equal protection of the laws.

Playing ducks and drakes with legislative language is not unprecedented. The California initiative was modeled on the federal Civil Rights Act of 1964 which, beginning with the *Weber* case in 1979, has been knowingly and willfully misread by the Supreme Court. For proof of this assertion, consider the comment made by Justice Sandra Day O'Connor in a 1987 case: "As Justice Scalia illuminates with excruciating clarity, [this section of the Act] has been interpreted by *Weber* and succeeding cases to permit what its language read literally would prohibit." She then proceeded to join not Scalia in dissent but the majority in its deliberate misreading of the Act. To paraphrase Shakespeare's *Hamlet,* "What is law to her or she to law that she should weep for it?"

As I said, Neuhaus is right about the judges, but he is wrong about almost everything else. Our Founders—"the patriots of '76," as Lincoln called them—did not justify their taking up of arms by claiming that George III had violated the principles of morality, "especially traditional morality, and most especially morality associated with religion" (to use Neuhaus's words). To have done so would have involved them (Jefferson, Adams, Franklin, and the rest) in a dispute with a king who represented "traditional morality, and most especially morality associated with religion." After all, George claimed to rule by the grace of God (*Dei gratia rex*), and, in support of this claim, he (or his schoolmen supporters) referred to the Bible, beginning with the first chapter of Genesis. To have disputed him on religious grounds would have required the Founders to engage in the kind of scriptural exegesis that Locke employed against Sir Robert Filmer, the defender of divine right; and this, quite obviously, they did not do.

Traditional morality? On the contrary, immediately after adopting the Declaration of Independence on July 4, 1776, the Continental Congress appointed a committee—consisting again of Jefferson, Adams, and Franklin—to "prepare a device for a Seal of the United States of North America," and on that Great Seal appear these words (they are on every dollar bill), *Novus Ordo Seclorum,* meaning, a *new* order of the ages, new because it was the first to recognize the rights of man, and then to give them constitutional protection. In the words of James Madison, the Founders "accomplished a revolution which has no parallel in the annals of human society." It is the Constitution, the product of that revolution, and not a recondite "moral law," that the President swears to "protect and defend," the members of Congress to "support," and the judges to "support and defend."

The Founders were proud of their work. The Constitution, they said, provided a remedy for the "diseases" most incident to democratic government, and *The Federalist* (written to persuade the people to give it their consent) leaves no doubt as to what they understood to be a disease: zealous opinions "concerning religion," "tyrannical majorities," "angry and malignant passions," "a factious spirit," the dangerous ambition that "often lurks behind the specious mask of zeal for the rights of the people," and those who begin their careers "by paying obsequious court to the people, commencing demagogues and ending tyrants."

To guard against these democratic diseases, or vices, the Constitution, in addition to consigning religion to the private sphere by separating church and state, withholds powers, separates powers, and excludes the people *"in their collective capacity"* from any share in the exercise of these powers. In a word, republican (or limited) government would be possible under a Constitution that excluded, or at least inhibited, the zealous, the angry, the morally indignant; and this, in turn, depended on confining the business of government to issues that did not give rise to zeal, anger, or moral indignation.

Throughout most of our history—if we ignore the slavery issue and the Civil War—the Constitution succeeded in doing this. Calvin Coolidge was not altogether wrong when he said the nation's business was business. James Madison said much the same thing in *The Federalist*, Number 10. The government's business, he said, or at least its "first object," is the protection of men's "different and unequal faculties," especially those "from which the rights of property originate." The result would be a variety of interests—landed, manufacturing, mercantile, moneyed—and regulating these various and interfering interests is "the principal task of modern legislation." Although Madison acknowledged that republican government especially requires a "sufficient virtue" in the people, he said nothing about the power to inculcate it.

On the other hand, the Constitution was adopted by a people whose character was formed by, and would continue to live under, the laws and institutions of an older order, an order that was, to some extent at least, preserved in and fostered by state constitutions and state law. Whether out of habit or as deliberate policy, the states continued to foster family life and moral education, and to prohibit practices (the publication of obscene material, for example) that threatened or jeopardized them. No longer; the Supreme Court put an end to that, and by doing so provoked Richard Neuhaus's angry and morally indignant discourse.

But no good will come of it. On the contrary, he has already caused a breach in conservative ranks that is not likely to be closed, and, even worse, his call for direct (and unconstitutional) action will confirm the opinion, held by many Americans, some of them Republicans, that religious conservatives are extremists and are not to be trusted.

*Commentary*

## Midge Decter

W HEN I FIRST READ the editorial introduction to the symposium presumably devoted to the subject of judicial usurpation, I could hardly believe my eyes. *Mit Brennender Sorge*, indeed: it turned out that the symposium was not intended by you to be a discussion of the ills of judicial usurpation—hardly either a new or in any sense a controversial concern in the *First Things* community—but about nothing less than the legitimacy of the United States government. And to prove that raising the question of legitimacy is, so to speak, no mere slip of the ideological tongue, we are before we know it into mention of civil disobedience and even, for God's sake, "morally justified revolution"!

Could you not see, in the twentieth of all centuries, how profoundly offensive it is to speak this way when even the truly morally justified revolutions of our time—against Hitler, Stalin, Mao, and their acolytes and imitators—never, alas, took place? In your Introduction you warn us of the "growing alienation of millions of Americans from a government they do not recognize as theirs." Such a warning smacks of nothing so much as the kind of careless radicalism you and I not all that long ago prayed for our country to have put behind it.

Let me in the name of our long friendship presume to tell you what is the source of this eruption on your part. One certainly cannot deny that the Court has usurped powers rightly belonging to the political process, nor can one in all sanity deny that it has been using those powers to reach extraconstitutional and illegitimate decisions (encouraged if not positively required to do so in the present period, be it remembered, by the refusal of the political process to deliver to the blacks their long overdue relief from Jim Crow). But of course usurpation has been going back and forth among the three branches of government from the beginning, and the job of balancing and rebalancing involves a continuing and very difficult process of public persuasion. People, that is, must first be made to care. What we are dealing with is, in short, a cultural, rather than primarily a judicial, problem.

It used to be said of the Court that its decisions followed election results. But even in these less than attractive times nothing quite so cynical is the case: what the Court actually follows is the *culture*. And the condition of the culture, it seems odd for me to be reminding you, is in the end *our* responsibility, yours and mine. You threaten that millions of your fellow Americans have come to feel as alienated from this country as you claim to do. But there is in fact little or no evidence for that. Nor should you wish there were more. The truth is that the issues really driving this symposium, abortion on demand, euthanasia, and homosexual marriage, represent the most powerful and terrible of all temptations to people, i.e., the temptation of convenience and slothfulness. How much easier such measures all promise to make things! That is why the cultural battle over these issues will be a long and slogging and often thankless one. You may know that your fellow Americans will be better off both spiritually and psychically without these invitations to embrace what is after all the convenience of death, but millions upon millions of them do not. They do not understand what it is they are being tempted with, and it will be no simple work to convince them. So far there are simply not enough resisters of this temptation to influence the Court. I repeat: *so far*.

I presume in the name of friendship, then, to accuse you of growing impatient with your labors, and in your impatience, reckless. And I beg you: do not be impatient, and for heaven's sake do not be reckless about the legitimacy of this country (calling it a "regime" does not disguise what is at stake here). You will only end by strengthening the devil's hand.

*First Things*

## *James C. Dobson*

MY DEEPEST GRATITUDE to the editors of *First Things* for facilitating what history may reveal to be their most important symposium. The moral legitimacy of our current government and the responsibility of the Christian towards it are questions of tremendous moment. As I read each essay in the symposium, I could not escape the sense that Dietrich Bonhoeffer was watching over my shoulder. I wonder —do we have the courage to act upon the conclusions we may reach in these deliberations?

While your contributors wrote with a circumspection appropriate to the occasion, they have laid an indisputable case for the illegitimacy of the regime now passing itself off as a democracy. Our government has delegitimated itself in at least two ways. On a purely political level, Americans hold that our rulers derive their authority to govern through the will of the people. Only the most partisan supporters of the present regime could insist that we still live in a functioning democracy. On the most essential matters of human life and conscience, the courts have systematically invalidated the will of the people. Furthermore, they have done this by constructing a jurisprudence that leaves no doubt they intend to continue ruling by judicial fiat for the foreseeable future. Only questions of relative insignificance have been left to the people to resolve for themselves. This is no small development and before we accept it there ought to be some sort of national discussion. I doubt most Americans are aware of the current impotence of their vote.

But there is a far more serious consideration for those citizens who believe, as Christians do, that rulers ultimately derive their governing authority from God. The decisions now being rendered by our "robed masters" (to use George Will's phrase) violate the most fundamental of all moral laws. As Professor Hittinger observed, not only has our government chosen to base its own legitimacy on their refusal to protect the defenseless, it has thrown down the gauntlet to any citizen who tries to offer such protection. "Support the slaughter of the innocents," they have said, "or consider yourself an enemy of this regime." Furthermore, the Supreme Court has placed on notice all citizens animated by religious beliefs: participation will be allowed only to the extent that they refuse to act on those beliefs.

I stand in a long tradition of Christians who believe that rulers may forfeit their divine mandate when they systematically contravene the divine moral law. The accumulation of evidence, when combined with the lawless jurisprudence that produced it, should remove all doubt that our judiciary has, by act and intention, stepped out from under the moral law upon which governing authority depends. They have made it plain that they have no intention of regarding any higher law than themselves and that those who do will not be tolerated in the public square. Having tortured the First Amendment to exclude all but "secular" motives from public debate, Justice Kennedy, writing for the Court, goes on to include in the definition of religious belief those who hold that "there is an ethic and a morality which transcend human invention." Therefore, whether you believe government derives its legitimacy from the consent of the governed or from a higher source, our government has clearly transgressed its bounds in such a manner as to lose its authority. This is where we are. The pressing question is, where do we go from here?

I want to lend my voice to the call for serious prayer and deliberation among the Christian community as a whole before any course of action is established. There may yet be political remedies whereby restraints are constructed against this unbridled judicial tyranny. We must immediately examine every constitutional, legislative, and legal option at our disposal. Judge Bork has suggested two. We need concentrated work now on every conceivable strategy to return constitutional balance to this American experiment in democracy. Investing Congress with the power to overturn Supreme Court decisions is no guarantee of moral policies. But to the degree that democracy could be restored, it may be worth the fight. Christian people would again be free to pursue just government by winning a majority in the marketplace of ideas. Prudence requires that we investigate all such means before raising the prospect of more drastic measures.

It should be noted, however, that any institutional reforms will require a groundswell of public support. On this matter the editors are more optimistic than I. We have lost the Judeo-Christian consensus upon which our founders staked the success of this experiment. I quite agree with Professor Arkes when he says, "There may be atavistic moral reflexes, drawn from a Christian past, but they seem readily matched these days by the reflexes of a newer sensibility that is wary of anyone who seems 'judgmental.'" I doubt very much that our culture, having established tolerance as the new absolute, has the moral rectitude to insist that government move in the direction of traditional morality. The flaw in the design of our system of government has been revealed not merely because our courts (as well as our legislatures) are creating law *ex nihilo*, but because our culture is operating on the same philosophical premise, stated in *Casey*, that we all have a fundamental right to create and live by our own sense of reality.

And what of the church? My sense is that this will prove a defining moment for Christianity in the United States. Will American clergy be willing to risk the worst charge of our times —that of being intolerant or "mean-spirited"—to state clearly and unequivocally the standards of God in relation to these matters? Our hope of reform will only materialize with a vibrant church capturing the imagination of the American people for a tran-scendent moral order. Yet Thomas Reeves, in his article "Not So Christian America" (*First Things*, October 1996), describes Chris-tianity in America as "in large part, innocuous. It tends to be easy, upbeat, convenient, and compatible"—not the sort of faith likely to usher in anything like another Great Awakening.

And if all means of reform have been rebuffed? Will churches be willing to forfeit their tax-exempt status in order to make a stand against the immoral actions of this government? Will clergy and laity alike be willing to face cultural ostracism, imprisonment, or worse in order to defend the faith they now profess? We may rapidly be approaching the sort of Rubicon that our spiritual forebears faced: Choose Caesar or God. I take no pleasure in this prospect; I pray against it. But it is worth noting that such times have historically been rejuvenating for the faith. Modern Christianity's easy cohabitation with American culture has been crippling for both.

If pressed to give my own thoughts as to the future, I defer to the words of William Wilberforce: "The only solid hopes for the

well-being of my country depend not so much on her fleets and
armies, not so much on the wisdom of her rulers or the spirit of
her people, as on the persuasion that she still contains many who,
in a degenerate age, love and obey the Gospel of Christ, on the
humble trust that the intercession of these may still be prevalent,
that for the sake of these, Heaven may still look upon us with an
eye of favor."

*First Things*

## Mary Ann Glendon

NO ONE CAN ACCUSE *First Things* of ducking big
questions. But its editors, Bork, Hittinger, Arkes, Colson,
and George have been uncharacteristically reticent
in naming the causes of the decline of the democratic elements
in our republican experiment.

The regime question they raise is real. There is a good case to
be made that we are already living in a *de facto* oligarchy. It is less
clear, however, that the courts are, as all six writers seem to think,
principally to blame. To be sure, the judiciary has steadily usurped
power over matters that the Constitution wisely left to ordinary
political processes. But the courts could never have carried off
that power grab were it not for pathology in other parts of the
body politic.

For many decades now, control over the most important
decisions affecting the conditions under which Americans live,
work, and raise their children has flowed steadily from the people
most affected toward state and federal legislatures and administrative agencies. The courts were hardly the only agents in this
process, nor is it certain that they could have held it back. Yes,
legislatures are more representative than courts, but they too are
increasingly responsive to the interests and values of "elites." Yes,
the judiciary all too often mirrors the biases of the knowledge

class, but the legislative and administrative processes are all too often captured by the money class.

And look not to the political parties, as presently constituted, for help. It does not seem an exaggeration to say that we currently have a party of big business paying lip service to traditional moral values, and a party of big government paying lip service to the need of working people and the poor. Even that distinction is collapsing as Democratic Party leaders cozy up to big business, and Republicans discover the joys of big government.

The cracks in the democratic pillars of the republic, alas, may extend to the cultural foundations. Hittinger recognizes this when he questions whether the people have "tacitly consented" to the new regime. If the nation's courts, legislatures, and political parties are really out of touch with the needs and desires of the citizenry, why don't the American people rise up in protest? Unlike in Eastern Europe, the machinery of democratic government is here at hand. Why not repossess it, using ordinary political processes? Why not "Pass out a leaflet, call a meeting, speak your mind, decide to do something about it" in the words of the old union song? Why not organize to reclaim participatory government?

Well, one problem is that, as Michael Walzer once pointed out, "There's nobody here but us Americans." And most Americans are highly dependent on big business and government: about a fifth of the labor force are public employees; a third work for the central core of large corporations (many under government contract or subsidy); the pensions of retirees are invested in the same corporations; recipients of governmental largesse include not only welfare clients, but a substantial fraction of the middle class (through government-insured loans, medicare, and retirement income funded with general tax revenues). Most of these dependents have children or others who are in turn dependent on them.

On this neo-feudal landscape, we find precious little politics in Aristotle's sense of ordering our lives together. You might say of anyone who is looking for sturdy, independent citizens these days what Rousseau said of Diogenes with his lantern: The reason he failed is that the man he was seeking lived in a different age.

Sure, we feel restless in the "iron cage" that Max Weber predicted we moderns would occupy. But not so restless, apparently, that we are ready to undertake the hard work of becoming citizens rather than subjects. Parents have a high stake in the future, but most are kept busy trying to make ends meet. Then, too, countless Americans are caught up in consumerism, working to pay for things they accumulate. It's our duty to consume, we're told, because it keeps other people working.

For spare moments, when regime-threatening questions might come to mind, the oligarchs have authorized a modern form of bread and circuses, an array of new sexual freedoms to compensate for the loss of the most basic civil right of all – the right of self-government. With the democratization of vice, the man in the street can enjoy exotic pastimes once reserved to Roman emperors.

For society to sponsor consumerism and hedonism while government maintains a large class of dependents, civil servants, and clients is increasingly expensive. But abortion is available to thin out the underclass and the unfit, and euthanasia may soon take care of the burdensome elderly and sick.

Perhaps, just perhaps, it is the increasing official contempt for human life that will finally arouse Americans to demand more say in setting the conditions under which they live. It's hard for many individuals to empathize with an unborn child, but everyone can imagine getting sick or growing old. As suicide rapidly becomes a "right," more people are nervously wondering whether it will become a duty. When you can't tell whether the doctor in the doorway has arrived to kill you or cure you, you'll know the culture of death has come to your house.

It's an open question whether the United States can still provide the world with an example of a people that breathed new life into its historic democratic experiment. That would require reinvigorating the structures of civil society. Local governments,

families, religious groups, workers' associations, precinct organizations, and the like are our "schools for citizenship" as well as our
seedbeds of character and competence. They are the only real
counterforces to the excesses of market and state.

But can they be retrieved from disarray? Only, as Glenn Loury
has argued, if we start with change at the personal level, "one by
one, from the inside out." Let it be, dear Lord, let it be. But if it is
not to be, the United States will not be the first republic to slip by
small degrees into the form of government that, alas, has been
more common than any other in human history: tyranny by a
minority.

*First Things*

## Gertrude Himmelfarb

REVOLUTION, LIKE DEATH, concentrates the mind
wonderfully. Two years ago it was the "Gingrich revolution" that galvanized conservatives. Today it is the specter
of revolution that hovers behind the symposium in *First Things*,
raising the issue of the "legitimacy" of the American "regime."

The two "revolutions"—or near-revolutions, or visions of
revolution—tell us a good deal about the course of American
conservatism and the mood of conservatives in these two eventful
years. Two years ago, the more prudent spirits among us (Owen
Harries, most notably) warned conservatives against indulging
in the rhetoric, to say nothing of the reality, of revolution. That is
not, we were reminded, a proper mode of conservative discourse
or politics. Others, including myself, were so elated by the 1994
congressional elections and the spirited temper of our new
representatives that we defended the idea (oxymoron though it
is) of a "conservative revolution"—a revolution, we argued, that
was really a counterrevolution, reversing some of the baneful effects
of a long-entrenched welfare state.

A funny thing happened to that revolution on the way to the more recent elections. The revolutionary rhetoric was abandoned —was, in fact, discredited—while some of the reality was (or is in the process of being) fulfilled. By now the spectrum of political discourse and social policy has moved so far to the Right that liberals find themselves at the Left while conservatives approach the center. President Clinton's "vital center" is not the old liberal center described by Arthur M. Schlesinger Jr.; it is (to Schlesinger's dismay, I suspect) a more conservative center. Today it is liberalism that is on the defensive; indeed the very word is in disrepute.

In these few years, we have begun to think the unthinkable— about welfare, Medicare, even that "third rail" of American politics, Social Security. We have even begun to do the undoable. The welfare bill is more momentous than Bill Clinton likes to make it appear, or even than some conservatives seem to think. The "devolution" of relief to the states is not merely a considerable move toward federalism (which in itself is significant). It is a considerable step toward the abolition of relief as an entitlement, a right that has been hallowed for some sixty years and that has been the linchpin of the welfare state.

Perhaps even more important, it has begun to change the ethos of society. The press now touts stories celebrating the work ethic (single mothers gamely working for a living even though welfare provides greater financial rewards). The words virtue, shame, and responsibility can now be heard, without audible quotation marks around them.

We have, in this respect at least, accomplished something like a major reform, if not a revolution. It has been confined largely to the arena of social policy and achieved through the normal workings of the political process. It has not even required any constitutional amendment, which makes it all the more commendable.

Other areas, however—the culture, the media, academia, and, most notably, the judiciary—have resisted the conservative trend. Indeed, here the situation may be getting worse rather than better.

It is this, and particularly the condition of the judiciary, that is prompting a new call for revolution. And it is now that a counsel of caution is in order.

This new revolution, as the editors of *First Things* conceive it, differs from the old not only in its objective—the judiciary rather than the welfare state—but in its nature and scope. This is a revolution truly worthy of the name.

The question posed in the title of the *First Things* symposium, "The End of Democracy?," is "in no way hyperbolic," the editors assure us. "In full awareness of its far-reaching consequences," they propose to determine "whether we have reached or are reaching the point where conscientious citizens can no longer give moral assent to the existing regime." The "regime"—not merely the judiciary, not even the administration of the day, but the "regime," embracing the entire system of government.

That the editors believe the regime to be actually or imminently illegitimate is suggested again and again in the introduction to the symposium. We are told that "many millions of children" have come to believe that "the government that rules them is morally illegitimate," and that "perhaps even a majority" of Americans feel that they have to choose between "God *or* country." We are reminded of the "venerable precedent" of the American Revolution, and, most ominously, of Nazi Germany: "America is not and, please God, will never become Nazi Germany, but it is only blind hubris that denies it can happen here and, in peculiarly American ways, may be happening here."

The gravamen of the charge is the "judicial usurpation of power." It is this that accounts for the "crisis of legitimacy" and the "end of democracy." But the editors of *First Things* also invoke the principle—for which they cite the authority of Western civilization and two papal encyclicals—that "laws which violate the moral law are null and void and must in conscience be disobeyed."

At this point the argument becomes confused, for it is surely not the judicial usurpation of power that either Western civilization or the papacy takes to be a violation of the moral law; the division of powers in the American system of government hardly has so exalted a status in the moral order. The real issue, as some of the symposium's contributors (but not the editors) make clear, is abortion and euthanasia. It is this that is the affront to moral law. And it is this that conjures up the specter of Nazi Germany and the Holocaust. (A judicial usurpation of power was not one of Nazism's evils.)

It is quite true that in the United States the "oligarchic judiciary," as Robert Bork describes it, has been the worst offender in legalizing abortion and euthanasia, as well as in violating the Constitution in myriad other ways. (Although one of the most appalling cases in recent years puts the President, not the courts, in that role. It was Clinton who vetoed the congressional ban on partial-birth abortions.) But what if the legalization of abortion were the product not of the judiciary but of the legislature—if it betokened not the "end of democracy" but the very exercise of democracy? This is, in fact, the case in most Western countries, where duly elected representatives have enacted the statutes legalizing abortion (and, in some countries, euthanasia as well). Does this mean that all these regimes—democratic regimes like Britain, France, Germany, Italy, the Netherlands, Sweden—are also in violation of the moral law and hence illegitimate?

In America we are confronting two separate and urgent problems, the judiciary and abortion, which happen at present to coincide but which may well diverge in the future. It is the conflation of the two that gives this controversy the apocalyptic tone that it has.

If conservatives do take democracy and the Constitution seriously, if we are truly exercised by the usurpation of judicial power, we must also be prepared for the possibility that *vox populi* might differ from many of us on the subject of abortion. The polls suggest that the majority of the American people want to restrict abortion in various ways but not to criminalize it. If this is so, the conservative tone in this debate should be moral and exhortatory, to be sure, but also pragmatic, prudential, and incremental, seeking as many restrictions on abortion as the American people can be persuaded to accept, while at the same time denouncing the judiciary for flouting both the democratic will and the Constitution by prohibiting such restrictions.

Those who cannot, in good conscience, condone legal abortions have the moral as well as legal right to press their case and, if it goes against them in a properly democratic manner, they may, subject to the penalty of the law, have recourse to the alternatives mentioned in *First Things*, "ranging from noncompliance to resistance to civil disobedience to morally justified revolution." But they have neither the moral nor the legal right, *in the name of democracy,* to impose their view upon the polity, any more than the judiciary today has that right.

In posing the issue in apocalyptic, revolutionary terms, *First Things* has opened a rift among conservatives that threatens to become a major fault line. American conservatism has always been a coalition of diverse groups marching under separate banners while fighting a common enemy. In the last few years that improbable alliance—of economic conservatives and social conservatives, evangelicals and secularists, federalists, pro-lifers, flat-taxers, and a variety of one-issue partisans—has succeeded in bringing about important changes in the polity and social policy.

That alliance is now in peril. With undisguised *Schadenfreude,* a liberal commentator on the controversy (perhaps misreading the names of some of the critics) describes it as a falling-out between Jews and Christians, while a Jewish publication sees it as driving "a wedge into the 'Reagan coalition.'" One conservative (or paleoconservative) reporter is pleased to find in it a repudiation of neoconservatism, while another conservative reluctantly concludes that "the Right" has succumbed to the "anti-American temptation."

What has been accomplished by all this, except to provide fodder for journalists and promote dissension among conservatives? Have any problems been raised with regard to the judiciary that were not raised before (by Judge Bork, most notably)? Have any new practical remedies, reforms, or strategies been proposed, as distinct from the ultimate recourse to civil disobedience or revolution?

Amid all this high moral posturing, it may be useful to be reminded of the old distinction between an "ethic of ultimate ends" and an "ethic of responsibility"—a distinction all the more pertinent in a democracy, where there is less than total agreement about the ultimate principles or grounds of morality, but substantial agreement about mediate, practical principles. An "ethic of responsibility" is not as elevated as an "ethic of ultimate ends." But it is all that can be achieved—and the best that can be achieved—in a democracy, where the political process makes it *morally*, as well as practically, incumbent upon us to be patient, prudent, and responsible.

*Commentary*

## *William Kristol*

WE WERE ARGUING on TV about abortion—partial-birth abortion, to be precise. A fellow panelist, exasperated by my simple-mindedness, tried to explain that the issue was complicated. It involved, you see, a "clash between two of America's most cherished values, life and choice."

So this is what it has come to: life has been reduced to a value—choice has been elevated to a value; and they have the same status. Or do they? In a world of "values," there is, according to Justice Anthony Kennedy in *Romer v. Evans*, something questionable about laws based on "an ethic and a morality which transcend human invention." In such a world, choice is in fact the value that reigns supreme. Choice is the value of values. It is the core—the hollow core—of contemporary liberalism.

It was not ever thus. In *The Federalist*, Number 1, Alexander Hamilton suggested that Americans had the chance to establish "good government from reflection and choice." The American Founders were concerned to vindicate the dignity of human choice. But they knew they could do so only by grounding our choices in reflection about standards of good government. The task of conservatism today is to restore to our public life an understanding of such standards—of good government, of justice, of morality—that are not simply of human invention. Conservatives have not succeeded in this formidable endeavor; indeed, we have barely begun.

Beginnings are hard, as Republicans learned after their congressional victory in 1994. The American people were soon put off by the easy talk of a "Republican revolution." And who can blame them? The typical American attitude is a sensible one. We had a revolution 220 years ago; unlike almost all other revolutions, it worked out well; but most political leaders who promise revolution bring their countries to grief. Talk of a Republican revolution seemed at once misleadingly easy and dangerously extreme. Most Americans know that the task ahead is both too delicate and too fundamental for mere "revolution." What is needed is a reformation.

As it happened, the Republican revolution petered out within the year, though not before giving Bill Clinton an opportunity to stage a remarkable political recovery. His subsequent reelection stalled the conservative political realignment many of us had hoped for; but 1996 saw no resurgence of liberalism, either. The Left is, therefore, today more dependent than ever on advancing its agenda by stealth and indirection. Its preferred instruments of action are the least responsible and accountable institutions of our society. These include the courts. The contributors to the *First Things* symposium were right to be indignant about this attempt to circumvent self-government. The editors of the journal were wrong, I think, to indulge in loose-talk about the end of democracy, the moral illegitimacy of the regime, or Nazi Germany.

Conservatism's mandate in the years ahead is to repulse the last surges of liberal nihilism wherever they manifest themselves, including in the judiciary. But conservatism's more fundamental mandate is to take on the sacred cow of contemporary liberalism —choice. And the "choice" issue presents itself most directly, of course, in the area of abortion.

Now, all sophisticated people are supposed to wish that the abortion issue would somehow go away. At least we are supposed to urge that voices be lowered and that more moderate positions come to the fore. As a strategic matter, there is a strong case for the pro-life movement to focus more on incremental advances than on, say, a human-life amendment to the Constitution. But the truth is that abortion is today the bloody crossroads of American politics. It is where judicial liberation (from the Constitution), sexual liberation (from traditional mores), and women's liberation (from natural distinctions) come together. It is the focal point for liberalism's simultaneous assault on self-government, morals, and nature. So, challenging the judicially-imposed regime of abortion-on-demand is key to a conservative reformation in politics, in morals, and in beliefs.

If this reformation is to have any chance of success, it will have to proceed more in the spirit of Lincoln than of William Lloyd Garrison, whose fiery rhetoric was reprinted prominently in the November 1996 *First Things*. It will have to persuade as well as to hector. It will have to be serious about intermediate means as well as ultimate ends. And it will have to demonstrate sober understanding as well as burning concern. For at the end of the day, a conservative future requires a conservative political majority. Such a majority does not yet exist. One can assemble an anti-liberal majority, as we saw in 1994; one can produce an ambivalent majority, as we have seen in 1996. But there is as yet no conservative governing majority in this country. Creating such a majority is the radical task before us. The problem with the *First Things* symposium is that its "radicalizing mood" distracts from this truly radical task.

About a century and a half ago, John Stuart Mill famously described conservatives as the stupid party. Can they now become the intelligent party? Can they persuade Americans that choice and life cannot be equally "cherished values"? Can they restore the force of the traditional imperatives that contemporary liberalism scorns as politically incorrect? These imperatives are not complicated. They include: honor your father and your mother; be a man; choose life. It is fair to judge our social well-being by the resonance and authority of these simple commands. All, of course, are based on "an ethic and a morality which transcend human invention."

*Commentary*

## *The Editors of* NATIONAL REVIEW

C AN A CHRISTIAN, or a Jew, or any other thoughtful religious person, justify resistance to unjust laws passed by our modern American democracy? And if such laws seem permanently entrenched, can he abandon his general duty toward lawful authority and (though forswearing violent resistance) live as a kind of internal exile, refusing to obey certain laws, even obstructing their enforcement, and withholding a portion of his taxes on the grounds that they feed the immoral appetites of an illegitimate Leviathan?

These questions are raised not in the abstract by *National Review*, but in the concrete circumstances of today's judicial decisions on abortion, physician-assisted suicide (a.k.a. euthanasia), gay marriage, and social institutions and morality in general, by *First Things*. To oversimplify, it offers two broad and (we would contend) not fully compatible judgments. The first argument—advanced by Robert Bork and Hadley Arkes—is that the federal courts have abused judicial review to the point of usurping the powers of elected legislatures and thereby eroding American democracy—and that something should be done about it. *National Review* fully endorses that argument and would like to see judicial review severely curbed. But the second claim—which appears in the essays of Russell Hittinger, Robert George, and Charles Colson—is more dubious. It is that, because politicians and people have acquiesced in these judicial decisions (in effect, by not rising up to reverse them), American democracy itself has embraced a moral neutrality in the law that is oppressive toward religious citizens, hostile to any morality that can be shown to have religious roots (i.e., all of them), destructive of social institutions like marriage and family which have until now been shored up by religious morality embodied in law, and literally murderous toward the unborn—and that therefore the American democratic regime may be "illegitimate."

Of course, the stronger the first argument, the weaker the second. If the courts are our unelected rulers, then American democracy cannot be held responsible for what are undoubtedly the crimes and misdemeanors they commit. All is not yet lost, moreover. The people have allowed sovereignty to slip from them partly from an undue respect for the Supreme Court, partly from an ignorance of judicial arrogance fostered by elite journalism and the law schools, partly because they don't have all day to devote to legal questions on which they feel a sensible humility, and—to be sure—partly because they have been corrupted by decisions that have transformed sins into rights and virtues into bigotry. They may yet rise up and restore majority rule. Conservative argument should concentrate on encouraging them to do so.

Suppose, however, that Professor Hittinger's pessimism is justified. What if the American people have surrendered to a court-imposed libertinism and made it their own? Suppose American democracy is "illegitimate" not because it is undemocratic, but because it has embraced a cold amoral legalism that tramples over the rights of religious people and traditional communities. What then?

"Render unto Caesar the things that are Caesar's . . ." was addressed by Christ to the subjects of a tyrannical and unjust empire whose moral and religious views (not to mention their nationalist sentiments) were outraged daily by its edicts and practices. Christ was not, of course, counseling acceptance of morally objectionable laws—He completed the injunction ". . . and to God the things that are God's"—but He was discouraging rebellion against Rome's general authority. The grounds on which a Christian may legitimately resist lawful authority are few and hard to establish—genuine oppression, positive legal injunctions to enforce a moral evil, etc. The methods he may use are narrowly circumscribed—refusal to enforce an objectionable law sometimes, organized physical resistance to it rarely, armed uprising almost never. And his aims should be appropriately modest—the withdrawal of the law rather than the overthrow of the government.

Note that these conditions do not depend upon a government's being democratic. Our general obligation to obey the laws rests upon the fact that the laws protect us (against our fellow man), not upon the ultimate justice of the government's founding, still less (fortunately) upon its general moral character. When law and government seriously oppress us (under despotism), fail to protect us (in conditions of anarchy), or threaten our very lives (Nazism, Bolshevism, Pol Pot), then our obligations to them are correspondingly relaxed, negated, or replaced by a duty of resistance. But these circumstances are happily rare. In most times and places, we have a simple moral duty to obey the law.

If democracy is not required to justify this obligation, it nonetheless strengthens it. For democracy provides legal avenues of protest and reform which remove the justification for resistance to specific unjust laws—or at least shrink it to the level of conscientious objection and modest civil disobedience (which, to be sure, is all that Professor Hittinger *et al.* are claiming). Yet the principle is clear: because a democracy never finally makes up its mind but allows indefinite debate, it cannot be said to have embraced a crime or entrenched a sin. Our aim now should be to reclaim our democracy from the courts.

*National Review*

### *Norman Podhoretz*

I AM AMONG THOSE who interpret last November's elections as a victory for conservatism. This is obviously the case with Congress, where the Republicans held onto their control of both houses. Moreover, most of the highly conservative members of the freshman class of 1994 were reelected to the House (despite the massive amounts of money spent by the AFL-CIO to dislodge them), and in the Senate the Republicans not only increased their margin but did so in a way that on balance left it even more conservative than before.

But of course what was perhaps even more significant was the fact that Bill Clinton won the presidency by running not as a liberal but as a conservative. To rehearse what has by now become a familiar litany: Clinton declared that "the era of big government is over"; he endorsed the conservative approaches both to welfare and crime; he came out for a balanced budget; and he signed a bill designed to head off the prospect of same-sex marriages. The great exceptions (payoffs to his two most loyal constituencies, women and blacks) were his veto of legislation banning partial-birth abortions and his intransigent support of affirmative action. Yet on neither of these issues did Bob Dole, and still less Jack Kemp, take him on, and so for all practical electoral purposes, they hardly affected his newly conservative image. On another cluster of issues that might have compromised that image—Clinton's drastic cuts in the defense budget and his opposition to missile defense—the Republicans also chose to remain silent, as they did too on questions of foreign policy in general, and especially his kowtowing to China (not that they would have had anything much to say if they had spoken up).

Many conservatives predicted that Clinton, having paraded around in stolen conservative clothes in order to appeal to an electorate that he knew had moved to the Right, would discard them after winning and, with no future elections to worry about, would execute a sharp turn to the Left. Thus far, however, they have been proved wrong. The leading liberals in the White House (Harold Ickes and George Stephanopoulos) are gone and Leon Panetta has been replaced as chief of staff by Erskine Bowles, who is markedly to his right. So too, though possibly to a lesser extent, with Clinton's new cabinet, which seems less liberal than the old.

The upshot is that conservatism showed itself alive and well in the elections of 1996. But does this mean that those who hailed the 1994 elections as a "revolution" were right? Well, I for one have always thought that "counterrevolution" was a more precise term. The demand of the voters in 1994 was for a rollback of the liberal policies and institutions that had been shaping the country for more than half a century, and that counterrevolutionary demand clearly remains in force. On the other hand, there is no comparably clear revolutionary idea of what the new shaping policies and institutions should be, and defining these will be the work of the next phase of American political life.

In this context the splits in conservatism become very troubling indeed. A unified conservative movement would have played a greater role in the work ahead than the currently fractious state of conservatism will permit it to do. Yet here I disagree with the generally accepted description of the crucial fault line.

In my judgment, the really dangerous division is not the one between the "economic" and "social" conservatives, who have after all managed against all expectations to cooperate politically for quite a long time now. Nor does the real problem lie in the disagreements within the conservative community over immigration, where the two sides are beginning to find more and more common ground. The divisions on foreign policy are harder to bridge, but the debate among the interventionists, the isolationists, and the realists has thus far proceeded without generating excessive rancor. Not so the split among the "social" conservatives that has been opened up by Father Richard John Neuhaus through the *First*

*Things* symposium and that I consider the most consequential of all.

An effort has been made by Jacob Heilbrunn, writing in *The New Republic*, to represent this split as one between Jews ("neocons" or Straussians, as he alternately describes them) and Catholics ("theocons" and Thomists). This is not the first time Heilbrunn has attacked the neoconservatives for the heinous crime of associating with Christians. A couple of years ago he laced into us for allying ourselves politically with Pat Robertson and the Christian Coalition; now we are placed in the dock for having gotten mixed up with Catholics as well (in both cases for the same politically "cynical" reasons). To Heilbrunn, Christians are evidently either anti-Semitic or anti-American or both, and as such they are the "natural enemies" of Jews.

The bigotry here is as morally repulsive as Heilbrunn's incitement to a war between Christians and Jews is politically and socially pernicious. Like most other forms of bigotry, it is also based on ignorance and intellectual shoddiness.

Thus (as one grows weary of pointing out), neoconservatism is not and never has been an exclusively Jewish phenomenon. From the very beginning it included among its leading figures Protestants like Jeane Kirkpatrick, Peter L. Berger, Richard John Neuhaus, and James A. Nuechterlein, and Catholics like James Q. Wilson, Michael Novak, William J. Bennett, and George Weigel. Nor (until the *First Things* symposium) did Neuhaus's conversion from Lutheranism to Catholicism affect his identification with neoconservatism.

As for the Straussian-Thomist labels, they are equally ignorant. Very few neoconservatives were or are followers of the political philosopher Leo Strauss, and very few of the "theocons" involved in the dispute in question—including Neuhaus himself—were or are Thomists. Indeed, to the extent that the Thomists are distinguished by their belief in natural law, I myself am closer to them than I am to the Straussians. And as another prominent Catholic neoconservative, Michael Joyce of the Bradley Foundation, points out, Thomas Aquinas "in no way stood, as Heilbrunn charges, for a quick and impulsive resort to revolutionary violence in the face of non-Christian government conduct." In other words, whatever else may be animating the more heated participants in the *First Things* symposium, it is not the true spirit of Thomas Aquinas.

No, the split that has been created by the *First Things* symposium is not between Jews and Catholics, or between "neocons" and "theocons," or between Straussians and Thomists. Nor is it, as certain defenders of Neuhaus have in their own ignorance taken to declaring, between conservatives who are concerned about judicial usurpation of legislative prerogatives and those who are insensitive to the threat it poses to democracy. Far from having discovered this threat, *First Things* has merely joined in a clamor over the imperial judiciary that some of us have been raising for over twenty-five years. The only new contribution *First Things* makes is to suggest that this development has finally brought us to "the end of democracy" and that it has drained the American "regime" of "legitimacy," from which it follows all but explicitly that civil disobedience and even outright rebellion are warranted and even morally required.

My own reaction to all this was a letter to Neuhaus in which I stated that his position was reminiscent of "the extremist hysteria of the old counterculture of the 1960s" which had driven both of us out of the Left in the first place. "Speaking of the 1960s," I went on,

> back then a professor of philosophy at Columbia named Robert Paul Wolff (remember him?) said that anyone who still believed that America was a democracy belonged in an insane asylum. I responded by charging him with implicitly inciting and justifying the violent tactics of the Weathermen. Now I have to tell you in all candor that I see no significant difference between Wolff's position and the one espoused by you. . . . I am appalled by the language . . . you use to describe this country, especially your own reference to Nazi

Germany; by the seditious measures you contemplate and all but advocate; and by the aid and comfort you for all practical purposes offer to the bomb-throwers among us.

In short, if you ask me (and you have), it is not this "regime" (horrid term) that is illegitimate; it is your position.

To be sure, in another tactic reminiscent of the 1960s, when incendiary anti-American declarations were invariably given a liberal spin to make them more palatable (the radicals were only "criticizing the government," or they were usefully "calling attention to a problem"), Neuhaus now denies (in his answer to his critics in the January 1997 *First Things*) that the symposium said what so many of us understood it as saying.

Perhaps, like some of my more irenic conservative friends, I ought to take this denial as a prudential retreat under fire from an extremist position that Neuhaus finds himself unable to continue defending; perhaps I ought to welcome it as an attempt to undo the damage the symposium did to the conservative cause. But in my unreconstructed opinion, it will take much more than a 1960s-style spin to repair that damage. Nothing less than a frank and forthright recognition of error (or should I say an act of contrition?) will suffice, and of that, alas, I see no sign so far.

I have already suggested that the mandate of conservatism in the years ahead is to pursue its counterrevolutionary project (which includes, as it always has done, the fight to roll back the imperial judiciary) while striving to work out the details of a more self-respecting and a more humane alternative to the social and political depredations of the liberal ethos. The anti-Americanism of the *First Things* symposium has served to undermine and besmirch this project, just as the anti-Americanism of the Left ultimately did to the ambitions of liberalism in the post-1960s political wars. It is a wonder to me that my old friend Richard Neuhaus has forgotten what we learned while fighting those wars as comrades-in-arms against the radicalism we had both formerly espoused, and I can only hope and pray that he will (to wrap him ecumenically in a phrase from Jewish liturgy) "speedily and in our day" once more undergo a process of deradicalization and re-emerge as a born-again neoconservative.

*Commentary*

# Irwin M. Stelzer

T HAT THE CENTER OF GRAVITY of American politics has shifted to the Right, the November elections leave no doubt. Republicans held the Congress; more important, they captured the President, if not the presidency. To say that Clinton moved Right less out of conviction than of necessity is merely to prove the point: he had to move Right, undoubtedly taking flak in the cabinet room and in the bedroom, in order to survive. His finely attuned political antennae told him to get with the conservative program or contemplate an early return to Arkansas.

So conservatism is alive and well—or perhaps merely alive. For it is threatened from without with death by 1,000 cuts, and from within by the willingness of some—how many, and what proportion of all conservatives, no one knows—to expand the reach of the government they profess to distrust.

The threat from without stems from the President's proclivity to practice liberalism by stealth. Unable to raise taxes lest he give the lie to his calls for the end of welfare as we know it and to the era of big government, the President proceeds with social engineering in a barely noticeable way—by imposing on business the costs once borne directly by taxpayers, in the knowledge that businesses will pass those costs on to consumers in the form of higher prices. Thus, while espousing both tax cuts and a balanced budget, the President retains within his gift such favors as time off for child-rearing or to take the cat to the vet. He need simply order businesses to extend these benefits. Meanwhile, regulation can proceed apace, unhindered by the newly conservative mood of the voters: within days of his reelection, the President had the Environmental Protection Agency (EPA) issue expensive new regulations on air quality, and the Corps of Engineers tighten restrictions on the use of so-called "wetlands." No legislation required; no new taxes required; no fear that too many voters will wonder where the money will come from to pay for the government's new largesse.

It is this expansion-by-stealth that concerns economic conservatives. They know that there is no free home leave, no free improvement in environmental quality. The bill will be paid in the form of higher prices or of reduced profit margins, which in turn will reduce investment in productive assets. They know, too, that any hope for shrinking the government goes a-glimmerin' when agencies like the EPA effortlessly expand, or when the government increasingly sets working conditions that were once the subject of private negotiation between employer and employee, or when the Corps of Engineers can decide what a citizen can and cannot build in his back yard if he is afflicted with a small puddle that might lead his plot to be classified as a wetland.

But the moral authority of economic conservatives to resist such an expansion of government power is undermined by social conservatives who would transfer government intrusions from the boardroom into the bedroom. How to argue that the government should not be telling people what they may or may not build on their private property while at the same time arguing that it has every right to tell them what they may or may not watch on their television sets in the privacy of their homes? How to argue that the Democrats should not use the tax system as an instrument of social engineering, while at the same time demanding a child tax credit to reward parents for having children?

In short, the social conservatives, with their grand view of the role of government, drain the moral legitimacy of the program of economic conservatives who pursue the more limited goal of reducing the size and reach of government, thereby reducing the tax burden and unleashing new energies to stimulate economic growth.

There is some hope, of course, that these two camps, with such opposite views of the proper level of government intrusion in daily life, still have enough in common to forge an alliance that would be to the benefit of both factions. After all, nothing unites groups so much as a common adversary. And the President and his party represent just such a unifying force. Economic conservatives know in their hearts that the President will employ every stratagem he and his team can devise to preserve activist government, to prevent further shrinkage in the welfare state, and to keep revenues flowing into the federal coffers. And they know, too, what is in store for their dreams of rolling back the regulatory state if Messrs. Bonior, Rangel, Dingell, Waxman, and their friends in the Congress regain the committee chairs they so effectively used to pile regulation on regulation, and to urge administrators on to more and more intense paroxysms of enforcement.

Social conservatives, for their part, share their economic brethren's fear and loathing of the Clintonites. They view with more than skepticism the call of a non-inhaling pot user and MTV aficionado for a return to family values and school uniforms. Besides, for them the litmus test is abortion, and the President is so far out of line with mainstream thinking on this subject that even the most tolerant anti-abortionist has no way of cutting him any slack on this issue.

But alas, even if a working alliance can be brokered between the social and economic conservatives—and that is far from certain, as witness the former's desire to channel available funds into a child tax credit and the latter's desire to use those same monies for supply-side tax cuts—it will not permit the conservative revolution (or evolution, if you prefer; I will come to the real line-'em-up-against-the-wall revolutionaries in a moment) to proceed. For deference by economic conservatives to a group with so opposite a view of the degree to which government can properly intrude into our lives will inevitably scare off the great mass of voters who spend less time than the true believers in thinking about how they want to be governed.

Most people, instead of eagerly awaiting reports on the doings at weekend retreats for the liberal or conservative elite, examining the latest effusions of the myriad think tanks, or studying the Federal Register to learn the latest news from the regulation-writers, go about their daily lives and rely on what generally proves to be a rather shrewd appraisal of who will more or less give them what they want from government. They want to keep more of the money they earn, but not if they have to elect a movie censor to do it; they want to "get the government off of my land" (remember the old Westerns?), but not if they have to elect someone who will decide on the design of record covers; most of all, they want to be left alone, not badgered by a well-intentioned big brother to accept his notion of what separates the merely raunchy (if, indeed, merely raunchy is acceptable to the social Right) from the unacceptably obscene.

So the outlook for the conservative movement is not as bright as it might be. But it is brightened considerably by the decision of the denizens of *First Things* to come out of the closet and 'fess up to their immortal longings for a society that derives its legitimacy solely from their divinely informed approval. It has always seemed strange to me that neoconservatives, long aware that intimate relations with the totalitarian Left could only end in tears, should think they could live easily in close proximity to *First Things* conservatives who, in the end, share their hard-Left brethren's contempt for the democratic process. It is even stranger that Jewish neoconservatives should have thought they could pitch an intellectual tent broad enough to attract the prototypical former Jewish liberal "mugged by reality" and many Catholics brought up in a tradition that does not welcome dissent from its revealed truths. Jewish intellectuals may be useful exponents of some of the positions of *First Things* Catholics, but they should not expect to be partners in a governing theocracy.

Perhaps—and it is only a perhaps—the unraveling of the alliance between the neoconservatives and the *First Things* crowd will liberate the former to seek the support of more natural allies.

If so, conservatism has a bright future. If not, we may be in for a Gore-y 2000.

*Commentary*

## George Weigel

CONFRONTED YET AGAIN by a weak and vacillating liberal mistrusted by the electorate, economic conservatism in 1996 managed to garner less than forty percent of the presidential vote for the second election in a row—in no small part because the Republican nominee failed to ignite the enthusiasm of social conservatives and exploit the liberal candidate's most glaring vulnerability. In the wake of this political failure, might we revisit in a less wooden way the question of the relationship between conservatives whose primary concern is governmental intrusion into the market and conservatives who are chiefly motivated by questions of culture? Tensions between these groups are to be expected, especially in matters of tactical politics. But they need not be mortal enemies.

The reason has to do with the relationship between free economies and the moral culture of the societies in which those economies function. The market is not an independent variable in the free society, as we have been reminded by Michael Novak, Francis Fukuyama, and other analysts of the cultural preconditions essential for the flourishing of a free economy. Absent a public moral culture capable of disciplining and channeling the explosive human energies set free by the market, the virtues—the moral habits—essential to making the market work will wither and die. But the idea that a people's capacity for self-command has a lot to do with their ability to make the market work did not originate with contemporary social conservatives (although these conservatives have deepened and broadened our understanding of that nexus). Adam Smith, the author of *The Theory of Moral*

*Sentiments* as well as *The Wealth of Nations,* was no intellectual schizophrenic.

What happens when the state legitimates behaviors that erode the moral foundations of civil society, and then declares those behaviors and that legitimation beyond the reach of democratic process? When the state attempts to establish, as the official national creed, a crudely utilitarian ethic based on a distorted notion of freedom as radical individual autonomy, the free economy is in serious trouble. So is the democratic polity. Does anyone deny this? If so, to what historical warrants would they appeal in arguing for the possibility of sustaining democratic capitalism on a foundation of decadence?

Contemporary American conservatism seems less a "movement" to me than a complex community of conversation built around certain commonly shared premises. Principled anti-Communism, which regarded Marxism-Leninism not only as a political and military threat but as a moral perversion, was one of those binding premises during the cold war. Then, sharply chiseled moral judgments were not regarded as inimical to conservative political effectiveness. On the contrary, they were regarded as essential: first, because the judgments were true in themselves; and second, because they were crucial in combating a soft liberalism and a radicalism of "moral equivalence" which could not comprehend, much less withstand, the Communist threat. So within the living memory of this symposium's participants, conservatives seem not to have been indisposed to moral argument as a part of the core, not the periphery, of public affairs.

A second premise I had assumed to be part of the conservative intellectual patrimony also had thick moral content: the premise that neither democracy nor the market was a machine that could run of itself. Put positively, the premise was that, in addition to a market economy and a democratic polity, the free society included a public moral culture that was crucial to the proper functioning of both free economics and free politics. I trust that that premise is not now being denied in some conservative quarters. If it is, then we really do face a parting of the ways. There is room for reasonable debate about the state's role in fostering that public morality; we can also debate which specific bricks are necessary to the free society's moral foundation. But the premise itself seems to me essential, and its recognition in the way we conduct our politics is crucial for American democracy. The American people have historically believed themselves to be engaged in a moral enterprise when they did their public business and when they defended their country from its enemies. To deny them the capacity to act publicly on that conviction is undemocratic.

As someone "present at the creation" of the discussion that led to the *First Things* symposium in that journal's November 1996 issue, I can speak with some authority about its intentions. The intention, briefly, was to sharpen our sense of urgency about the present establishment of three interrelated ideas as a government-sanctioned ideology in the United States—ideas which one had assumed to be repugnant to conservatives. The first of these ideas is philosophical-anthropological: that the human person is an autonomous, self-constituting Self. The second idea is ethical: that freedom is a matter of doing what I choose precisely because I choose it. The third idea is political: that democracies must protect the exercise of freedom-as-license by autonomous selves so long as nobody in whom the state declares a "compelling interest" gets hurt.

None of these ideas has any tether to the American Founding and the Founders' understanding of republican virtue. Mixed together, they form a lethal ideological cocktail. For on this account of democracy, the only relevant actors in society are the autonomous individual and the state. Conservatives used to have a word for what lay at the end of that particular road: we called it "totalitarianism." The totalitarian temptation seems built into modernity. Democracies are not preternaturally immune to it. Our immunization comes from the moral culture that makes democracy possible.

There is a lesson to be learned here from contemporary American conservatism's most notable achievement: the collapse of Communism. Communism failed for many reasons; stupid economics was married to brutal politics and legitimated by philosophical nonsense. But the latter, the philosophical absurdities, were the key to the rest. Yes, the Communist project collapsed because of Western grit and Western military capacities and the heroism of the human-rights resistance in East Central Europe. But, at bottom, Communism failed because it was *wrong*: because it was based on a defective concept of the human person and human community—including political community and economic interaction.

A similar failure in the public philosophy of the democracies, eroding public moral culture and the virtues essential to transforming raw plurality into genuine pluralism, would have the gravest results. Autonomous selves cannot be democrats indefinitely. Autonomous selves can give no compelling account of their commitment to democratic civility, religious tolerance, or the procedures of democratic self-governance. Autonomous selves cannot imagine making the sacrifices necessary to defend freedom from its enemies.

The language of "regimes" and "regime legitimacy" is not well-fitted for getting at these issues, for this vocabulary takes insufficient account of America as a "proposition country," a distinctive democratic experiment conceived as the working-out of a set of truth-claims. But disagreements over the vocabulary for accurately describing our circumstances ought not mask this fact: the *First Things* symposium raised questions that are unavoidable for the future of conservative politics.

Has the Supreme Court, in its increasingly bizarre attempts to justify its policy preferences in the matters of abortion and homosexuality, "established" by fiat a national creed incompatible with the religious and moral convictions of biblically formed Americans? Is that creed now being imposed on individual citizens and local communities by the federal regulatory apparatus and the educational bureaucracies of the federal and state governments? Does the fact of that establishment—does the content of that ersatz creed—attack the moral-cultural foundations of Ameri-can democracy? Is America merely a republic of procedures —increasingly, procedures of litigation and judicial legislation— by which autonomous selves regulate their conflicts? Or is America a substantive moral experiment in a people's capacity for self-governance? These are "radical" questions, not in some debased 1960s sense of "radicalism" but because they force us to think through, once again, the basic ("root," *radix*) truths to which the Founders pledged their lives, fortunes, and sacred honor in creating this *Novus Ordo Seclorum* called the United States of America.

Speaking in Baltimore on October 8, 1995, Pope John Paul II suggested that Lincoln's question at Gettysburg—whether a nation conceived in liberty and dedicated to the proposition that all men are created equal could long endure—was a question for every generation of Americans. I think that is exactly right. To press that Lincolnian question into public debate today does not demean the many virtues of the American people, manifest in millions of individual lives and in what the legal scholar Mary Ann Glendon has called "communities of memory and mutual aid." Nor is it to hold the United States accountable to an abstract moral standard that no real-world polity could possibly achieve. Nor is it to declare oneself ready to engage in insurrection (which the editors of *First Things* have explicitly denied was their inten-tion). It is, however, to acknowledge that there is nothing "given" about the success of American democracy, and that securing the future of democratic politics and free economics requires us to strengthen, steadily, the nation's moral-cultural foundations. Because democracy is not, and cannot be, an infinite series of pragmatic accommodations, made on vulgarized utilitarian grounds.

This is reminiscent of Burke's conservatism in his critique of Jacobinism and his defense of the small platoons and their essen-tial social function. Those functions, when they are not being declared illegitimate by the Supreme Court, are increasingly usurped by a Court-driven federal government which imagines itself the defender of enlightened opinion against the unwashed masses and their stubborn adherence to traditional virtues and values. That kind of conservative critique of the functioning of our democracy, rooted as it is in an affirmation of the moral value of the American experiment, has about as much to do with Tom Hayden and Stokely Carmichael as it does with the public philosophy of Genghis Khan.

*Commentary*

## *Correspondence,* FIRST THINGS

I ENTIRELY AGREE with those contributors to the symposium who maintain that the judiciary has vastly exceeded its proper powers and that this is a very serious problem for our polity. But I do not at all agree that this raises the specter of the illegitimacy of our government.

Slavery did not illegitimize the Founding, as some radical historians suggest. Nor did the Vietnam War (an "unjust war," many claimed) illegitimize the government at that time. By the same token, the appalling errors of the present judiciary (in respect to abortion particularly) do not illegitimize the government today. If abortion is the litmus test of a moral law that cannot be violated by positive law, then all of the Western democracies that legalize abortion—and do so by the legislative rather than the judicial process—are illegitimate. (Indeed, the only legitimate governments would be Iraq, Iran, and the like.)

The Editors' Introduction cites the American Revolution as if we are now in a similarly revolutionary situation—an analogy that, in my opinion (and that, I believe, of the overwhelming majority of Americans), is absurd and irresponsible. It also cites a papal encyclical affirming the supremacy of the moral law. But the pope did not declare Nazi Germany or the Soviet Union illegitimate, despite the genocide and mass murders, which were surely as much violations of the moral law as abortion.

The use of the word "regime" compounds the problem, for it suggests that it is not the legitimacy of a particular institution or branch of government that is at stake but the very nature of our government.

This is not, it seems to me, a proper mode of political discourse, still less of conservative political discourse. Indeed it discredits, or at the very least makes suspect, any attempt by conservatives to introduce moral and religious considerations into "the public square"—as if morality and religion necessarily lead to such apocalyptic political conclusions. It can only confirm many Americans in their suspicion that cultural conservatism is outside the "mainstream" of American politics, that it is "extremist," even subversive.

I am not reassured by the promise that this is only the opening round of the discussion, that this magazine (and other journals as well) will continue to explore this theme and present different points of view. On the contrary, in my opinion this aggravates the problem, for it focuses attention even more on a subject that is not and should not be a subject of contention. It makes it sound as if the legitimacy of the government is a major concern of conservatives, and this is precisely the idea that I find unacceptable.

It is with great regret that I am resigning from the Editorial Board of *First Things*, a journal with which I have been proud to be associated. But you have raised so grave and, in my opinion, irresponsible an issue, and given it such prominence, that I cannot, in good conscience, continue to serve on the board.

*Gertrude Himmelfarb*

YOU DO NOT SPEAK FOR ME (a member of the Editorial Advisory Board since the inception of the journal) when you say that the government of the United States is morally illegitimate and come close to advocating not only civil disobedience but armed revolution. I don't care to engage in an argument with you; I want simply to announce my resignation from the advisory board. Please remove my name from the masthead.

*Walter Berns*

WHILE I DO NOT RETRACT a word of my criticism of the judiciary's usurpation of democractic powers, I wish that my remarks had not been preceded by the Editors' suggestion that we may "have reached or are reaching the point where conscientious citizens can no longer give moral assent to the existing regime." My criticism of the courts was not intended to support any such proposition. The necessity for reform, even drastic reform, does not call the legitimacy of the entire American "regime" into question.

*Robert H. Bork*

## *The Editors of* FIRST THINGS

THE SYMPOSIUM on the judicial usurpation of politics has generated an intense debate about many things, as is evident in the above responses. Obviously, this is a debate that will continue. William Bennett is right: the stakes are indeed high. They are too high to indulge any desire to score debating points. Our hope is to move toward a conversation that is calm, deliberate, and keenly aware of the implications of conclusions reached.

We deeply regret the resignations of valued friends who believe this entire discussion is out of order. Their distress no doubt reflects honest disagreement, but also, we believe, misunderstanding. Neither the editorial introduction nor the essays in the symposium asserted that the government of the United States is illegitimate. We thought that was made clear, but apparently not. The editorial distinguished between the judicial usurpation of politics, which we called the current regime, and the polity defined by the Constitution. The editorial said: "What is happening now is the displacement of a constitutional order by a regime that does not have, will not obtain, and cannot command the consent of the people."

What we called the regime is an aberration. We do not agree that the judicial usurpation of politics is inevitable or irreversible, that it is, in fact, to be equated with the government of the United States. It is this regime of the judicial usurpation of politics that is illegitimate. We are sorry that this crucial distinction was not clear to some of our readers. It seems part of the difficulty is in the use of the term "regime," which in some political theory has a very definite and comprehensive connotation. In order to avoid confusion, we suggest the term should be used with caution, if at all, as the discussion continues.

Of course, the question inevitably arises as to whether the aberration is somehow inherent in the constitutional order itself, in which case some may argue that it is not, properly speaking, an aberration. In the symposium, Judge Bork writes: "On the evidence, we must conclude, I think, that this tendency of courts, including the Supreme Court, is the inevitable result of our written Constitution and the power of judicial review." An aberration that is, in retrospect, seen as an inevitable result is still an aberration.

The Founders may be accused of a lack of prescience, but it is certain that they did not intend a government by what Bork calls judicial oligarchy. All the participants in the symposium, with the editors, believe that the aberration of a nation governed by judges is not irreversible. Different remedies are suggested and varying degrees of hopefulness are expressed about the likelihood of their being adopted or, if adopted, whether they will be effective.

But there should be no doubt that the symposium is an urgent call for the American people to reassert the theory and practice of democratic self-government and thus revive the republic bequeathed us by the Founders.

It is said that the question of illegitimate government is not and should not be a subject of contention. That, some contend, is a question that was agitated in the radicalisms of the 1960s, and should now be consigned to the past and declared undiscussable. While the editors are not of one mind as to how the discussion should proceed, the question was a subject of contention, also in our pages, before the November symposium, and will continue to be a subject of contention, whether or not we want it to be. The question of legitimate and illegitimate government, and what it means for the governance of this country, *should* be a subject of contention. It has been that since the founding of this republic, and will be so long as it endures. To give the experience of the 1960s veto power over the democratic discourse of today is to grant the madnesses of that time a victory that they do not deserve.

Respondents remind us that the problem is more with the culture than with the courts. We wholeheartedly agree. The operating premise of *First Things* is that politics and law are, most importantly, aspects of culture. At the heart of culture is morality, and at the heart of morality is religion. No one can fairly accuse this journal of neglecting our cultural crisis. Professor Glendon and others render an important service by placing this discussion in the context of what she calls the several "pathologies in the body politic." The question of the judicial usurpation of politics is not the most critical question facing our country. The most critical question is that of spiritual and moral reawakening. The judicial usurpation of politics was, however, the question posed for discussion in the November issue. And, as that symposium amply demonstrates, it is a question closely related to the spiritual and moral, as well as political, health of the body politic.

We did not choose this controversy. It was started by a judiciary, and most particularly by a Supreme Court, that has increasingly arrogated to itself the legislative and executive functions of government. In more recent years, the judiciary has disregarded and nullified the democratic deliberations and decisions of the American people on how we ought to order our life together, which is the subject matter of politics. That is what is meant by the judicial usurpation of politics. The Supreme Court itself, notably in the *Casey* decision of 1992, has raised the question of the legitimacy of its rulings, and called upon the people to ratify that legitimacy by following its lead. We believe the governed have not given their consent to being governed by the courts, unless ignorance and indifference are construed as consent.

At question here is not merely a series of errors, even appalling errors, in particular court decisions. *If* the judiciary continues on its present course, *if* it does not restrain itself, and *if* there is no way to restrain it, we are witnessing the end of democracy. And when we speak of the end of democracy it is not inappropriate to allude to the authoritarian and totalitarian alternatives to democracy, no matter how uncomfortable such allusions may be. In no way do the editors assume that such restraint of the judiciary is impossible. We wrote in our introduction, "We hope that more people know and more people care than is commonly supposed, and that it is not too late for effective recourse to whatever remedies may be available. It is in the service of that hope that we publish this symposium." That was and is our earnest intention. We probably cannot do much about critics who choose to think that we do not intend what we say we intend.

Judicial activism, as it is called, is nothing new. The problem today is not one of degrees in judicial activism. There has been a qualitative change. It is not a matter of the judiciary stretching its authority in order to act when action is necessary and the other branches of government are paralyzed, as was arguably the case with racial segregation. Robert Bork, among many others, has made the constitutional case that the *Brown* decision of 1954 was rightly decided, and it has, in any event, been effectively ratified by the consent of the people.

In subsequent years, something very different has been happening. Judges, no doubt emboldened by the moral aura emanating from *Brown*, routinely assume that it is their prerogative to make the big decisions about how we ought to order our life together. On issue after issue, government by judicial fiat is no longer the exception but the rule. Arbitrary judicial preferences are speciously constitutionalized. Among the virtues of democracy, Justice Antonin Scalia has written, is that it allows the people to argue with one another, persuade one another, and to change their minds. "That system is destroyed," says Scalia, "if the smug assurances of each age are removed from the democratic process and written into the Constitution. Our ancestors left us free to change. The same cannot be said of this most illiberal Court."

This most illiberal Court and the judicial system for which it sets the pace are set on a course that has done serious damage to democracy and will, unless checked, result in the end of democratic government in this country. Again, we believe the courts can be checked and hope they will be checked. But perhaps not. If not, we should be reminded that most people have lived and do live under governments that are not democratic, and we Americans might get used to it as well. Yet the loss of democratic self-government is not just a political loss.

The development of Christian thought over time has led to an understanding that democracy is morally imperative. It was very deliberate that, in the issue immediately preceding the November symposium, we published the declaration "Christianity and Democracy," which sets forth the case for that imperative. Not all Christians share this understanding of the democratic imperative, but it is powerfully supported also by Catholic social teaching, as witness in particular the 1991 encyclical *Centesimus Annus* ("The Hundredth Year"). In this view, there is an important connection between democratic government and legitimate government.

Democracy can assume different forms, and governments that do not style themselves as democratic are not necessarily illegitimate. Remember, too, that the Communist totalitarianism of our century spuriously claimed to be democratic. For a discussion of the institutions and practices that mark authentic democracy, we refer the reader to the above-mentioned "Christianity and Democracy." For present purposes, we note only that a government, such as ours, that makes its claim to legitimacy on the basis of democratic theory and practice raises a question about its legitimacy when it violates democratic theory and practice. The judicial usurpation of politics is a grievous violation of democratic theory and practice.

Our position, our hope, is that this violation has not been perpetrated by the government of the United States. It does not have and will not obtain the consent of the executive and legislative branches nor of the sovereign people. The people and their representatives have not, in the words of Lincoln's First Inaugural, addressing the Supreme Court's decision in *Dred Scott,* "practically resigned their government into the hands of that eminent tribunal." The problem before us is precisely one of judicial *usurpation.*

Anarchy and despotism are indeed to be greatly feared, but it is not we who are raising that prospect. That prospect is raised by the courts that deny the democratic deliberation of vital questions affecting the whole people. Lincoln in the same address: "A majority, held in restraint by constitutional checks, and limitations, and always changing easily, with deliberate changes of popular opinions and sentiments, is the only true sovereign of a free people. Whoever rejects it, does, of necessity, fly to anarchy or to despotism. Unanimity is impossible; the rule of a minority, as a permanent arrangement, is wholly inadmissible; so that, rejecting the majority principle, anarchy, or despotism in some form, is all that is left."

Permanent rule by the small minority that is the judicial elite is wholly inadmissible. It is our hope that the people and their political leaders will come to share that conviction and give it public effect. Some object that there have been many wrongs in the past—for instance, slavery and the Vietnam War—that did not raise the question of legitimacy. Distinctions are in order. The toleration of slavery was an ominous and deliberate compromise in the founding. Many people, with Lincoln, believed that the eventual extinction of slavery was intended by the Founders. The Vietnam War, whatever one may think of its justice, was a failed policy of the executive and legislative branches. The judicial usurpation of politics is qualitatively different. In *Roe, Casey, Romer*, and other decisions, this most illiberal Court has imposed not only what we believe are wrong policies, but has imposed them in the form of unchallengeable constitutional principles.

The sense of crisis is intensified because these illegitimate impositions, both past and in prospect, are on matters of great public gravity. The legal killing of millions of unborn children, the extension of that license to kill the sick and elderly, the redefinition of marriage and family, the unlimited tolerance of pornography, the exclusion of religion from public life—these and others are what Lincoln called vital questions affecting the whole people. The judicial removal of these public questions from democratic deliberation and decision is the more insidious and difficult to resist because it is frequently done in the name of enhancing privacy and the rights of the autonomous self. Moreover, many politicians who prefer not to address difficult and morally laden questions, or who share the policy preferences of the courts, are actively complicit in the judicial usurpation of politics.

Government by the judiciary and the waning of democratic politics should not be viewed as an exclusively conservative concern. Writing in *Dissent*, Michael Walzer, a prominent liberal philosopher, cautions that the nation's rules are increasingly made without regard to what the majority thinks the rules should be. Because of the role of judicial and other elites, Walzer writes, "there is a sense in which the 'left' or some vulgarized version of the left [has] dominated the culture" for the last several decades, although "many Americans experienced this left culture as something alien, frightening, or deeply disturbing." Liberals who care about the American democratic experiment, and many do, should take Walzer's warning to heart, recognizing that, despite the attraction of short-term gains for their policy preferences, the tyranny of the minority is in accord neither with their beliefs nor their long-term interests.

Perhaps the most ominous development is the growing explicitness with which the judiciary rejects any moral law superior to the law of the state, as defined by the courts. The Supreme Court decisions analyzed in detail in the November symposium would seem to declare that the Judeo-Christian moral tradition has no standing in our polity. More than that, the Court suggests in *Romer* that citizens whose vote is motivated by "an ethic and morality which transcends human invention" are illegitimately imposing their religion upon others. That claim figures prominently also in circuit court decisions on assisted suicide that are now before the Supreme Court.

Almost all Americans claim adherence to an ethic and morality that transcends human invention, and for all but a relatively small minority, that adherence is expressed in terms of biblical religion. By the strange doctrine promulgated by the courts, Christians, Jews, and others who adhere to a transcendent morality would, to the extent that their actions as citizens are influenced by that morality, be effectively disenfranchised. It is a doctrine that ends up by casting religious Americans, traditionally the most loyal of citizens, into the role of enemies of the public order. We cannot help but believe that the courts do not intend that consequence. They must be given every possible encouragement to abandon the reckless course they are presently pursuing.

In this discussion, a number of legal remedies have been proposed. They should be carefully examined and, where possible, urgently pressed. The symposium also includes a survey of possible responses if or when remedies fail, ranging from noncompliance to civil disobedience to organized resistance to justified revolution.

That reflection is part of a very long tradition of moral and political thought about legitimate responses to illegitimate government. As explained above, we do not believe that the government of the United States is illegitimate. Ours is not a revolutionary situation and, please God, will never become that. Like those who signed the Declaration of Independence, we are today confronted by a "long train of abuses and usurpations." We believe that the republic that emerged from their revolution has the means to redress today's abuses and usurpations.

Nor have we issued a call to civil disobedience. Individuals cannot in conscience obey laws that contravene the moral law, but that is very different from an organized program of civil disobedience on the model of, for instance, the civil rights movement led by Martin Luther King Jr. And both are different from Robert Bork's suggestion in the symposium that an elected official might refuse to obey a decision of the Supreme Court. Bork writes, "To the objection that the rejection of a court's authority would be civil disobedience, the answer is that a court that issues orders without authority engages in an equally dangerous form of civil disobedience." As Lincoln insisted, public officials who are sworn to uphold the Constitution have a duty to interpret the Constitution. To give the judiciary a monopoly on constitutional interpretation is an abdication of public responsibility.

Yes, there is a danger that the very discussion of these matters could be exploited by the violent who do not share our devotion to this constitutional order and the rule of law. As the specter of illegitimacy is raised by justices in black robes who replace the rule of law with their personal predilections, so the specter of violent revolution is raised by angry men in army fatigues playing war games in the woods of Idaho. We believe, however, that the delusions of weekend revolutionaries should not set the boundaries of political discussion. Indeed, acquiescence in judicial usurpation, far from warding off extremism, would likely increase the number of Americans who believe there is no alternative to violent change. We therefore call for the vigorous pursuit of every peaceful and constitutional means to return our country to its democratic heritage, and to encourage its people to take up again what Professor Glendon calls the hard work of being citizens rather than subjects.

Some critics claim that the symposium and its reverberations prove once again that religion in the public square is a subversive force. There is a strong element of truth in that. Certainly authentic religion cannot be captive to any political or ideological movement, whether of the right or of the left. The crisis of the judicial usurpation of politics is not created, however, by religion's problem with the judiciary. It is created by the judiciary's problem with religion. Indeed, it is created by the judiciary's problem with being held accountable, in accord with the will of the people, to any judgment other than its own. In *Casey* the Court worried about the legitimacy of the law that it is making. It is right to worry. It should be more worried than it apparently is. If, as we hope, we are not on the way to the end of democracy, the judiciary will restrain itself, or it will be restrained.

# PART III

# THE WAR OF THE ROSES

## *The Editors of* NATIONAL REVIEW

SOME OF THE ISSUES raised by *First Things* point to ultimate divisions; others derive from temperamental reflexes. In the abstract, the point is obviously reachable when a rogue society forfeits the loyalty of responsible and courageous citizens. It is not always easy to recognize that point, which often passes by societies that wake to find a despotism in power. Norman Podhoretz was greatly disturbed at the sentence in Father Neuhaus's introduction in which he spoke of Hitler Germany. Father Neuhaus was complaining about a society that yielded critical authority to a Supreme Court that openly disavows higher law than that of its own making. But surely the point to reflect on, especially between scholars as engaged intellectually and personally as Richard John Neuhaus and Norman Podhoretz, is the uses of simile. That Hitler is different from the Supreme Court of the United States does not disable the analyst whose purpose is to point out what similarities there are—in this case, moral usurpation; indeed, a denial of moral language. What Colson and Arkes and Hittinger and George and Bork, and *First Things* editor Neuhaus, are saying is that the time has come to reformulate one's compliance with a democratic society whose laws are no longer set by the people.

The problem is in part temperamental because there are different orders of historical patience involved. The way to look after and dispose of the problem of the Supreme Court, the neocons are telling us, is to batter its decisions intellectually, arouse moral protest, discipline the Court with a symbolic constitutional amendment, and get back on that historical trajectory of American exceptionalism that has given the Republic a general congruity with enlightened views of human behavior. It took us almost one hundred years to free the slaves, but that is what we ended up doing. Another hundred to translate legal freedom into sociological freedom, but we did that also. Along the way we discovered the rights of women, and acknowledged some basic international responsibilities. Though Neuhaus is hardly preaching the way of John Brown, some of his critics speak as if that were the ultimate meaning of the *First Things* manifesto.

Most conservatives see it as something else, namely a call to focus on what has been happening. First, the Court described (*Roe v. Wade*) a human right to terminate life by abortion, then it refused (*Planned Parenthood*) to acknowledge any right to political interposition, then it denied society's right (*Romer*) to pronounce on homosexuality, now it threatens (*Baehr*) to sanction homosexual "marriage" and dallies with euthanasia (*Glucksberg*). The *First Things* essays ask not for revolutionary defiance, but for organic thought given to the attenuation of loyalties. The moment can come when loyalty is severed.

*National Review*'s position is intellectually combative, temperamentally pragmatic. We sanction, and indeed have given space to, the fine thinking of such as Hadley Arkes and Father Neuhaus on the terrible exercises of judicial enactments. But we have never condoned protests in any other form than political and intellectual. There are those (none of them associated with *First Things*) who would shoot the abortionists and bomb buildings as expressions of defiance. The world is familiar with hardy expressions of protest, as with the monks in South Vietnam who served themselves up in flames to protest Diem. Martyrdom can be a noble calling, but it is not a regimental maneuver. Most conservatives will acknowledge the usefulness of sharpening the discriminating faculties that allocate loyalties; but they will decline a war against our political regime, and most emphatically decline a war against our brethren, the neocons.

*National Review*

# THE ANTI-AMERICAN
# TEMPTATION

### David Brooks

THE *FIRST THINGS* CONTROVERSY is more than just a tempest in a conservative teapot. It raises one of the more interesting questions of the moment: Is the Right about to go anti-American? Already, many conservatives are profoundly disturbed by the calm way the American public seems to have accepted Bill Clinton's character, and find themselves asking the same questions as Ross Perot: "Is there no sense of decency in this country?" And now, along comes *First Things*, questioning the legitimacy of the American government itself.

*First Things* is a magazine about religion and the public square, and Richard John Neuhaus is a leading proponent of the idea that religion must play a larger role in political life. A certain number of people who regard the symposium as alarmist or worse will say it proves how dangerous it can be to bring a religious sensibility into close contact with politics. Those who apply religious principles directly to politics, their opponents will say, measure the political realm by moral criteria that are inappropriately abstract. They consider declaring government morally illegitimate when decisions don't go their way. Thus, religion can breed apocalyptic extremism and zealous outbursts.

Neuhaus argues that no topic should be out of bounds for discussion and that the radical nature of the recent court crisis demands new types of thinking in response. This symposium is only the beginning of the discussion, he maintains. "Most people throughout history have lived under dubious regimes," Neuhaus says. "It may well be that the end result of this discussion will be that we will have to get used to asking how you live in an order that is morally dubious and not amenable to change. This symposium will look like the last gasp of American exceptionalism."

Modern American conservatism rose by changing its character. What had been a prosaic, incrementalist political clique became a visionary, ideological creed. So it's perhaps fitting that if conservatism rose to political power by wedding itself to abstract ideas, it should also withdraw from political power because of that tendency.

Long gone is the thing that used to be known as the Conservative Temper. This is the mood that fears change, distrusts abstract notions, reveres the here and now, and is obsessed by historical continuity. That style of conservatism was extinguished, many conservatives would say, when the unconscious assumptions upon which it was based were challenged by the 1960s. Suddenly the just prejudices that nobody had much thought about—for example, that the two-parent heterosexual family is naturally superior—were called into question. Conservatives could no longer just mutely cherish and preserve. They had to argue for propositions that had previously been unquestioned. They needed to put into words things that had been accepted as given, and they needed to apply abstract ideals to political debate. Some secular conservatives took the ideals of the free market and applied them to politics. Some religious conservatives brought their religious beliefs more closely to bear on political issues.

The new conservative style, based on conscious fealty to abstract ideals and beliefs, is not necessarily bad. But it does contain its own dangers. What happens, for example, when the nation doesn't live up to the high ideals and shows no prospect of doing so? Maybe the people themselves are corrupt. Maybe they have become morally deadened, quite untroubled by the fact that 1.3 million abortions are performed every year. Or maybe the people are not corrupt, but are still in the sway of a corrupt elite whose hold on the leading institutions gives it the power to determine the course of the nation. What happens, in short, when the conservative finds he loves his ideals more than his country?

The first thing that happens is that the conservative (maybe it is more accurate to call him "orthodox" because of his love of abstract ideals) starts proposing radical solutions in an effort to jerk his country back to where he thinks it should be. Radical revolution is the opposite of the original Conservative Temper. But revolutionary talk has become common in conservative circles. Robert Bork has a proposal that would radically alter the constitutional order, one that would allow the Congress to overturn by majority vote any Supreme Court decision. Other conservatives would pass a constitutional amendment doing away with judicial review.

The other thing such people do is hold debates about whether they can support their government. "Jefferson was too reckless when he said the ground of democracy needed to be watered every thirty years by the blood of revolution," Neuhaus says, "but we should raise fundamental questions and look things over from time to time." That sentiment in favor of a return to first principles is the antithesis of the Conservative Temper.

Religious thinkers who are active in the public square do not want to avoid debates about first things. And they *will* dwell on when the sovereignty of God demands breaking off loyalty to nation. They will cite, as the contributors to the *First Things* symposium do, the many different ways theologians have addressed this question over the centuries. They will declare, as Neuhaus does, that the phrase "God and country" should not come tripping off the tongue because the two are not necessarily linked.

If conservatives feel that they love their ideals more than their country, then you will see them withdrawing from public life, as Charles Colson warns religious conservatives will. If they find that the revelations about Bill Clinton's character produce no response in a public too deadened to care about certain standards, then they will become more interested in preserving small communities of virtue than in influencing the entire nation. If they decide that the political elites are impervious to reason, or simply ignore reason, then they will abandon reasoned argument and simply deliver caustic commentaries on their opponents' unreason.

That is the trend *Washington Times* columnist Tod Lindberg noticed in Antonin Scalia's recent dissents. Such a conservatism won't present a very happy face to the world. It would console itself with the glories of transcendence and hope these could compensate for its abandonment of the here and now.

American conservatism is far from going down this road. Many conservatives still think history is moving in their direction. They interpret Clinton's resurgence as an odd confirmation of the conservatism of the time; he has adopted many conservative-sounding policies and is more comfortable with being religious in public than any president since Jimmy Carter. They note that while the judiciary is headed in the wrong direction on abortion and gay marriage, it has been handing down comforting judgments on school choice and the role of religion in public (and on affirmative action). They retain faith in the wisdom of the American people, in their ability to eventually correct the errors of their courts, and in the basic health of the American government.

But the *First Things* symposium, while still an outlier, may also be a harbinger. American conservatism is based on abstract ideals, and if there is a wave of disenchantment on the right it will take the form we see here. It will call America into question in the name of higher things.

The Republican party proudly calls itself the party of ideas. Well, Republicans had better learn to take the good with the bad. Idea-driven people are quick to abandon political parties. They have been known to fly off the handle. And intellectuals sometimes blithely engage in discussion of civil disobedience and revolution, as if talk of these horrendous subjects had no real-world consequences.

Two years ago, in the midst of the controversy over *The Bell Curve*, one writer did warn his fellows that not all subjects are fit for public discussion. "America is not an academic seminar limited to a few utterly dispassionate and socially disengaged intellectuals interested only in 'the truth'," he declared. That writer, of course, was Richard John Neuhaus.

*The Weekly Standard*


## Samuel Francis


R ECRIMINATIONS AMONG neoconservatives are always amusing, if only for the polemical nastiness with which they are conducted. Yet the significance of the controversy over the *First Things* symposium reaches well beyond mere irony. Its meaning was to some extent elucidated by David Brooks, who noted that it exuded "a tone of crisis, a sense that history itself is moving in the wrong direction," and that this "is a tone mainstream conservatives have not used in a long while."

Of course, what Brooks means by "mainstream conservatives" is neoconservatives. Among paleoconservatives, the view that history is moving in the wrong direction is and always has been a commonplace. One of the basic assumptions of almost all schools of paleoconservative thought has always been that something—in America, the West, or the Modern Age—has gone wrong.

This is not true for the neocons, whose adoption of a species of conservatism is predicated on the essential rightness of modern

American government and society, the direction of its historical course, and the Modern Age in general. Indeed, it was the anti-American thrust of the New Left that precipitated the neocons' break with the left, and as they have made clear over the years, the neoconservatives are unable to distinguish the anti-Americanism of the left from the conservative and fundamentally patriotic critique of American history and culture mounted by paleoconservatives. At peace with the direction of history, the neoconservatives emerge not as serious critics of the current regime, but rather as its inveterate defenders and apologists. Thus their contributions to political debate have been largely limited to policy prescriptions that merely build on or seek to ameliorate the current structures of the American state and society, and anyone, on the left or right, who suggests a more radical deviation from those structures is denounced as an "extremist," a "bomb-thrower," and an "anti-American." Neoconservatism is thus fundamentally a defense of the status quo, a political formula with which the dominant left can be content because it does not seriously challenge the premises and power structure that the left has constructed and uses for its own hegemony.

When the neocons at *First Things* arrive at the conclusion that something really is wrong in America, and when they start muttering about the possible "illegitimacy" of the "regime," then what they are driving toward is something very close to paleo-conservatism. What the dispute reveals is the emergence of a paleoconservative tendency among the neoconservatives at Neuhaus's magazine, and what the hysterical reaction of the senior neocons to the symposium represents is a determination to squelch this tendency before it begins to blossom into a full-blown paleo-conservative defection that would leave the neocon sagamores perched on the roofs of their own wigwam while the waters of right-wing dissidence swirl ever higher and ever closer to their noses. When Podhoretz writes to Neuhaus that "I did not become a conservative in order to be a radical," that he has no intention of discussing the legitimacy of the regime – "not again, not twice in a single lifetime, not after going around and around that track twenty-five and thirty years ago"—he is not talking merely about his break with the left but also about his and his fellow neocons' decade-long effort to housebreak the American right into a tame running dog of history.

Yet, to be sure, Podhoretz and his friends have a point. A good deal of the discussion of "legitimacy" in the *First Things* symposium is careless, if not outright ignorant, of elementary political theory. In the first place, the whole symposium is couched in terms of the Henry David Thoreau–William Lloyd Garrison–Martin Luther King concept of legitimacy, whereby any deviation of a political order from a privately perceived and vaguely defined "higher law" or "dictate of conscience" justifies disobedience, if not outright resistance. Throughout its pages the symposium sports sidebars of quotations from King and Garrison, and several of the contributors assume the validity of a dubious equivalence between abortion and slavery or segregation. Most of them seem to be unaware that in classical political philosophy, such subjective standards for resistance are impermissible. Classical as well as traditional Christian political theory holds that disobedience is incumbent on the subject only when the regime commands *him* to violate generally known and accepted divine, natural, or human law, and instances of such passive disobedience are known in both history and literature—Socrates, commanded by the Thirty Tyrants to commit murder, simply ignored their order and went home; Antigone, in Sophocles' tragedy, insisted on obeying the divine law of burying her brother, despite Creon's explicit command not to do so; Sir Thomas More, commanded to take the Oath of Supremacy to Henry VIII, refused and was executed; and in our own time, one might cite the example of Private Michael New, who, ordered to wear a foreign military uniform, refused to obey on the grounds that doing so would violate his own oath of loyalty to the U. S. Constitution.

In none of these cases did any of the principals maunder on about the "legitimacy of the regime," try to instigate general disobedience, or seek to raise rebellion against it. In all of them they did what they believed God and law commanded and refused to violate those commands at the behest of earthly powers, and all of them were willing to pay the price of their disobedience. As More himself put it on the scaffold, "I die the King's good servant —but God's first."

Nowhere does the symposium dwell on the important distinctions between these cases and those of contemporary America. Today, no one is commanded to have or perform an abortion or to suffer or perform euthanasia. The laws to which the symposiasts object are permissive, not compulsive, and how one might "resist" such permissive laws is never clear. Pour chicken blood on abortion clinics? Kill abortionists? By embracing the subjectivist doctrine of disobedience of Garrison and King (to whom Neuhaus himself was an aide), the contributors come very close to embracing the very dangerous logic of that position. Once you have decided that the state does not conform to the "higher law" as revealed to your own conscience (which is easily confused with your own interests, preferences, and passions) and that you have the duty to make it conform, then there is no limit to how far you will go. Thoreau and Garrison lead ineluctably to the terrorism of John Brown; King leads unavoidably to the real bomb-throwing of the Weathermen.

Finally, for all the tremulous insinuations of desperate deeds in the symposium, none of the contributors bothers to explore very seriously the obvious legal and political remedies for the woes of which they complain. Judge Bork does indeed comment on the futility of both reason and reform in trying to restrain the courts in recent decades, and he suggests some constitutional amendments to correct the courts, but he is none too sanguine about the prospect of doing so. Yet in truth there are many corrective measures that neither the neoconservatives nor the Republican Party has ever attempted to sponsor. They could seek to limit the appellate jurisdiction of the courts; they could encourage governors and local officials simply to ignore and disobey illicit court mandates; they could impeach justices and judges; they could even muster more opposition to judicial nominations that the Republicans in the two years of their majority in Congress have shown any disposition to do; and they could also make life very unpleasant for the courts, reducing judges to salaries of one dollar a year, terminating their clerical support, and throwing them out of their offices into the streets. The fact is that judges, like the Pope, have no battalions, no instruments of force with which to back up their decrees, and without such instruments, they can construct a tyranny only with the passive or active cooperation of the slaves they seek to rule.

Indeed, many of the complaints lodged against the courts by the *First Things* crowd are hardly new. The courts have been abusing the Constitution and handing down illicit commands to states and localities for at least fifty years, and while paleoconservatives have developed an extensive and sophisticated critique of these trends, neoconservatives have been largely silent. Where was Richard John Neuhaus when conservatives were peppering the countryside with billboards demanding the impeachment of Earl Warren? He was at the side of "Dr." King, helping that fanatic destroy the fabric of constitutional government at the behest of the Warren Court and its twisted reading of the Constitution. If it's an "illegitimate regime" you're looking for, you don't have to wait for court decisions on abortion and euthanasia; we have had nothing but an illegitimate regime in the United States for the last fifty years, a government dedicated to destroying the Constitution, gutting the restraints on federal power, and subverting the cultural norms and institutions of American society. Now, when the courts have at last touched on the religious dogmas that Father Neuhaus and his symposiasts find untouchable, they have finally concluded that the "regime" really is illegitimate and are full of all sorts of ill-considered instructions as to what they and the rest of us must do about it. But the principles of Constitutional subversion invented by the Warren Court in its decisions in the 1950s (and indeed the New Deal Court of the 1930s and

40s) are the very same principles applied in the cases to which Neuhaus and his colleagues object today. It's about time they arrived at what should have been clear and was clear to many Americans years ago. Their stumbling perception that something is wrong is welcome, but to tell the truth it's just a few decades too late.

Nevertheless, it is a perception to which more and more Americans, conservatives or not, are being driven. Father Neuhaus's neoconservative critics no doubt sense this and know where such perceptions will eventually lead, and that is why their response to the symposium sounds so much like the shrill screaming of a trapped and dying animal. The value of the *First Things* debacle is that it once again rips the mask away from the real face of the movement to which the American right has attached itself, and it offers some hope that in the future those who remain wedded to that movement will be exposed as the apologists for the regime that they are. As the socially destructive and politically repressive character of the federal leviathan becomes increasingly obvious to more and more Americans and to more and more "mainstream conservatives," those who insist on standing with Podhoretz and his allies as defenders of a power structure that everyone else has come to reject will find their footholds increasingly slippery and their company increasingly small.

*Chronicles*

## *Tom Bethell*

FIRST THINGS CAUSED A STIR with its symposium. Quite an achievement. Normally, such abstractions indulge the authors more than they interest the readers. But Richard John Neuhaus has the knack of liveliness, and this symposium was read. The heated reaction to it tells us something about contemporary politics.

The tone of the symposium was above all moderate and academic. But the response was strong. The news of that response came in *The Weekly Standard*. Headlined "The Right's Anti-American Temptation," the article by David Brooks quoted Peter Berger, a sociologist of religion, and the historian Gertrude Himmelfarb, both of whom had resigned in protest from the *First Things* editorial board. "To explore whether the American gov-ern-ment is legitimate is a slippery slope," said Berger, while Himmelfarb thought that any analogy with the American Revolution was "absurd and irresponsible." Another protester was former *Commentary* editor Norman Podhoretz, who saw the symposium "as an outburst of anti-Americanism reminiscent of the anti-Americanism found among left-wing intellectuals in the 1960s."

Was there not a certain disparity of tone between the symposium participants, murmuring mildly in their dependent clauses, and this vehement response? Richard Brookhiser in his *New York Observer* column used the word "overreaction," and Neuhaus thought that was the right word. But Himmelfarb told me that she found the symposium "very nearly hysterical." It was a "very passionate statement," and if abortion is to be the litmus test, then Iran and Iraq, which both prohibit abortion, become "the only legitimate regimes." We all rejected the radicals' claim that America was illegitimate in the 1960s, she said, appealing to unity, and we shouldn't adopt their arguments now "on this one issue of abortion." In discussion with Neuhaus, Podhoretz had also brought up the 1960s, a battleground he did not want to revisit.

Richard Neuhaus responds: "We cannot let the madness of the 1960s set the agenda for public discourse today." I would put it somewhat differently. We, too, disagree with the 1960s radicals. But it was their agenda that we disliked, not necessarily their methods. Conjuring up "the 1960s" as a mad time that we do not want to revisit confuses methods and goals.

Oddly, perhaps, Himmelfarb accepts the moral legitimacy of civil disobedience, which she regards as a proper response for those who feel strongly about some issue. But "you do that as an individual, and you take the consequences." Neuhaus and company "want to suggest that we all should be taking that position." She approves of rebellious *action*, it seems, but fears (some) verbal persuasion, which may be irresponsible precisely because it is constitutionally protected. Neuhaus should have broken the law himself—that would have been "the moral thing." You do whatever it is that is illegal, Himmelfarb said, "and then you go to jail, the way some of those people in the 1960s did—Berrigan or whoever." Here that decade reappears as a moral model.

Martin Luther King and the Berrigans did want others to join their cause, of course. Neuhaus was in the civil rights movement, and proudly "went to jail with Martin Luther King." But he claims that his symposium was not a call to civil disobedience. "If and when that such a call is appropriate, then I certainly expect that I would be involved in the response," he adds. One great difference between the civil rights movement and the restlessness provoked by today's judiciary is that the former was vast, and hugely popular with the intellectual classes; the latter is very small and unpopular.

The *First Things* contretemps suggests that the neoconservative agenda now diverges quite considerably from that of the conservative mainstream. The shared agenda provided by the Cold War is a thing of the past. Neoconservatives may not much like the Court's activism, but they do not much mind it, either. Furthermore, the Court's persistent tendency is to centralize power (they overturn state laws, almost never federal laws), and that the neocons do not mind at all. Above all they fear the disorder that questions of legitimacy might stir up. They want to preserve a strong central government that is interventionist both at home and abroad.

Meanwhile we should be realistic enough to see that the Left has utterly triumphed in the cultural war. Many conservatives don't want to hear this bad news, and they have been too busy going to victory parties to notice. Note well: the *New York Times* never gloats, but always warns of a resurgent right, however phantasma-gorical. The first order of business is to appreciate that we are losing slowly—even if Bill Clinton was forced to adopt "our rhetoric" in the election. It's a tiny triumph for the sheep to claim that the wolf must wear sheep's clothing.

"Decline runs across our entire culture," Robert Bork warns in *Slouching Towards Gomorrah*. Having described a book burning at Yale, he ends with the comment that "the charred books on the sidewalk in New Haven were a metaphor, a symbol of the coming torching of America's intellectual and moral capital by the barbarians of modem liberalism." The radicals, since tenured, are now engaged in dismantling intellectual life at the universities. The media quietly applaud. A majority of the Supreme Court seeks the approbation of the intellectual classes.

Neoconservatives disagree with this analysis. "I think we have won," says Himmelfarb. "The 1960s did not win. Those people had to retreat." Was Bork too pessimistic, then? No, she liked his book, and wrote a blurb for it. But it is important for people like Bork to be able to write a "resounding critique" of our current situation without being put in the position of saying "that America has gone . . . what? Fascist?" as Himmelfarb put it.

Neuhaus cannot see where we are supposed to be having the better of it. "Look at education, look at family policy, look at abortion, look at doctor assisted suicide, look at affirmative action. Where are we winning?" We win some arguments, perhaps, but in terms of policy outcomes, liberal victories are almost never rolled back. Welfare reform? Let us see what happens when they try to thrust pregnant moms into the work force. Government jobs programs will expand, and they will turn out to be more programs than jobs.

"Steady as you go," say the neocons. You're winning already. Don't rock the boat, don't risk being labeled extremist. Don't delegitimize yourselves by moving over into that dark terrain off to the right. The neocon position in this regard is congruent with that of the liberals, who forever warn of right-wing victories and an imminently resurgent Christian right. Sometimes it's not clear who applies the labels and who warns of their application. In any event most conservatives like being told they are winning and obediently troop off to their victory parties. Meanwhile the liberals take their numerous and all too real judicial victories to the bank.

One consequence of the neoconservative policing of opinion is that the spectrum of respectable opinion creeps ever leftward. So does the political debate (now we have reached gay marriage). Neocons wield no influence over the Left, which is too vast and variegated an entity. In any event it rejects rules of ideological etiquette and is unperturbed by such cries as "distasteful!" (leveled at Neuhaus). Liberals say: No enemies to the Left. Conservatives are told: No friends to the Right. This asymmetry is to be found all over the Western world—the Christian world in particular. Liberals understand elementary mechanics. Those further from the center enjoy greater leverage, and make the liberals look moderate by comparison. Guilt by association does not exist on the Left. Those on the Right, on the other hand, are afraid of being labeled. This political asymmetry explains the drift toward cultural dissolution.

*The American Spectator*

# Neocons vs. Theocons?

*Jacob Heilbrunn*

O N SEPTEMBER 26, 1997, after the Senate failed to overturn President Clinton's veto of a ban on partial-birth abortions, Paul Weyrich, Gary Bauer, and other members of the religious right assembled in the antechamber of Senate Majority Leader Trent Lott's office. The rhetoric could not have been more firey. As Lott looked on approvingly, Watergate felon and evangelist Charles Colson declared, "a nation which sanctions infanticide is no better than China, no better than Nazi Germany." Richard John Neuhaus, a Catholic priest, went even further. "It is not hyperbole to say that we are at a point at which millions of conscientious American citizens are reflecting upon whether this is a legitimate regime," Neuhaus said. "That is the solemn moment we have reached."

Despite the apocalyptic tone of what was, after all, an open meeting convened by the most powerful Republican in Congress, the gathering in Lott's chambers attracted little notice. But this meeting was not an isolated or aberrant event. It was a harbinger of a political development that has now reached fruition: a full fledged war between two leading groups of conservative intellectuals over the basic question of what constitutes a moral society.

This war is deeply personal. On one side are the mostly Jewish neoconservatives, a fairly small group of ex–New York leftists who have wielded influence greatly beyond their numbers through sheer intellectual energy. Since the conservative renascence began in the late 1970s, the neocons have given it much of its form and heft; building on the earlier work of William F. Buckley Jr., they provided most of the ideas and arguments that allowed conservatism to compete with (and in many areas triumph over) liberalism. As conservatism benefited from the neocons, so did the neocons benefit from conservatism. They made conservatism intellectually respectable, and conservatism made them intellectually important. Now challenging the neocons is an equally small (and equally ambitious, and equally disputatious) group of what might be called theocons—mostly Catholic intellectuals who are attempting to construct a Christian theory of politics that directly threatens the entire neoconservative philosophy. This attempt, in the eyes of at least some of the neocons, also directly threatens Jews. What makes the matter all the more painful for both sides is that, until recently, the neocons and the theocons were, for the best of political reasons, the best of friends.

And this war is fundamental. It is rooted in a battle over the identity of the American nation. The neoconservatives believe that America is special because it was founded on an idea—a commitment to the rights of man embodied in the Declaration of Independence—not in ethnic or religious affiliations. The theocons, too, argue that America is rooted in an idea, but they believe that idea is Christianity. In their view, the United States is first and foremost a Christian nation, governed ultimately by natural law. When moral law—moral law as defined by Thomas Aquinas and enunciated by John Paul II—conflicts with the laws of man, they say, the choice is clear: God's law transcends the arbitrary and tyrannical decrees of what the theocons increasingly refer to as an American judicial "regime."

The war between the neocons and the theocons first broke into the open in November, when Neuhaus published a symposium in his magazine *First Things* titled "The End of Democracy?" The symposium made explicit for the first time the central point of the Catholic intellectuals' thesis: that the government of the United States (in particular the judiciary) had become so debase—so, essentially, un-Christian and therefore so illegitimate—as to threaten the existence of America as a nation under God, and that this crisis might require a revolutionary response. The ultimate paradox: a conservative revolution.

In the introduction to the symposium, the editors likened the United States to Nazi Germany and cited an encyclical from Pope John Paul II to justify entertaining the possibility of revolution against a judicial tyranny: "Law, as it is presently made by the judiciary, has declared its independence from morality." The editors asked point-blank whether "we have reached or are reaching the point where conscientious citizens can no longer give moral assent to the existing regime." They went on to observe that "America is not and, please God, will never become Nazi Germany, but it is only blind hubris that denies it can happen here and, in peculiarly American ways, may be happening here." The same issue contained quotations from the theologian Dietrich Bonhoeffer on resisting the Nazi regime.

Three court cases form the foundation for the theocons' assertion that the judiciary has usurped power and assaulted the values of its host society: the 1992 Supreme Court decision in *Planned Parenthood v. Casey*, when the Court refused to overturn *Roe v. Wade*; the 1996 Supreme Court decision *Romer v. Evans*, when the Court declared that Coloradans voting against gay-rights statutes were driven by animus; and the 1996 Ninth U.S. Circuit Court of Appeals decision upholding euthanasia, a decision written by the liberal judge Stephen Reinhardt, which the Supreme Court seems likely to overturn.

Robert Bork cites approvingly the suggestion of his staunchly Catholic wife that the high court's rulings were essentially illegal: "My wife said the justices were behaving like a 'band of outlaws.' . . . An outlaw is a person who coerces others without warrant in law. That is precisely what a majority on the present Supreme Court does." Bork calls for stripping the Court of the power of judicial review or subjecting its decisions to a vote in the Senate and House of Representatives. (In his new bestselling book, *Slouching Towards Gomorrah*, Bork sees the root of the evil in the Declaration of Independence.) Russell Hittinger, a professor at the University of Tulsa who has published a book on natural law theory, maintains that "civil disobedience" may be necessary as a weapon against "despotic rule" of the courts. Robert P. George, in "The Tyrant State," advises readers that the "doctrine of the necessary conformity of civil law to moral truth long predates the rise of modern democracy. It . . . was given careful, systematic exposition by Thomas Aquinas. It has been a central feature of the tradition of papal social teaching."

These ideas are not entirely new. In one way or another, the right has been inveighing against the judiciary since the Warren Court and against the immorality of the government since *Roe v. Wade*. And in recent years these arguments have gained political strength, as the Christian Coalition became a power, as Patrick Buchanan rose to national political prominence, and as the idea of the government as an illegitimate occupying power gained greater currency among a wider population increasingly alienated from Washington. But what *was* new about the *First Things* symposium was the attempt to fashion a cogent, serious and popular intellectual framework for these ideas—to render respectable ideas that intellectuals had come to regard as the province of the radical right and the booboisie. Pat Buchanan and Bob Dornan and Phyllis Schlafly had never threatened the neoconservatives because they didn't compete on the same plane. This, though, was an attempt to do just that.

The neocon response was as impassioned as it was swift. Neoconservative heavies such as Gertrude Himmelfarb, Walter

Berns and Peter Berger immediately resigned from the editorial boards of *First Things*. Norman Podhoretz, the chief popularizer of neoconservatism, entered the lists to denounce Neuhaus for the "aid and comfort you for all practical purposes offer the bomb throwers among us." Podhoretz declared, "I did not become a conservative in order to be a radical, let alone to support the preaching of revolution against this country." The furor caused by the November symposium begat a second symposium in *First Things*, published in the January issue. This time, the thoroughly alarmed neoconservatives went ballistic, employing the language of the old right against the old left and the new right against the new left, invoking the ghosts of anti-Americanism and radicalism and "subversive" activity. And Gertrude Himmelfarb warned that Catholics threatened to undermine the very thing they claimed to want, the ordering of American society according to Judeo-Christian ethics. The theocons' radical rhetoric, she wrote, "discredits, or at the very least makes suspect, any attempt by conservatives to introduce moral and religious considerations into the 'public square'—as if morality and religion necessarily lead to such apocalyptic conclusions. It can only confirm many Americans in their suspicion that cultural conservatism is outside the 'mainstream' of American politics, that it is 'extremist,' even subversive." William J. Bennett, who is both a Catholic moralist and a sort of neoconservative, weighed in with a rejection of the Catholics' core notion: "We are still America, not 'Amerika.'"

The battle that was joined in November and continued in the January issue of *First Things* has spread to other publications of the right. David Brooks, writing in the neoconservative *Weekly Standard*, warned of "the right's anti-American temptation," a play on the title of Bork's book *The Tempting of America*. *The Wall Street Journal* and *National Review* have weighed in on the controversy. In late November, a group of conservatives from both sides, Neuhaus, William Kristol, and Buckley, met in an attempt to reach a truce. They got nowhere.

To understand why the dispute is likely to resist further efforts at peacemaking, it helps to consider briefly the core beliefs of both neoconservatism and American Catholic conservatism on the nature of America. The neoconservative understanding of the United States is strongly influenced by the works of the political theorist Leo Strauss. Strauss began his greatest book, *Natural Right and History*, by praising the Declaration of Independence as embodying man's natural rights. He argued that contempt for natural rights and the Declaration had led to the spread of relativism and nihilism in the West, but his solution was not religion. The virtues of religion, Strauss believed, should inform a properly constructed society, but the state must not explicitly endorse any religious code. The formula is reminiscent of Gibbon's famous observation that "the various modes of worship, which prevailed in the Roman world, were all considered by the people, as equally true; by the philosopher, as equally false; and by the magistrate, as equally useful." Strauss believed that America was founded on the idea of the natural rights of man, but his vision of those natural rights was not that of the Thomists. Strauss maintained that Aquinas's conception of natural law could not be reconciled with Aristotle's vision of natural rights, and that it was the Athenian vision of democracy that must prevail in an America comprised of diverse people: "the divine law is not the natural law, let alone natural right," wrote Strauss.

The theocrats will have none of this. They are Thomists, would-be prophets of a new Age of Aquinas; their properly constructed America would, like the America of the Straussians, be based on an idea. But for theocons that idea is the natural law of Thomas Aquinas. Like the Straussians, they decry relativism and cultural decadence, but their solution is to embrace explicitly the notion of a Christian nation: a nation that accepts the idea of a transcendent divine law that carries universal obligations even for nonbelievers.

The founding father of the new Thomist movement is the theologian Germain Grisez, a Christian ethics professor at Mount St. Mary's in Emmitsburg, Maryland. Grisez, who helped persuade Pope John Paul II to force the Catholic University of America to expel Charles Curran in 1986, is the author, among other works, of the standard two-volume guide to Catholicism *The Way of the Lord Jesus: Living the Christian Life*. In it, Grisez develops a comprehensive natural law theory in opposition to modernity. In his preface, he observes that culture now influences Christianity rather than Christianity influencing culture. Most notably, Grisez points out that obligations to a higher law as defined by the Catholic Church can supersede laws of the government: "sometimes, too, a government which on the whole is just has laws which unjustly permit the violation of a certain group's fundamental human rights, for example, laws permitting abortion. Now, in general, if citizens observe one person killing another they may use the minimum force necessary to defend the victim's life, and in such a case, laws against trespassing, the destruction of property, and so forth should not keep anyone from doing what is required." Among Grisez's followers are Princeton professor Robert P. George, who serves on the U.S. Civil Rights Commission, and John Finnis of Oxford University Law. Finnis, one of the most prominent opponents of homosexuality, draws on natural law to argue that society must publicly discourage "waverers" from joining the ranks of homosexuals and that homosexuality "disposes the participants to engage in an abdication of responsibility for the future of mankind."

The most comprehensive explication of natural law theory, however, comes in two volumes published by Oxford's Clarendon Press and edited by Robert P. George. In *The Autonomy of Law*, for example, Finnis argues that though "human law is artifact and artifice ... both its positing and the recognition of its positivity ... cannot be understood without reference to the moral principles that ground and confirm its authority. . . ." George declares that law is a "cultural object that is created for a moral purpose." He concludes by quoting Bork on the need for judges not to presume that they can dictate natural law.

For many years, as conservatism gained strength in America, the natural gulf between the neocons' Straussian view and the theocons' Thomism was ignored for a number of reasons. One was that modern American conservatism was greatly defined by William F. Buckley Jr., and Buckley, though a devout Catholic, initially took a phlegmatic view of doctrinal disputes. In the 1960s, as the conservative Catholic movement split over the issue of pragmatic political decisions versus doctrinal considerations in the matter of such issues as abortion and homosexuality, Buckley chose pragmatism. In 1966, he outraged many Catholics when he stated that non-Catholics were not bound by Church teachings: "Surely the principal meaning of the . . . pronouncements of Vatican II is that other men must be left free to practice the dictates of their own conscience." Buckley's brother-in-law, L. Brent Bozell, broke with *National Review* to co-found with Frederick Wilhelmsen a Spanish Carlist movement called "Sons of Thunder" and a magazine called *Triumph.* "The Catholic Church in America," he declared, "must forthrightly acknowledge that a state of war exists between herself and the American political order." In what Patrick Allitt in *Catholic Intellectuals and Conservative Politics* terms "the first anti-abortion drama of a type made familiar two decades later by Operation Rescue," Bozell and his followers, dressed in red berets and carrying papal flags, stormed a George Washington University clinic that was supposedly conducting abortions, and were arrested.

But by and large, Catholic conservatives, like conservatives in general, chose Buckley's way, not Bozell's. Then came 1973 and the Supreme Court decision of *Roe V. Wade*, a radicalizing event for many Catholics. Since then, the United States has seen a more or less continuous debate over the old and new moral order, and this debate has further radicalized many Christians. It has also further eroded the dominance of Buckleyite pragmatism.

Another reason for the rise of Thomism is that the old cultural divide between Catholics and Protestants has been shrinking for years. As this has occurred, the moralist Catholics and evangelical Protestants have discovered more and more that they share a natural affinity of ideas, and they have been moving steadily closer together. The first great step took place almost two decades ago, when religious right leaders such as Jerry Falwell adopted the right-to-life stance espoused by the Catholic Church. Falwell declared that Protestants had "joined the fight" and lauded Pope John Paul II as the "best pope we Baptists ever had. It was a little-noticed but important moment in political history: northern Catholics and southern Baptists—two powerful blocs that had traditionally shared an allegiance to the Democratic Party but had also traditionally viewed one another with cultural suspicion —had joined hands in cultural conservatism.

In May 1994, *First Things* issued a declaration titled "Evangelicals and Catholics Together." The declaration was signed by Neuhaus, Colson, Pat Robertson, Bill Bright of Campus Crusade for Christ, and Jesse Miranda of the Pentecostal Assemblies of God. It stated that "there has been in recent years a growing convergence and cooperation between Evangelicals and Catholics" and that "we will do all in our power to resist proposals for euthanasia, eugenics, and population control that . . . betray the moral truths of our constitutional order."

The alliance has grown ever since, lending strength to both groups. As the neocons provided the intellectual muscle for Reagan conservatism, so now the Catholic Thomists are providing the brainpower for the Christian Coalition. George and Finnis were the star witnesses on behalf of the state of Colorado in the *Romer v. Evans* gay rights case. The ballot, which would have permitted local communities to discriminate on the basis of homosexuality, had originally been funded by evangelist James C. Dobson's organization. And Supreme Court Justice Antonin Scalia invokes Catholic teachings in his public speeches and has written with approbation of a culture war in his court dissents. "The court," he wrote in its review of the *Romer* case, "has mistaken a *Kulturkampf* for a fit of spite."

The final reason for the rise of the theocons is the one perhaps most painful to neocons. It is the work of the neocons themselves. For years, figures such as Gertrude Himmelfarb, Irving Kristol, and Norman Podhoretz have hailed religious populism and denounced liberals for viewing it as a threat. And for years, the neoconservatives have been arguing, in tones frequently of despair and anger, precisely the theme espoused by the Catholic intellectuals they now denounce: that the American cultural elite and the American Judiciary constituted an overclass both alien from and largely hostile to the values of the nation as a whole. It was Kristol who concocted the theory of a "new class" of intellectuals hostile to its own country. In recent years, and to this day, the neoconservatives have embraced and defended the Christian right. Writing in *Commentary* in August 1991 Kristol argued that the danger to the republic was not Christian fundamentalism, but the secular humanism of the new class. "American Jews, alert to Christian anti-Semitism," he wrote, "are in danger of forgetting that it was the pagans—the Babylonians and the Romans—who destroyed the temples and twice imposed exile on the Jewish people." In the October 1996 issue of *Commentary*, Podhoretz compared the "liberal *culturati*" to the "Stalinists of the 1930s," and bemoaned the "bigotry with which the Christian Coalition itself is routinely discussed in liberal circles." And it was the neoconservatives, in their arguments, who laid the groundwork for the Thomists' portrayal of the United States as a captive nation under an illegitimate judicial "regime." The idea of the Supreme Court as the aggressor in the culture wars, while conservatives are simply the beleaguered minority, belongs to the neocons at least as much as it does to the theocons. As Cornell professor Jeremy Rabkin recently wrote of the Supreme Court justices in Kristol's *Public Interest*: "In an age of confusing transitions, the justices are the last dogmatists. It requires such dogmatists to sustain a culture war."

In the second of the *First Things* symposia, Midge Decter wrote a poignant plea to the theocons to stop pushing their doctrine. "I could hardly believe my eyes," she wrote of her readings in the first symposium. "I presume in the name of friendship, then, to accuse you of growing impatient with your labors, and in your impatience, reckless. And I beg you: do not be impatient, and for heaven's sake do not be reckless about the legitimacy of this country. . . .You will only end by strengthening the devil's hand." Her essay was followed immediately by what amounted to a response and flat rejection from Dobson. Dobson declared that he stood in a long tradition of Christians who believed that rulers may "forfeit their divine mandate" when they contravene "divine moral law," and he concluded by asking whether "clergy and laity alike [will] be willing to face cultural ostracism, imprisonment, or worse."

When Neuhaus and Dobson and Grisez hear Podhoretz and Kristol and Decter accuse them of not acting like true conservatives—of being radical and subversive—they must be at least a little tempted to laugh. Well, yes. Of course they are radicals and subversives. That is what they intended to be all along; that is what they have always been. They see America in 1990 as the abolitionists saw it in 1860—as a state that is violating God's law and must be resisted, by any means necessary. They suspect the neocons of mouthing the rhetoric but not having the stomach for the consequences of their own talk, and they regard them with attitudes ranging from exasperation to contempt. Hadley Arkes, a professor of political theory at Amherst, speaking of neoconservatives and abortion, laments that in "their heart of hearts," the neoconservatives "don't think people are being killed in these surgeries. They think we're going to the edge of fanaticism." Paul Weyrich, who heads the Free Congress Foundation, is openly dismissive. "I resent the political correctness of some of the neocons who suggest that you can't discuss something." He asks: "If a government is illegitimate, do you stop paying taxes, do you stop serving in its armed forces? These are all questions which need to be thoroughly thought through."

If the Thomists have a public face that is at all nationally known, it is that of Alan Keyes, who this year made his second quixotic run for the presidency. Last summer, in a half-filled hotel ballroom, in the midst of the otherwise content-free Republican

National Convention, Keyes gave the inaugural address of a group he calls The Declaration Foundation. The foundation is the Thomists' first attempt to organize politically, and Keyes's speech was the first speech by an articulate conservative to present an intellectually cogent argument on behalf of Thomism.

"I believe that it is absolutely clear, in everything the Founders did, that they intended the Declaration to be a bridge between the Bible and the Constitution, between the basis of our moral faith and the basis our political life," Keyes said. "The Declaration constitutes a definition of the source and limits of our freedom. The source is God. And the limits are quite clearly defined: we cannot use the freedom in such a way as to claim unto ourselves the authority which is the basis of our freedom."

Keyes knows this is a radical doctrine in the context of the American experience. That's why he likes it. He maintains that he is not preaching revolution, and seemed surprised by the controversy surrounding the *First Things* symposium. "How can that be anti-American?" he asked. It is a question that the neocons must wish they had never helped raise.

Keyes's campaign was a failure. The "Republican moneybags," as he puts it, shut him down. But there does seem to be some grass-roots receptivity to his message, which Keyes booms away at on his daily radio show. The very success of Keyes and his fellow theocons in propagating their doctrine inside the GOP would, however, condemn the party itself to failure. A Catholic tradition that attempts to infuse a religiously neutral Constitution with divine right is a recipe for political disaster. Thomism is an ideology to which only the faithful can subscribe. It is not so much anti-American as un-American.

Until now, the neoconservatives have preferred to tune out the message and embrace the messenger. These intellectual operatives have operated on the comforting assumption that a common interest animates evangelicals, Catholics, and neocon-servatives. Father Neuhaus has not: in the December issue of *First Things,* he praises the declaration of the Southern Baptist

Convention last summer in favor of evangelizing the Jews. "[T]he Baptists," he writes, "were responding to Christian theologians who had singled out Jews as being exempt from the otherwise universal need for the Gospel." That's not the sort of overture you expect from an old friend. It has begun to dawn on the neoconservatives what can happen when, to borrow a phrase from Midge Decter, you strengthen the devil's hand.

*The New Republic*

## Ramesh Ponnuru

TO LIVE AS A RELIGIOUS BELIEVER in the terrestrial city is necessarily to experience divided loyalties. Short of the Kingdom of God, complete justice can never reign, and all temporal allegiances must be provisional. The modern American social order is sufficiently benevolent that we are usually only dimly aware of this tension. For the editors and contributors to the symposium in *First Things*, however, recent judicial decisions have put the issue in stark relief.

What troubled most of those who have commented on the symposium was the editors' introductory statement that we may "have reached or are reaching the point where conscientious citizens can no longer give moral assent to the existing regime." The very legitimacy of the "regime," they argued, was in question, and those conscientious citizens might eventually—perhaps soon—have to consider civil disobedience or even "morally justified revolution." This use of the word "regime" was confusing: some critics took "regime" to mean something illegitimate by definition, like "junta." Further, did illegitimacy attach to the Federal Government itself, as some paramilitary groups suggest, or merely to the practice of judicial rule? This confusion caused many commentators to miss the conditionality of the editors' position: that "we are witnessing the end of democracy" and will have to consider lawbreaking *if* the courts are not restrained, by themselves or others.

The reaction to the symposium was as sharp as it was swift. Garry Wills, attentive to nuance as ever, claimed in a *New York Times* op-ed that the symposiasts "made arguments indistinguishable from those advanced by the militias." (Evidently Mr. Wills knows militias that cite classical philosophers and papal encyclicals and worry more about assisted suicide than gun control.) It was probably inevitable that some journalist would take the caricature a step further.

Which brings us to Jacob Heilbrunn. According to him, *First Things* brought into the open "a full-fledged war between two leading groups of conservative intellectuals." In one corner are "the mostly Jewish neoconservatives," followers of political theorist Leo Strauss, who believe that "America was founded on an idea—a commitment to the rights of man embodied in the Declaration of Independence." The "theocons," on the other hand, are

> mostly Catholic intellectuals who are attempting to construct a Christian theory of politics that directly threatens the entire neoconservative philosophy. This attempt, in the eyes of at least some of the neocons, also directly threatens Jews. . . . The theocons, too, argue that America is rooted in an idea, but they believe that idea is Christianity. In their view, the United States is first and foremost a Christian nation, governed ultimately by natural law.

Heilbrunn describes the theocons as "Thomists, would-be prophets of a new Age of Aquinas." Their "founding father" is the theologian Germain Grisez, their public face that of Alan Keyes.

Heilbrunn's piece is directed not so much against the "theocons" as against the neocons. Michael Lind, Heilbrunn's sometime collaborator, has cast crafty neoconservative Jews as having opportunistically ascended to the intellectual leadership of a conservative movement whose rank-and-file is made up of anti-Semitic evangelical Christians. Heilbrunn's article is perhaps best seen as the second installment of this "sellout of the neoconservative Jews" thesis: now they've opportunistically allied themselves with even craftier anti-Semitic Catholics.

It's a well-constructed story line: gripping, coherent—and entirely fictional. The *First Things* symposiasts included two Catholics (Hittinger and George), true, but also two Protestants (Bork and Colson), and one Jew (Arkes). Heilbrunn doesn't mention that Bork is not a Catholic, but takes note of "his staunchly Catholic wife." (George's staunchly Jewish wife doesn't make an appearance.) The editors responsible for the introduction to the symposium included one Catholic (editor in chief Father Richard John Neuhaus), one Lutheran (editor James Nuechterlein), and one Jew (managing editor Matthew Berke).

A more central flaw in Heilbrunn's story is his utter (and at times laughable) incomprehension of Thomist natural-law theory, which is a branch of philosophy and not of theology. Indeed, it reminds me of the classic academic put-down to empty arguments: "That's not right; it's not even wrong."

Adherents of natural law believe that moral truths can be discovered through reason alone. As Professor George puts it, "What people like me are arguing is that the standard of public policy should be what reason can understand. So a view should stand or fall based on its reasonableness. Biblical tradition can be the carrier of wisdom on matters like same-sex marriage, as can the Talmud. But we don't appeal to the authority of the Bible or of the Catholic Church in making our case. We appeal to principles of rationality that are available to all people." So, for instance, when George and John Finnis of Oxford University testified in *Romer*—an incident Heilbrunn records—not once did they invoke the Bible or any authority other than reason itself. Their reasoning was available to, and arguable by, non-believers. Indeed, natural law's Protestant critics have disparaged it precisely for its reliance on human reason in matters of moral consequence. If Thomism were merely a stalking horse for a "Christian nation," then people like David Novak—a rabbi who is also a natural law theorist, student of Grisez, and member of *First Things*' editorial board— shouldn't exist.

Similarly, Heilbrunn's account of the conservative "battle over the identity of the American nation" doesn't even rise to the level of being wrong. If there is a distinctively conservative theory of American nationhood, it isn't any sort of "idea nation" thesis, let alone a "Christian nation" idea, but rather the culturalist view of nationhood adumbrated by *National Review* and in particular by John O'Sullivan (a Catholic, for those keeping score). Heilbrunn provides no evidence for his claim that the "Christian nation" thesis is central to "American Catholic conservatism," because there isn't any. Perhaps R. J. Rushdoony or John Lofton believes in religious tests for office, but no prominent mainstream conservative intellectual does. *National Review*'s David Klinghoffer, in some of his writings, seems to endorse the view that divine law should some-times be imposed on non-believers; I can't think of a contemporary conservative Christian intellectual who agrees. Father Neuhaus and Professor George both subscribe to the "neoconservative" view that the principles of the Declaration of Independence constitute American nationhood. It is Heilbrunn who can't make up his mind about the Declaration. Judge Bork and the theocons are damned for rejecting it, Alan Keyes for embracing it too closely. (It does, after all, speak of people being "endowed by their Creator with certain inalienable rights.")

The attempt to cast Germain Grisez as the *eminence grisez* of the Catholic conspiracy against democracy is singularly inappropriate, since Grisez isn't primarily a political theorist and indeed did not hear of the *First Things* symposium until after publication. Moreover, Grisez, George, and Finnis (who believe moral truths can be derived from self-evident first premises) are heterodox among Thomists (most of whom think moral truth can be derived from human nature). Hittinger wrote an entire book, *A Critique of the New Natural Law Theory*, rebutting Grisez.

And Father Neuhaus belongs to neither camp. As one might expect of a convert from Lutheranism, he's drawn more to Augustine than to Aquinas. Meanwhile, Alan Keyes, the supposed champion of the Catholics who are supposedly at odds with Jewish Straussian neocons, *is* a Straussian—and one who devoted a pre-primary speech in New Hampshire to blasting the idea of a "Christian nation." Finally, Norman Podhoretz—who is surely a neocon if the term means anything any more—is no Straussian. Heilbrunn's map of the Right just doesn't do justice to the intellectual geography he tries to cover. It's rather like those early maps of Africa that, though topographically unreliable, confidently declared: "There be lions here."

Heilbrunn's journalistic malpractice extends to his use of quotation and paraphrase. He describes Miss Himmelfarb's letter as having "warned that Catholics threatened to undermine the very thing they claimed to want, the ordering of American society according to Judaeo-Christian ethics." In fact, her letter said *nothing* about Catholics; Heilbrunn was putting words in her mouth to make it seem that she accepted his *Jews v. Catholics* framework. He deploys his shoddiest tactic, however, on George. In his *First Things* essay, George wrote that the "doctrine of the necessary conformity of civil law to moral truth long predates the rise of modern democracy. It is present in both Plato and Aristotle, and was given careful, systematic expression by St. Thomas Aquinas. It has been a central feature of the tradition of papal social teaching." George's reference to Plato and Aristotle is inconvenient to Heilbrunn's argument that Catholic "theocons" are trying to impose their religious views on the nation. So he simply uses ellipses to eliminate it. (In his article, the second sentence of the passage reads, "It . . . was given careful" etc.) Heilbrunn also chooses not to quote George's comment a few paragraphs later: "These are no mere sectarian teachings. Belief that laws and the regimes that make and enforce them must be evaluated by reference to universal standards of justice is shared by people of different faiths and of no particular faith."

Heilbrunn's cascading confusions would matter little (except to those whose views he distorted) were they not coupled with astonishingly reckless charges. Take the claim, quoted above, that the so-called "theocon" enterprise "in the eyes of at least some of the neocons, also directly threatens Jews." No on-the-record or even off-the-record comments are provided for that incendiary remark; nor is any argument for the plausibility of the underlying claim.

Toward the end, Heilbrunn casually slanders Thomists, about whom he demonstrably knows nothing, as "not so much anti-American as un-American." Insinuations of Catholic disloyalty to America, reckless charges of Catholic anti-Semitism, slanderous portrayals of Catholic elites plotting to build a theocracy: Heilbrunn traffics in the most cliched forms of anti-Catholic bigotry. Perhaps he should have entitled his article *Protocols of the Elders of Rome.*

Presumably almost all conservatives, and other people of good will, will reject *The New Republic's* attempt to drive a wedge between Catholics and Jews. But that is not to deny that the *First Things* controversy has revealed real intra-conservative divisions. One of these divisions has less to do with Leo Strauss or Thomas Aquinas than with Thomas Hobbes, the early modern theorist of absolute sovereignty. The Hobbesian streak among conservative critics of the symposium was most evident in *National Review's* piece, which argued, "Our general obligation to obey the laws rests upon the fact that the laws protect us (against our fellow man), not upon the ultimate justice of the government's founding, still less (fortunately) upon its general moral character." Whatever else might be said of this view, it does seem at the very least in tension with the principles and spirit of the American Revolution, in particular with the principle of majority consent.

But the influence of Hobbesianism can also be detected in the insistence of many conservatives that the "legitimacy" of a political status quo should not be the subject of sustained public argument. To be sure, not every proposition is worth discussing.

But once one has been raised, to say that it should not be discussed is self-defeating. More importantly, as *First Things* has noted, the Supreme Court has itself raised the question of the legitimacy of the law. As Notre Dame Law Professor Gerard Bradley observes in his brilliant essay "Shall We Ratify the New Constitution?" recent Supreme Court decisions (most notably *Casey* and *Lee)* can reasonably be construed as asking the American people "to ratify and thereby legitimate" a constitution of the Court's devising. In that light, the *First Things* symposium was simply a resounding "No!"

The editors' reference to Nazi Germany—which outraged many of the critics—is a dicier issue. Quoting the papal encyclical *Evangelium Vitae* on the general point that a law's binding force on the conscience depends on its morality, they noted that the footnotes in the encyclical refer to earlier papal statements that specifically condemned Nazi crimes. The editors add, "America is not and, please God, will never become Nazi Germany, but it is only blind hubris that denies it can happen here and, in peculiarly American ways, may be happening here." The passage, in other words, was intended as an antidote to an uncritical version of American exceptionalism that denies the possibility that human rights could ever be tyrannically violated in this country. Whether or not the argument was tactfully made, it ought to be openly debatable.

For many of the neoconservative critics of the symposium, the anti-American rhetoric of the 1960s was a formative, and traumatic, political experience. But the parallel is weak, the result of analyzing arguments formally rather than materially. Quips Bradley, "Except for the hair, Hadley Arkes doesn't have much in common with Abbie Hoffman. Nor is Jerry Rubin the same as Dietrich Bonhoeffer." Or as Father Neuhaus puts it, "There is nothing so elementary as that there are criteria for just and unjust government. It astonishes me that people think that we came up with something new or something retrieved from the ash heap of the 1960s."

A very mild anti-American strain does indeed exist on the Right—think of the number of conservatives who interpreted President Clinton's re-election as a verdict on the intellect or morality of the American public – but conservatives remain more likely to make the opposite mistake of uncritically embracing populism. I'll get worried about anti-Americanism on the Right when I see Neuhaus burning a flag.

If anything, the symposium could be faulted for laying insufficient stress on the *permanent* nature of the tension between the demands of God and those of Caesar. Putting the symposium in such a context would have raised the needed alarms without being alarmist. It might then have reminded conservatives that liberty requires eternal vigilance—without apocalyptic rhetoric.

Meanwhile, if the Right is repeating an error of the late 1960s. Left, perhaps it's factionalism: a tendency for intellectuals to get caught up in theoretical disputes while ignoring points of concordance that have far more practical relevance. Almost all conservatives agree that the federal judiciary has needlessly and destructively intervened in the nation's social and moral controversies. Almost all conservatives agree that it's important to address the problem. If this debate concentrates the conservative mind on a program to rein in the courts and a strategy to advance that program—if it makes efforts to curtail judicial review respectable—all conservatives would have reason to cheer. Some conservatives may balk at delegitimizing the courts, but an aggressive campaign to *demystify* them is long overdue. Justice Scalia's recent dissents offer a model of how to do this.

*First Things* may also have performed another public service. After more than sixteen years of sitting in the back of the Republican bus, social conservatives are getting restive. Already, important players like Gary Bauer and Phyllis Schlafly are taking shots at Ralph Reed's accommodationism and moving into Pat Buchanan's orbit—which is to say, out of their alliance with the rest of the Right. Something good will have come of this debate if conservative intellectuals are awakened to grassroots discontent with the party's handling of moral issues, most importantly abortion. If the conservative coalition is to be kept together, that sentiment is going to have to be responsibly accommodated.

*National Review*

## *John J. Reilly*

L ET ME FIRST MAKE some personal admissions. I write occasionally for *First Things*. I was not part of the symposium, but I wrote an essay that appeared in the July/August 1996 issue of *Culture Wars* dealing with much the same topic. The piece was entitled "How to Prevent a Civil War." My argument was not so different from that of Robert Bork's contribution to the symposium, in which he suggested various mechanisms for limiting the scope of constitutional judicial review. I too used the term "regime" to describe the current jurisprudential system, though I picked up the usage not from the right, but from Michael Lind's *The Next America*. I too think that contemporary constitutional theory is damned and doomed. If I differ from the symposium's participants, it is only in believing that the current jurisprudential regime is not just wicked but rotten, and that it will collapse under very little pressure in a fashion not at all dissimilar to Soviet Communism. I am thus not a wholly impartial observer.

Objectivity notwithstanding, the action in the weeks that followed the symposium was manifestly explosive. The piece by Jacob Heilbrunn is worth considering in some detail. Heilbrunn's thesis is that the neoconservatives (the necons) are mostly New York–based Jewish intellectuals who broke with leftist politics in the 1970s. They remade conservatism by articulating serious intellectual critiques of liberalism and the welfare state. When the conservative revival began about twenty-five years ago, the concerns of cultural conservatives were not much represented among this group. Therefore, they were not much represented in government or the academy, despite the fact it was cultural conservatives, mostly evangelicals and ethnic Catholics, who provided the growing electoral muscle of the Republican Party. Recently, however, the neocons have been joined by a new breed of conservative intellectual, for whom Heilbrunn has coined the nifty term "theocon." The theocons, by his account, are predominantly Catholic, and, unlike their Jewish colleagues, have a tendency to frame political questions with a theological twist. The theocons, in fact, are seeking to restructure American society in accordance with Thomistic natural law. Their efforts are intellectually sophisticated, far more so than anything conservative populists from George Wallace to Pat Buchanan have been able to formulate. However, according to Heilbrunn, "Thomism is an ideology to which only the faithful can subscribe. It is not so much anti-American as un-American."

Well, so much for John Courtney Murray and the decades-long attempt to establish the compatibility of Thomism with the American enterprise. For that matter, so much for the more recent debate about the natural law assumptions of the Founding Fathers. The only kind of natural law Heilbrunn seems to feel to be appropriate for American political discourse is the post-Kantian theories of Leo Strauss, who did indeed influence many neoconservatives.

I for one find Helibrunn's assessment more odd than offensive. Whatever else you may think about Thomism, it is difficult to think of it as a subversive political ideology. Images rise up of a Senate Subcommittee on Neo-Scholastic Activities. Could its jurisdiction be challenged on the ground that subcommittees offend against Occam's Razor? C-Span is not ready for this. For that matter, it is misleading to characterize *First Things* as a hotbed of Thomism. Richard John Neuhaus is indeed a Catholic priest, but before that he was a Lutheran pastor. Much of his social thinking is informed by the Lutheran model of the "orders of creation," which is analogous to natural law but by design non-theological. The magazine's editor, James Nuechterlein, remains a Lutheran and delivers himself of a no-popery declaration every few months to make sure that no one forgets. The managing editor, Matthew Berke, is Jewish.

The contributors to the magazine are all over the lot in terms of denominational affiliation. *First Things* is perhaps most noted for its "Evangelicals and Catholics Together" initiative, announced in its May 1994 issue, which went far toward providing a common roof for all cultural conservatives. St. Thomas is indeed much quoted and praised in the pages of *First Things*, but then it defines itself as a "Monthly Journal of Religion and Public Life." One thing it is not is a Catholic magazine, much less an organ of creeping international Thomism. Of course, there is no lack of prominent proponents of natural law on the national scene, many of whom are Thomists. The most prominent, no doubt, is Justice Antonin Scalia, who often makes himself unpopular with his Supreme Court colleagues by critiquing their more incoherent decisions from the bench. There is former presidential candidate Alan Keyes, a brilliant speaker who would have transformed the 1996 election campaign if he had been featured at the Republican convention. (Keyes, by the way, is a former student of Allan Bloom, who was in turn a student of the influential Leo Strauss. In Keyes's mind, at least, Aquinas proved more persuasive.)

On the other hand, the ranks of Thomists do not include people such as Robert Bork, whose objections to judicial activism arise from a historically-based interpretation of the powers of the courts. "Theocon" might not be a bad term for describing many cultural conservatives. It might not even be a bad term for describing me. However, it is misleading to suggest that all or even most theocons are Thomists, or that opposition to the current state of constitutional law is a crank enthusiasm of religious sectarians, Catholic or otherwise. (For that matter, with all due respect to the Podhoretz and Kristol clans, neoconservatism is not a Jewish monopoly, even if you confine the term to subscribers of little magazines.) Granted that Heilbrunn's criticisms are misdirected, nevertheless it seems to me that all sides to this debate, neocons, theocons and the liberals who mock them, are overlooking some important things about it. What we are seeing now is a drama that has been played out more than once before in American history, when the chaos created by a radical episode was repaired a generation later by much the same people who caused the commotion in the first place. We have all heard that the 1990s are the 1960s turned upside down. In the neocon-theocon flap, perhaps we see an instance of 1960s style turned against the institutionalized vestiges of 1960s substance.

The short explanation for the radical tone of the *First Things* symposium is that the Supreme Court does bad work in important areas of the law and will not admit its mistakes. It does not help that in such ill-reasoned decisions as *Planned Parenthood v. Casey*, for instance, we find such language as, "If the Court's legitimacy should be undermined, then so would the country be in its very ability to see itself through its constitutional ideals." What nonsense. The country can see its constitutional ideals in the constitution. The court's "legitimacy" (perhaps Justice O'Connor meant "credibility"?) stands or falls by the court's competence, the lack of which has been the problem.

This explains the exasperation, but why does the exasperation take the form of a bunch of parsons and college professors making noises like students circa 1968 threatening to storm the math building? Partly it's because the parsons and college professors came through the 1960s themselves, though they were for the most part too old to be students at the time. The style of some generations, as William Strauss and Neil Howe argue in their book *Generations*, dominates cultural and political life for decades. The substance may change, but the manner is tenacious. Father Neuhaus, for instance, once famously marched into Henry Kissinger's office with other prominent opponents of the Vietnam War and read him the Riot Act. The *First Things* symposium is not quite as dramatic, but the spirit is the same.

These remarks apply even more to neocons than they do to theocons. The neoconservatives became neoconservatives, after all, because they were appalled by the extremism of the language and behavior of the far left of twenty or thirty years ago. The theocons of today, or at least the ones at *First Things,* have few violent tendencies, but once again the neocons are put off by language that seems to suggest that questions of civil order are at issue. The difference this time around is that the "radicals" have a better chance of winning. The radicals of the 1960s had no prospect of success. On the other side of the victory of, say, the Weathermen there was a world of re-education camps and political dictatorship that few Americans could imagine. Of course, the kids of the 1960s have "won" in the sense of outliving their elders. One of them is actually in the White House as I write. However, he got there by abandoning some of his youthful beliefs and dissimulating about the rest.

The task of today's conservatives is the relatively modest proposition of repairing the damage many of them did themselves twenty or thirty years ago. On the other side of the victory of today's cultural conservatives, there is a world sort of like the Eisenhower Administration but without racial discrimination. Many people might not like this outcome, but it is not hard to visualize and few people find it actually repulsive. Thus, we may be in for a larger than average historical irony. The very attitudes and rhetorical style that did so much to institutionalize the 1960s in our law and popular culture may also be among the chief instruments by which that era is finally dismantled.

*Culture Wars*

# Crossing the Threshold

*Hadley Arkes*

W E HAD INTENDED to sound an alarm in public, and sure enough, we managed to produce, as Henry James would say, a "minor tremor of the public tail": Five writers and professors joined in a symposium, "The End of Democracy? The Judicial Usurpation of Politics." I happened to find a place in this band of incendiaries, along with the likes of Robert Bork, Russell Hittinger, Charles Colson, and Robert George. Our arguments also were amplified, with a certain edge, in an introduction written by Father Richard Neuhaus.

The concern of the writers was with the steady aggression of the courts in reshaping the matrix of our laws on the matter of abortion, assisted suicide, gay rights, and the meaning of marriage. Under the direction of the courts, the law would withdraw from its central mission in casting protections on human life: There would be a new license to take life as a kind of "private right," and all legislation to the contrary—all public votes and referendums— would be swept away. And when legislators were stripped of the power to legislate, there would be no point in arguing over these matters in the course of electing people to the legislatures. One by one, then, these subjects would be withdrawn from the arena of public discussion, from the deliberation and judgment of citizens. In a "regime of consent," the power of consent is being withdrawn from those who are governed. In the name of the "rule of law," this regime is being converted into something else.

It was explained in the Declaration of Independence that governments may lose their legitimate claim to govern when they become "destructive" of those "ends" for which governments are established in the first place. Those ends involved, at their core, the protection of our natural rights. And standing first in the list was the protection of life. The writers in the symposium spoke no treason, and they took care not to incite people to a course of lawlessness. But as Russell Hittinger put it, we come to the very edge when our government tells us that the killing of unborn children must be regarded as a private right; that we may have no proper concern about the terms on which killing is carried forth in our neighborhoods; and that the meaning of "homicide" is no longer part of the business of people living together in a republic. Father Neuhaus took note of the alternatives that spring to mind, "from noncompliance to resistance to civil disobedience to morally justified revolution." He would endorse none of them, but he wrote, darkly, of "a growing alienation of millions of Americans from a government they do not recognize as theirs; what is happening now is an erosion of moral adherence to this political system."

From passages of this kind, the controversy seemed to burst into flame. Of course, the symposium was meant to jolt and to launch a discussion. But we were rather surprised that so many of our usual allies seem more alarmed by us than by the offenses that we had sought, in detail, to describe. As the saying goes, attacks on us "come with the territory." Still, some of those attacks have been bizarre. But the real tremors have been generated by the concern that we were challenging the legitimacy of the

American regime. In point of fact, we thought we were trying to *vindicate* the American regime, against a pattern of moves that threatened to replace the regime with something else. We were, as I say, sounding an alarm, but perhaps we assumed, all too readily, that seasoned readers, reading a serious journal, would recognize that we were writing with a certain restraint and shading. We expected then that urbane readers would be cautious in flying, from our words, to the most extravagant implications. We had been raising a serious question about judges violating the principles that were at the core of the political order. And yet, even to raise that point was taken as a virtual incitement to the militia groups to take up arms against the government. But one does not entail the other. And we cannot be restrained from speaking of serious questions of principle because the lawless in spirit might be moved to become lawless in fact. As Richard Neuhaus put it, "the delusions of weekend revolutionaries should not set the boundaries of political discussion."

There is no need to soften the point: The charge made by most, if not all, of the participants in the symposium was that the usurpation of the judges, on matters of the gravest moral consequence, has created a corruption in the political order. But in that sense, we said nothing more damning than what could have been said of this country in the nineteenth century, when the republic incorporated in its laws the acceptance of slavery. The wrong of slavery ran back to the very premises of a regime that held it wrong to rule another human being without his consent.

But as long as slavery was sustained through the consent, or the suffrage, of the people, there was no remedy for the problem consistent with the character of the regime: The problem could not be "solved" by calling off elections, for that remedy would violate the very principle that the opponents of slavery were trying to vindicate. In the same way here, the acceptance of abortion on demand may constitute a corruption running deep, but it cannot justify the resort to force in a regime in which people are still free to persuade, and seek support, in free elections.

But the problem would remain, with the same predicament in principle, if we found an elected government that was willing to preside over a regime of death camps. The willingness to mount a resistance, with acts outside the law, would be portentous for the same reasons. And yet, with all of our reservations about acting outside the law, could we strictly say that it would be wrong for any citizen to throw his body in the way of the killing machine and rescue people where he could? Such an act would be outside the law, but in resisting the killing of the innocent, it might have the effect of administering, to fellow citizens, a bolt of recognition.

Happily, we are so constituted that no elected government in America could sustain itself while presiding over an Auschwitz. The American people may be growing duller in their moral reflexes, but they are likely to react with outrage if they had any evidence that real persons were getting killed, systematically, in large numbers. The difference between this case and the problem of abortion is that many ordinary people, with decent reflexes, simply do not have the same sense that real human beings are getting killed in these surgeries.

And so our dilemma persists. It is a portentous thing to say in public, even in guarded ways, that certain acts outside the law may be justified. But the dilemma in principle is intractable: If we know that human lives are being taken in abortions, what is the honest answer to be given when people earnestly ask us whether they would be doing a justified thing, overall, if they actually saved innocent lives? How could we hold back, or avoid the straight, honest answer, on grounds other than prudence?

In the end, then, we bite our lips and counsel people to accept the restraint of the law. But discreetly covered over here is the fact that we cannot really explain why we should be constrained, in principle, from rescuing the innocent from the arbitrary taking of their lives. Lincoln once wrote to his friend, Joshua Speed, "You ought . . . to appreciate how much the great body of the Northern people do crucify their feelings in order to maintain their loyalty to the constitution and the Union."

Our symposium sought to convey our sense of the depth of the problem, even as we preserved our commitment to lawfulness. Our friends do not quarrel with our assessment of how bad, in fact, things are, but they seem to condemn us for a want of prudence in saying so. Of our forbearance they say nothing. What they apparently find disturbing—to the strain of their own tolerance—is that we should be artless enough to say, in public, that the regime is truly in crisis because certain thresholds of principle have already been crossed.

*Crisis*

# PART IV

# THE ANATOMY
## OF A CONTROVERSY

BY RICHARD JOHN NEUHAUS

# I

# BROTHERS OFFENDED

"DISAGREEMENT IS a rare achievement," the late Father John Courtney Murray was fond of saying. "Most of what we call disagreement is simply confusion." Murray knew this from personal experience. For many years he was attacked, sometimes harshly, for his scholarly efforts to demonstrate the compatibility of Catholic teaching with American democratic theory and practice. Before his death in 1967, Murray worried that America's theory and practice were disintegrating and called on Catholics to help defend what he called "the American proposition" against a growing number of "radicalized" detractors. Thanks in large part to Murray's work, Catholics were equipped to do just that by the teaching of the Second Vatican Council, which laid a firm theological and philosophical foundation for the democratic experiment in sustaining a free and virtuous society.

---

EDITOR'S NOTE: References in this essay to items listed in the Bibliography are preceded by the letter "B" (e.g., "B27" would indicate item 27 in the Bibliography). Other references indicate page numbers in this volume. Citations of works not directly related to the controversy appear in footnotes.

This essay is an effort to achieve disagreement and agreement, rescuing both from the frequently passionate controversy initiated by the November 1996 symposium in *First Things*, "The End of Democracy? The Judicial Usurpation of Politics." This is surely not the last word on the controversy. In addition to the numerous commentaries already published, there appears to be no end in sight of the debate over what has gone wrong with our experiment in ordered liberty and how it might be set right. While I expect the Founders would be distressed by what has gone wrong, one may hope that they would be pleased to know that their constituting ideas are so vigorously debated two centuries after the launching of their experiment, and ours.

Columnist Steven Hayward writes that "it is hard to recall a single edition of a magazine that has caused as much discussion as the *First Things* symposium" (B108). That claim may be overstated. One readily recalls, for instance, the February 1963 issue of *Commentary* with Norman Podhoretz's "My Negro Problem, and Ours" or Francis Fukuyama's "The End of History" a few years ago in *The National Interest*. It is hard to explain why an article or symposium ignites such widespread discussion. I expect it has only a little to do with editorial sagacity, although as Tina Brown of *The New Yorker* inelegantly puts it, editors do want to create a "buzz" around their publications. There is no point in publishing if nobody is going to pay attention.

Among the many laudatory responses to the *First Things* initiative is that of *New Oxford Review* editor Dale Vree: "Richard Neuhaus is an excellent controversialist. He gets into a lot of scrapes. But this one is different—he's lost some of his allies. He's paid a price. I salute his courage in doing this. He must have known what the consequences would be" (B138). My appreciation of this compliment is tempered by the fact that my editorial colleagues and I did not anticipate the consequences. More precisely, we did not anticipate that some friends and allies would object quite so strongly to the argument we were advancing.

Achieving agreement and disagreement can be made more difficult when friendships and alliances are engaged. In the flood of mail received, almost all of it strongly supportive, is a letter from a law professor in the midwest who simply cites a passage from Proverbs 18: "A brother offended is harder to be won than a strong city: and their contentions are like the bars of a castle." There is indeed something to that. A professor of forensics tells me that the Speech Communication Association will devote a session to the *First Things* controversy at their convention in Chicago this year. No doubt the controversy is a fascinating case study for the scientific examination of argumentative discourse, but I expect such an exercise will be quite incomplete without an intimate understanding of its personal dimension. While I know the principals in the controversy and have thought about it long and hard, I do not claim to possess a satisfactory explanation of why people have reacted as they have. It is the better part of wisdom, I believe, to resist the temptation to psychologize; rather, one should attend to what people have actually said and try to credit the reasons they give for saying it. That way also holds greater promise for locating genuine agreements and disagreements.

Although I do enjoy a good argument, I do not relish controversy, and I undertake this essay with considerable reluctance. Some very unpleasant things have been said since the appearance of the November symposium. In private relationships, it is usually better to ignore such unpleasantnesses, especially when they are eruptions of passing pique, in the hope that bonds of affection and shared loyalty will be restored in time. There are different, although not necessarily conflicting, responsibilities in public debate. Having initiated a debate, one has a responsibility to see it through. Having engaged the attention of an audience, one cannot then dismiss their interest in subsequent exchanges as idle curiosity. The purpose of writing and publishing is to contribute to public discourse. Part of that job is responding to critics, even when they are friends, and even when their criticism is less than civil. I am resolved not to respond in kind, and withal to court a lightness of tone that does not put additional pressure on relationships already strained. Whether or not I keep that resolve is for the reader to judge.

In the first part of this essay I address misunderstandings and, in some instances, misrepresentations that have contributed to confusion in the discussion to date. This task will require a certain amount of brush-clearing, so to speak. The problem in such an exercise is that one is tempted to rebut every criticism and distortion that has cropped up in the course of the controversy. That would be both tedious and quarrelsome. The chief objection to a quarrel, Chesterton said somewhere, is that it interrupts an argument. So I will try to be selective, clearing away only the brush that has most obscured the argument to date. I turn then to the question of why the symposium has caused such strife, whether what is happening portends a break-up of "the conservative movement," and the very different understandings of conservatism that are in contention. We will want to ask the unavoidable question, Where do we go from here? And we will want to ask that question with specific reference to the threat that sparked the controversy in the first place, the judicial usurpation of politics. Finally, we will reflect on how this dispute illuminates both the difficulty and necessity of appeals to moral truth in public discourse.

ONE PARAGRAPH in our January 1997 editorial requires repeating:

> At question here is not merely a series of errors, even appalling errors, in particular court decisions. *If* the judiciary continues on its present course, *if* it does not restrain itself, and *if* there is no way to restrain it, we are witnessing the end of democracy. When we speak of the end of democracy it is not inappropriate to allude to the authoritarian and totalitarian alternatives to democracy, no matter how uncomfortable such allusions may be. In no way do the editors assume that such restraint of the judiciary is impossible. We wrote in our [November] introduction, "We hope that

more people know and more people care than is commonly supposed, and that it is not too late for effective recourse to whatever remedies may be available. It is in the service of that hope that we publish this symposium." That was and is our earnest intention. We probably cannot do much about critics who choose to think that we do not intend what we say we intend (117; B71).

The painful truth of that last sentence has been forcefully brought home to me as this controversy has continued to rage. In his *Commentary* essay and in interviews, my friend Peter Berger has repeatedly stated that our real concern is not judicial usurpation but the unlimited abortion license. As he told *The Chronicle of Higher Education*, "I do not share their position on abortion. And when one does not share it, the radical questioning of the legitimacy of American democracy becomes totally implausible. I don't want to be associated with it" (B143). It should be noted that on the question of abortion Berger considers himself more pro-life than pro-choice, as those terms are currently defined. But long before the November symposium, he complained that *First Things* was giving excessive attention to the abortion question.

There is no doubt that it makes a very big difference whether one really believes that abortion is the killing of an innocent human being. This is not the place for a thorough discussion of abortion, clearly the single most fevered, unsettled, and unsettling question in our public life. Suffice it that *First Things* is editorially committed to the frequently stated goal of "every unborn child protected in law and welcomed in life"—a goal that we well know will never be perfectly achieved in this very imperfect world. But does our commitment to this goal warrant the claim that our symposium's driving concern was not really judicial usurpation but abortion?

This much may readily be granted: If the courts usurped jurisdiction over relatively minor questions—for instance, the federal regulation of highway laws—it does seem very doubtful that we would have published a symposium of the title "The End of Democracy?" But the questions on which the courts have actually usurped power strike at the very heart of American democracy, challenging the right of a supposedly self-governing people to deliberate and decide how to order our life together. Preeminent, but by no means alone, among those questions is abortion, which is, among other things, the inescapably political question of who belongs to the community for which we accept common responsibility. So if all that critics mean to say is that we would not be as concerned about trivial offenses by the courts as we are about monstrous offenses, the point is so obvious as to hardly require discussion.

Critics who do not credit our stated intention allege that our concern about judicial activism is selective. If court decisions supported the judgments we favor, they say, we would not be raising an alarm about judicial usurpation. Berger, for instance, proposes a "thought experiment" in which it is Congress that establishes abortion on demand and the Supreme Court that rules it unconstitutional. The first thing to be said in response to his challenge is that nobody should claim immunity—certainly I do not claim immunity—from the temptation to approve the use of questionable means to achieve a good end. On the question of abortion and much else, I am not a disinterested observer.

A second and more pertinent response is that his hypothetical is wildly contrary both to fact and possibility. It is doubtful that there is a constitutional means by which Congress could have abolished the abortion law of all fifty states. If, notwithstanding, Congress had done what the Court did in *Roe v. Wade*, we would obviously be living in a very different America, so radically disordered in its morals and laws that government would likely be unsustainable. We would then be facing a crisis much greater than the crisis of judicial usurpation. Contrary to pro-abortion propaganda, the fact is that prior to the Court's preemption of the question in *Roe* the country was moving in the opposite direction as state legislatures were rejecting the pro-abortion position and reaffirming the legal protection of the unborn.[1]

The third and most pertinent response to Professor Berger's thought experiment is that if the Court had declared the hypothetical Congressional action unconstitutional it would only be doing its duty. Along with many constitutional scholars, I believe the Fourteenth Amendment protects unborn children when it declares "nor shall any State deprive any person of life, liberty, or property without due process of law; nor deny to any person within its jurisdiction the equal protection of the laws." Prior to *Roe*, that is what most scholars, courts, and legislatures believed, as the abortion laws of all fifty states reflected. Had the Court declared—in accord with the plain language of the Constitution, the legal tradition of the country, and the express will of the people—that abortion on demand is unconstitutional, it would not have been an act of judicial usurpation but of faithfulness to its legitimate function in our constitutional order. Moreover, even scholars who doubt that the Fourteenth Amendment applies to unborn children recognize that the great "innovation" (read: usurpation) of *Roe* was to nationalize a question that is rightly a concern of the states. Had this been done by Congress, as in Berger's thought experiment, we might have had a symposium on congressional usurpation. In any case, the thought experiment is no more than an effort to deny the stated intention of the *First Things* symposium.

Other critics have attempted to score debater's points by claiming that if permissive abortion law makes a government illegitimate, then there are very few legitimate governments in the world. The simplest answer to that ploy is to note that none of the editors or writers of *First Things* claims that the government of the United States is illegitimate. We do say that the regime of judicial usurpation is illegitimate and, if it is not rem-

---

1. See Russell Hittinger, "Abortion before Roe," *First Things* 46 (October 1994): 14-16.

edied, it will increasingly throw into question the legitimacy of the government as such. I don't know why some people find that distinction so difficult.

There is another distinction that seems to be lost on some critics. The question of illegitimacy arises not because of the abortion license but because judicial usurpation violates the proposition that "Governments are instituted among men, deriving their just powers from the consent of the governed." This statement of the Declaration of Independence is the foundational proposition of the American constitutional order. In our republican form of democratic government, powers that are not derived from the consent of the governed are not just, which is to say they are not legitimate. The Court's most egregious, but by no means only, violation of this proposition happens to be on the question of abortion, but it could have been in connection with some other question. In the nineteenth century it was the *Dred Scott* decision and the national establishment of slavery.

Specific laws, even when enacted by legitimate authority, may be deemed illegitimate because they violate "the laws of nature and of nature's God." I believe that *Roe* is such a law because it prohibits what is morally mandated, namely, the protection of unborn children. The question of the illegitimacy of the judicial regime, however, arises not because of abortion but because the Court does not have the legitimate authority to make such a law about abor-tion or anything else. It is, as Robert Bork suggests, outlaw law (16), and outlaw law can only encourage lawlessness. The Court exercised a power that is not derived from the consent of the governed, and in the instance of *Roe* made law contrary to the evident will of the governed and—I would argue, knowing that not all agree—contrary to the plain language of the Constitution.

That other nations have permissive abortion laws is, I would suggest, quite beside the point. Our business is with the American constitutional order. Nonetheless, it is worth noting, as the scholarship of Mary Ann Glendon of Harvard has definitively established, that the United States under *Roe* has the most permissive abortion license in the democratic world.[2] (Although some claim that Canada now has that dubious distinction.) Further, in countries such as France and Germany, abortion law is still within the political arena where it can be reconsidered and revised through the normal political process. In this country, the Court has declared that the abortion license is constitutionally entrenched and therefore beyond the bounds of political debate and decision. As Russell Hittinger's essay in the original symposium demonstrates (18-29), the Court has gone further by suggesting that those who oppose its abortion edict are guilty of undermining the constitutional order and indeed the rule of law.

*First Things'* position does not, as some critics suggest, reflect unlimited confidence in the *vox populi*. It does reflect a firm commitment to this constitutional order. And I for one am confident that, were it left to the people to decide through their representative institutions, we would have much more protective abortion law than we have at present. On the basis of the relevant survey research data of the last thirty years, it would appear that approximately 75 percent of the American people think abortion should not be permitted for the reasons that 95 percent of abortions are obtained. No more than 20 percent of the citizenry thinks that abortion should be legal for any reason at all during the entire nine months of pregnancy, which is of course the law (or lawlessness) of *Roe*.[3]

Nevertheless, one knows that opinion research does not translate directly into protective laws. The point here is that nobody—at least nobody in *First Things*—is saying that the government is illegitimate because of permissive abortion. We are saying that the abortion regime established by *Roe* and subsequent decisions is illegitimate, both because it violates higher law (as in "the laws

2. Mary Ann Glendon, *Abortion and Divorce in Western Law* (Cambridge, Mass.: Harvard University Press, 1989).

3. For a lucid analysis of the relevant research see James Davison Hunter, "What Americans Really Think about Abortion," *First Things* 24 (June/July 1992): 13-21.

of nature and of nature's God") and because it rests on decisions that the Court does not have the authority to make. One must hope that the governed have not entirely acquiesced in the judiciary's making law that does not have and will not obtain their consent.

Another constantly repeated charge is that *First Things* has adopted a radical and radicalizing posture reminiscent of the madnesses of the 1960s. This charge is supported by items large and small. For instance, in a discussion generally sympathetic to our argument, James Bowman, writing in the *Times Literary Supplement* (B171), regrets the "incendiary" fillers that accompanied the November symposium. Numerous others have made the same point. In fact, there were three quotations: one by Dietrich Bonhoeffer, the Lutheran pastor martyred by the Nazis; one by Martin Luther King Jr.; and one by abolitionist William Lloyd Garrison. They were carefully selected to demonstrate the range of Christian reflection on obedience to illegitimate law. Of the three only Garrison might be described as incendiary. King's "Letter from Birmingham Jail" is surely part of the canon of the American story and in the section quoted he cautions against anarchy and emphasizes the need to accept the penalty for selective civil disobedience. In the quotation from his *Ethics*, Bonhoeffer contends that, even under the provocation of tyrannical acts by a government such as the Third Reich, one must not conclude "that this govern-ment now possesses no claim to obedience in some of its other demands, or even in all its demands."

That is hardly "incendiary," "reckless," or "apocalyptic"—to cite but a few of the dismissive terms employed by critics. In 1970, Peter Berger and I published *Movement and Revolution*, in which Berger observed that the only revolutionary to be trusted is a reluctant revolutionary.[4] I agreed then and I agree now. In a time when talk about revolution was loosely bandied about, my part of that book was a cautionary examination of the criteria

---

4. Peter Berger and Richard John Neuhaus, *Movement and Revolution* (New York: Doubleday & Co., 1970).

that must be met for a "justified revolution," based on centuries of Christian reflection about "justified war." I am not surprised when leftists eager to divide their opponents caricature my colleagues and me as the Abbie Hoffmans or Tom Haydens of the 1990s, but I admit to disappointment when they are fed their lines by people who actually know what we are saying and, at least in some cases, have been saying for many years.

*Forward* (formerly known as the *Jewish Daily Forward*) ran the headline, "Neuhaus' Call for Revolution Touches Off Storm" (B28). The story asserted that the conservative coalition "is coming unglued over whether America is beginning to resemble Nazi Germany." "Father Neuhaus suggests," readers were told, "that no response [to the crisis of judicial usurpation] would be too extreme." In his distinctive contribution to elevating the level of public discourse, Walter Berns is quoted as saying that I "should see a psychiatrist." The story notes that the *First Things* editorial cites a papal encyclical, and then immediately follows that, curiously enough, with this: "Not that anyone would accuse Father Neuhaus of being insensitive to the Jewish cause; his split with the Rockford Institute [in 1989] was triggered by his suggestion that the right-wing think tank was not being alert enough to the dangers of anti-Semitism." So citing a papal encyclical is not necessarily an anti-Semitic act. It is good to have that cleared up. *Forward* was courteous enough to print my letter in which I pointed out that "the call of the symposium was not . . . for revolution but for a restoration of the constitutional order" (B32).

Such distinctions, which seemed so evident to my colleagues and me, were lost on many others. No doubt we could have made the argument more clearly. Anything human is subject to improvement. But at times one suspected a willful determination to misunderstand, to put the worst possible construction on what was said. At other times, the operative assumption appeared to be that some things simply must not be discussed. There is much to be said for the position that decency and prudence require reticence on some topics. But we cannot rule out of order or consign to a memory hole large parts of our civilizational story. Critics leapt on the fact that one essay in the original symposium, that by Charles Colson, traced the history of Christian reflection on disobedience to illegitimate regimes. This was taken as evidence that *First Things* had gone over the edge, as though Augustine, Aquinas, Calvin, and John Knox are not part of the mainstream of the Western experience.

Locating the "mainstream" is, of course, a tricky business, and many are tempted to assert, *Le* mainstream? *C'est moi!* Among some who presume to represent the mainstream, nothing was stronger evidence of our "ideological deviationism" (to employ a Marxist term) than the reference to Nazi Germany. Recall the allegedly notorious sentence: "America is not and, please God, will never become Nazi Germany. . . ." (6; B1). Here is a remarkable thing: In the numerous published references to that sentence not one—not even one—mentioned that the reference was to John Paul II and the encyclical *Evangelium Vitae*. Repeatedly it was asserted that Neuhaus—always "Neuhaus," never "the editors"—compared, perhaps even equated, America with Nazi Germany. The fact is that the previous sentence refers to *Evangelium Vitae*, and our statement intends to make clear that the Pope is *not* saying that America is comparable to Nazi Germany.

Yes, yes, but what about the rest of our infamous sentence, ". . . it is only blind hubris that denies it can happen here and, in peculiarly American ways, may be happening here"? What about it indeed? As any fair reading of the passage will show, the antecedent to "it" in that sentence is John Paul's assertion that laws that contravene the moral order "undermine the very nature of authority and result in shameful abuse." Does any sensible person deny that that can happen and may be happening here? Such a denial requires, it seems to me, a dangerously inflated belief in American exceptionalism. And to the degree that "it" does happen here, is it not, although in peculiarly American ways, similar to what happened in Nazi Germany?

All right, someone might respond, but why bring up Nazi Germany at all? The answer is that our subject was the relationship between positive law and moral law, and in the brilliant essay by Robert George, the teaching of *Evangelium Vitae* on that subject was examined. In the encyclical, John Paul II makes the connection with Nazi Germany. Immediately following our much-attacked sentence we wrote that "it is the Supreme Court that has raised the question of the legitimacy of its law, and we do not believe the Pope is an alarmist" (6). As I said, not one critic to date has mentioned the encyclical in connection with the Nazi reference, perhaps because they do not want to say publicly that they do think he is an alarmist. For that matter, few among those who have decried our discussing "legitimacy" have mentioned that the question was very explicitly raised by the Court. The line is that *First Things* is irresponsibly provocative, incendiary, apocalyptic, etc., in raising these questions. To paraphrase Lincoln on the fellow they rode out of town on a rail, if it weren't for the honor of the thing, I'd just as soon they would read what we wrote.

If any one person represents the mainstream of American conservatism, I suppose it is William F. Buckley Jr. He has made several valuable interventions in the discussion. In the *Commentary* symposium, he defends *First Things'* "thinking out loud" about what cannot be declared off limits as unthinkable (B119). Buckley and the other editors of *National Review* expand on this point:

> In the abstract, the point is obviously reachable when a rogue society forfeits the loyalty of responsible and courageous citizens. It is not always easy to recognize that point, which often passes by societies that wake to find a despotism in power. Norman Podhoretz was greatly disturbed at the sentence in Father Neuhaus's introduction in which he spoke of Hitler Germany. . . . But surely the point to reflect upon, especially between scholars as engaged intellectually and personally as Richard John Neuhaus and Norman Podhoretz, is the uses of simile. That Hitler is different from the Supreme Court of the United States does not disable the analyst whose purpose is to point out what similarities

there are—in this case, moral usurpation; indeed, a denial
of moral language. . . . The *First Things* essays ask not for
revolutionary defiance, but for organic thought given to the
attenuation of loyalties. The moment can come when loyalty
is severed. . . . Most conservatives will acknowledge the
usefulness of sharpening the discriminating faculties that
allocate loyalties; but they will decline a war against our
political regime, and most emphatically decline a war against
our brethren, the neocons (126-27; B55).

I trust it does not detract from my warm agreement with what he
says if I observe that even an analyst so acute as Buckley fails to
mention that the Nazi simile was introduced by a source considerably more authoritative than myself.


*America*, THE JESUIT WEEKLY, devoted a long and thoughtful
article to the controversy, using the occasion to evaluate the
influence of the Catholic neoconservatives—meaning chiefly
Michael Novak, George Weigel, and myself. In "The 'Catholic
Moment' Under Siege" (B164), Father David Toolan says that the
Catholic neocons have been "broadly ecumenical" and have
"pioneered conversations with leading Jewish intellectuals,
Evangelicals, fundamentalist and Pentecostal Protestants—even
the editors of the *Wall Street Journal*." (For *America*, it seems, the
*Wall Street Journal* is a real reach.) "The Catholic neocon success
story is that they have pulled all these groups together—people
who haven't ordinarily talked to each other—in the ongoing task
of reflecting critically on what [John Courtney] Murray called
the 'American experiment in ordered liberty.'"

The question is whether that "success story" has now been
jeopardized by the *First Things* brouhaha. Toolan notes that the
January issue of the journal cites the encyclical *Centesimus Annus*
in support of the thesis that democracy is a moral imperative.
"[Neuhaus] remains, at least at this point, a reformer and has not
issued a call for civil disobedience, much less insurrection. But if

anything, he raised the ante, acknowledging that religion in the public square can be a 'subversive force' and wondering whether the judicial 'aberration is somehow inherent in the constitutional order itself.' If his former allies were expecting an apology or a recantation, this was hardly it." Toolan quotes the passage from Gertrude Himmelfarb's letter of resignation protesting the symposium: "Indeed, it discredits, or at the very least makes suspect, any attempt by conservatives to introduce moral and religious considerations into 'the public square'—as if morality and religion necessarily lead to such apocalyptic conclusions" (113). "Gertrude Himmelfarb's letter of resignation," Toolan writes, "evoked the neoconservative movement's worst fear—political suicide."

One form of political suicide is to incur guilt by association. If you are in the business of persuading, you want *almost* everybody to agree with you. There are some people whose agreement you definitely don't want. I confess that my own inclination is to say pretty much what I think needs saying, and not to be excessively inhibited by fears about who will agree or disagree. Which probably explains why I am so often in trouble. The fear of guilt by association reached a frenzy during what is called the McCarthy era. Arthur Koestler addressed the fear in a Carnegie Hall lecture in 1948. "Bad" allies, he told the audience, are unavoidable. "You can't help people being right for the wrong reasons. . . . This fear of finding oneself in bad company is not an expression of political purity; it is an expression of a lack of self-confidence."[5]

The pioneers of the neoconservative project have vivid memories of the McCarthy era, and indeed first honed their polemical skills in the ideological bloodlettings of the left in the late 1930s. In that world of political and intellectual struggle, location was everything. It mattered intensely where you stood and with whom you stood. Deviationism to the left or the right was mortal sin. It is entirely understandable that, in defining this new thing called neoconservatism, people who were moving from the left to the

5. Quoted in Tony Judt, "The Dualist," *The New Republic*," April 14, 1997:42.

right were self-consciously alert to their perceived location within the larger world of the politics of ideas. In the nineteenth century it was said that conservativism was the "stupid party." The great achievement of neoconservatism—both celebrated and deplored in many books and innumerable articles—is that, while not everyone agreed it had made conservatism the smart party, it had certainly succeeded in making conservatism intellectually respectable.

Needless to say, there are conservatives who were conservative "right from the beginning," as Pat Buchanan might put it, and many of them don't agree with this telling of the neoconservative story. In their worlds they thought themselves eminently respectable, and they do not take kindly to the suggestion that they had to borrow intellectual respectability from a band of refugees fleeing the madnesses of the left. More on those disputes later. For the moment we take note of the standard telling of the neocon-servative ascendancy, and why it is that some feared *First Things* was threatening to throw it all away.

It is hardly surprising when the likes of Richard Cohen of *The Washington Post* (B99), Frank Rich of *The New York Times* (B10), Jacob Heilbrunn of *The New Republic* (143-55; B53), and Garry Wills of, well, it seems almost everything (B78) gleefully depict the *First Things* argument as an incitement to bomb throwing. That is exactly what some neoconservatives feared, and in their rush to distance themselves they inadvertently ended up repeating the formulas of anathematization employed by their long-standing opponents on the left. Quite predictably, this circumstance has led to confusion about who stands where, and with whom.

No one doubts that Gertrude Himmelfarb is a cultural historian of great distinction. She has distinguished herself also by insisting upon the most exacting standards of accuracy in the exercise of the historian's craft. While she was never closely involved with the work of *First Things* and its sponsoring institute, we have been in friendly conversation for at least twenty years.

When I heard about her resignation, I called her and we discussed it in what I thought to be a friendly manner. I was not terribly surprised that she was unhappy with the symposium. She, along with Peter Berger, was unable to attend the editorial board meeting at which the symposium was planned. I was very surprised that she felt it necessary to resign from the board. I suppose the argument could be made that, had it not been for the resignations of Himmelfarb and Berger, the symposium would not have received the attention it has. Certainly there would have been no story for those who are so desirous of seeing a "conservative crack-up."

Writing in *Commentary*, Himmelfarb says that *First Things* is issuing "a new call for revolution," and "this is a revolution truly worthy of the name." She continues: "That the editors believe the regime to be actually or imminently illegitimate is suggested again and again in the introduction to the symposium. We are told that 'many millions of children' have come to believe that 'the government that rules them is morally illegitimate,' and that 'perhaps even a majority' of Americans feel that they have to choose between 'God *or* country'" (89; B124).

In Himmelfarb's version, a speculation that was cautionary and in the future tense somehow was transposed into an assertion that is descriptive and in the present tense. The editors were pondering what might happen if the judicial usurpation of politics is not remedied. The editorial passage in question began with, "What are the consequences when many millions of children are told and come to believe that the government that rules them is morally illegitimate?" And it ended with, "We do not know what would happen then, and we hope never to find out" (8; B1). Himmelfarb's rendering of the text is seriously in error.

There is a similar difficulty with her public statements in a number of forums that the editors of *First Things* believe the government of the United States is illegitimate and are calling for revolution, even though we have repeatedly said quite the opposite. If one is not careful, especially in the heat of polemical exchange, it can happen that he is so certain that he knows what people *meant* to say that he convinces himself that they actually said it. In any event, the editors said just what they meant to say and, since there could hardly be anything more on the public record than this controversy, it does seem necessary to respectfully offer these corrections for the sake of accuracy.

Peter Berger's resignation is a very different matter. There are few people in my life to whom I owe such a debt of friendship and intellectual stimulation. Over more than thirty years now, we have written books together, issued manifestos, directed all kinds of projects, and, perhaps most important, luxuriated in hours beyond numbering of eating, drinking, good argument, and bad cigars. I do not for a moment believe that has come to an end.

There are personal factors that do not belong in an essay such as this, but so much has been made publicly of Berger's resignation that perhaps a word of explanation is in order. He was unhappy with a number of important decisions I had made in recent years, and as discussed above, he thought the journal excessively preoccupied with the question of abortion. He knew that I thought his "more pro-life than pro-choice" position (73; B117) was intellectually and morally unconvincing, as well as being politically impracticable. But it was not over that issue that we had, very reluctantly, discontinued his monthly column in *First Things*. He had over time grown increasingly concerned about a number of matters, some of which I probably don't understand as well as I should, and the November symposium finally triggered his break with the journal, but not, I am confident, the breaking of our friendship.

The third resignation, that of Walter Berns, is again a very different matter, and not without its amusing aspects. I suppose I have met Walter Berns four or five times over the last twenty years and found him a congenial fellow. I recall that we once had a friendly public debate at Boston College on the role of religion in the American founding. His was a name carried over to the masthead of *First Things* from its predecessor journal, a quarterly called *This World*, which Irving Kristol had asked me to take over in the early 1980s. I was quite taken aback by the peremptory tone of his letter of resignation: "You do not speak for me (a member of the Editorial Advisory Board since the inception of the journal) when you say that the government of the United States is morally illegitimate and come close to advocating not only civil disobedience but armed revolution. I don't care to engage in an argument with you; I want simply to announce my resignation from the advisory board" (113-14; B62).

And so the news was disseminated near and far: "Three members of the editorial board resigned in protest against the editorial direction of *First Things.*" But of course Berns had never had the slightest involvement in the direction of the journal. He has made two contributions over the years. The first was a nice little opinion piece on same-sex marriage (he was against it), and the second was his letter of resignation. A further oddity in Berns's part in this controversy is that he believes that, as he writes in the *Commentary* symposium, the Constitution "consign[s] religion to the private sphere" (77; B118). One can scarcely help but wonder why for eight years he was even so marginally associated with a journal which has as its declared purpose the countering of that reading of the Constitution, and is published by an organization called the Institute on Religion and Public Life.

One cannot help but be amused by Berns's identification of *First Things* with the "paleoconservatives" in view of the fact that the last big public ruckus over conservative realignments was our 1989 break with the Rockford Institute, which is generally thought to be a bastion of paleocon orthodoxy. There is delightful irony, too, in the fact that Berns's garbled account should appear in *Commentary*, which, along with its then-editor Norman Podhoretz, played such a prominent and honorable part in those events. Less amusing is his treatment of the late Russell Kirk. "Rather rudely," he admits, he interrupted Kirk's presentation on the moral and religious basis of society, and suggests that Kirk's perfunctory response showed that the question of religious pluralism "had never occurred to him" (74-75). Many of us had substantive disagreements with Kirk, but this anecdote is an egregious insult to his memory. I expect that Kirk was, as Berns says, taken aback by the bad-mannered interruption and that the brevity of his response indicated his desire to overlook it. Russell Kirk was a gentleman.

On the main issue, judicial usurpation, Berns does not seem to differ with the *First Things* writers, although he might be somewhat more despairing of the future of our constitutional order. In a 1993 book published by the American Enterprise Institute, he favorably quotes Fred Baumann who wrote that "it becomes ever clearer that it is not the Constitution that lives but only its name; consequently neither the Constitution nor the Court deriving its justification from the Constitution can enjoy further legitimacy." "I know of no one who has put this better," writes Berns. While we have not reached the point described by Baumann, Berns writes, "The idea of constitutionality—and its converse, unconstitutionality—is still accepted by the American people but only, I suspect, because, in their commendable innocence, they continue to believe that it is the Constitution whose provisions the Court is enforcing." [6] If there is a disagreement with Berns, it might be on whether such popular innocence is commendable. In a book marking the bicentennial of the Constitution, Berns wrote: "If, as seems likely, we will not much longer have reason to celebrate these constitutional anniversaries, it will not be because of any failing on the part of ordinary Americans." [7] That doleful view of our constitutional future may strike many as a bit apocalyptic, but I would not call Walter Berns an alarmist.

Propriety protests discussing Norman Podhoretz in a section devoted to brush-clearing, for he is a towering figure of legendary status in the political journalism of the past four decades. I am

6. Walter Berns, "Preserving the Living Constitution," in *Is the Supreme Court the Guardian of the Constitution?*, ed. Robert Licht (Washington, D.C.: AEI Press, 1993), p.45.

7. Berns, *Taking the Constitution Seriously* (New York: Simon & Schuster, 1987), p.13.

pleased to count him as a friend, although our friendship does seem to have hit a rough patch. In his *Commentary* essay, Podhoretz complains: "Far from having discovered this threat, *First Things* has merely joined in a clamor over the imperial judiciary that some of us have been raising for twenty-five years" (95; B127). He is entirely right. Under his spirited editorship, *Commentary* raised many important clamors, and it is not fair that *First Things* should receive the credit for putting judicial usurpation so high on the political agenda. Podhoretz laid the groundwork for numerous questions being pressed today, and I am pleased to have had a small part by virtue of his having welcomed me as a contributor to *Commentary* over the years. Norman Podhoretz's editorship of *Commentary* will go down in the annals of political journalism, and credit is due.

I am puzzled by Podhoretz's saying in his letter to me, which he quotes in his essay, that he sees "no significant difference" between Robert Paul Wolff's position and mine (95). Wolff said that "anyone who still believed that America was a democracy belonged in an insane asylum." I would suggest that it is a significant difference that I think anyone who believes America is *not* a democracy belongs in an insane asylum, although I would not put it so rudely. Of course we can disagree about what constitutes a significant difference. Podhoretz writes, "Neuhaus now denies that the symposium said what so many of us understood it as saying" (95). In view of the fact that the symposium did not say what he and a few others said it said, he might consider the possibility that he *mis*understood.

I concede it is difficult being accused of "anti-Americanism," since I have over the years been attacked from the left for my excessive attachment to America and its constitutional order. I have written books and innumerable articles, not least of all in *Commentary*, in critical affirmation of the American experiment. *Time* magazine once observed that I hope to appear before the Throne of Judgment as an American. "It is a wonder to me," writes Podhoretz, "that my old friend Richard Neuhaus has forgotten what we learned while fighting those wars as comrades-in-arms against the radicalism we had both formerly espoused" (102). Wonder and worry not, dear friend, I have forgotten nothing.

It is new to me, however, that Podhoretz sees himself as my spiritual director. "Nothing less than a frank and forthright recognition of error (or should I say an act of contrition?) will suffice, and of that, alas, I see no sign so far." He concludes with the hope that I will "re-emerge as a born-again neoconservative" (103). I had always thought that Podhoretz agreed with me on the dangers of treating politics as a religion. My suggestion is that we leave aside talk about confession and conversion and just go back to being friends. As for explaining his explosive reaction to the symposium, I can do no better than agree with Buckley who wrote, "Norman Podhoretz was greatly disturbed" (127; B55).

One or two other critics in the *Commentary* symposium accuse *First Things* and me personally of being theocratic opponents of democracy, among other ludicrous charges. What is one to say? I am keenly aware that there are millions, even billions, of people on planet earth who know nothing about *First Things* and are entirely unfamiliar with my own writings. Such ignorance is no fault. But it baffles me why an editor would want to publish what such people have to say about the journal and my own views. As an editor, I would no more publish, say, Irwin Stelzer on these matters (103-07; B128) than I would an author who attacked Norman Podhoretz for not caring about the State of Israel or an author who deplored Peter Berger's ignorance of sociology. Such people simply don't know what they are talking about.

I was also taken aback by the intensely personal nature of attacks. It was "Neuhaus" this and "Neuhaus" that, with no recognition that the *First Things* initiative was a thoroughly collaborative effort involving such as editor James Nuechterlein, who is also, not so incidentally, a long-standing *Commentary* contributor. There was no discussion of the arguments in the original symposium of Hadley Arkes, Robert Bork, Charles Colson, Robert George, or Russell Hittinger. By no means were all the *Commentary* contributors critical of the symposium, but those who did rant against it did so without reference to the people and ideas that constituted the substance of the symposium. This too seemed very odd. It is as though, with the partial exception of Robert Bork, what the symposiasts said is of no consequence. The point is that Neuhaus, who was "one of us," must be punished for his alleged deviation. The dynamics are curiously reminiscent of those so nicely analyzed by Norman Podhoretz as he recounts his deviation from the Left in his instructive book, *Breaking Ranks*. Ideological excommunication did not stop Norman Podhoretz then, for which we can be thankful, and I expect it has considerably less potency in the present instance.

So far I have been discussing very atypical responses to the *First Things* initiative. In his *Commentary* essay, Robert Bartley, editor of the *Wall Street Journal*, writes, "It seems to be Neuhaus against everyone else" (B116). I suppose he wrote that very soon after the November symposium appeared, when he had had a chance to talk only with a few of his friends. The reality is that the response has been overwhelmingly favorable. Aside from critics on the left and a handful of conservatives, almost all of whom were included in the *Commentary* symposium, the *First Things* initiative has met with truly remarkable support. A month after *The Weekly Standard* attacked us, the editors acknowledged privately and with some surprise that they had received an unusual amount of mail and all of it, without exception, took the side of *First Things* (B29; B31). In addition, while it was certainly not our purpose, we cannot pretend to be displeased that the affair has had an excellent effect on circulation and, contrary to the predictions of some, financial support for the institute and the journal is, I am happy to say, encouragingly solid.

WHILE KEEPING IN MIND Arthur Koestler's sage counsel against worrying excessively about friends who may be right for the wrong reason, one has a responsibility to clarify also to friends what he is and is not saying. To cite one example of many, the syndicated columnist Cal Thomas has addressed the controversy on several occasions. Although the neoconservative world of, say, *Commentary* is far removed from Thomas, he is read by many millions of Americans; his writing runs neck-and-neck with George Will for the title of most widely syndicated opinion column in the nation. With particular reference to Charles Colson's essay (41-52; B5), Thomas suggested in an early column that the question of judicial usurpation forces a hard choice for religious conservatives (B13).

In decisions such as *Planned Parenthood v. Casey, Lee v. Weisman,* and *Romer v. Evans,* the Supreme Court has practically excluded religion and even morality that "transcends human invention" from standing in our legal system, says Thomas. He correctly anticipated that the Court would strike down the Religious Freedom Restoration Act, thus putting "the state in a position of supreme authority over all matters deemed to have religious origins." The 1996 election shows, he believes, that the Republican Party has abandoned the public questions that most clearly engage moral judgment. Thomas continues:

> Conservative religious believers are now faced with a clear choice. They can abandon their political interests and claim resident alien status in a land that has forgotten their God, no longer concerned, in Colson's worlds, "about the fortunes or misfortunes of a flawed republic, no longer consider this land their country." Or they can continue in frustration to try to restore a moral order from the top down, which seems to me like building the house before the foundation is laid. Or they can remember what the Founders said: "When, in the course of human events, it becomes necessary for one people to dissolve the political bands which have connected them with one another, and to assume, among the powers of the Earth, the separate and equal station to which the laws of Nature of Nature's God entitle them. . . ." Which course religious conservatives choose will have profound

political and social consequences for those living in the
twenty-first century (B13).

Thomas and others who speak in a similar vein should not
be dismissed lightly. Thomas's audience extends far beyond those
who are derisively called fundamentalists or members of the religious right. His view reflects an alienation from government that
is both deeper and more widespread than many commentators
appreciate. The conventional wisdom is that low voter turnout
and other indicators reflect a disillusionment with government
because government doesn't do things very well or because of
political scandals related to campaign financing and the such.
That is, I believe, a dangerously superficial analysis that fails to
recognize that millions of Americans are, albeit in varying degrees,
alienated because they perceive the government, and especially
the courts, as hostile to their deepest convictions and their hopes
for the world they want to pass on to their children.

Thomas is an evangelical. American evangelicalism is marked
by a high level of enthusiasm—religiously, as Monsignor Ronald
Knox described in his classic book *Enthusiasm*, but also politically.
Such enthusiasm is a great strength, and a great weakness. Of the
essays in the November symposium, some critics targeted Charles
Colson's as going over the top. Others thought Colson the very
soul of moderation compared with James Dobson's contribution
(75-78; B68). Who are these people? Where do they come from?
After publishing Dobson's article, I was struck by the number of
intellectuals and supposed opinion leaders who wanted to know
who this Dobson fellow is. He is, of course, the founding president
of Focus on the Family, which runs what is quite possibly the
largest network of communications in America.

Many years ago, I published an article in *Commentary*, "What
Do the Fundamentalists Want?" That was when the "religious
right" was in its first flush, and the best and brightest of our national commentators were emitting confused alarms about these
aliens from another planet who had invaded our cultural and
political space. As the current controversy testifies, elite opinion,

on both the right and the left, has over the last twenty years not become much wiser on this score. The chattering classes of our elite universities, opinion journals, and foundations have yet to be successfully introduced to a large number, perhaps a majority, of their fellow citizens.

What Richard Nixon called "the silent majority" is, to say the least, silent no more. In the context of the present controversy, one might cite many voices from within that world, but the voice of Cal Thomas usefully demonstrates both what is right and what is wrong in one kind of response to the crisis. Continued political engagement to "restore the moral order" along the lines attempted by the Christian Coalition is, says Thomas, "like building the house before the foundation is laid." He proposes three possibilities: alien resident status, continued political participation, and revolution. If, as I think is the case, revolution is not an option, the third possibility is the same as the first, the only question being whether one's period of alien residency will be spent in a prison cell. Our task is to persuade Thomas and those of like mind that the "foundation" has been laid, and it has been well laid by those we call the Founders. Our current contestation is over defining that foundation—whether it is the Puritan-Lockean synthesis of those who wrote and ratified the Constitution or whether it is the "living constitution" of those who have declared the first constitution dead. That is the choice, and about that choice the contest is by no means over.

Yet some secular commentators are uneasy even about referring to the original understanding as a Puritan-Lockean synthesis. Any reference in public to transcendent truth (as in "Puritan"), except when limited to the purely ceremonial, gives them the heebie-jeebies. In this connection, the initial reaction by *The Weekly Standard* is instructive (129-33; B24). It is a masterpiece of decorous ambivalence, an ambivalence inspired in significant part by the fact that Gertrude Himmelfarb is editor William Kristol's mother and Norman Podhoretz is deputy editor John Podhoretz's father. Further, their contributing editor, J. Bottum, is our associate editor, and other *First Things* contributors are also close to *The Weekly Standard*. Author David Brooks was walking on eggs, and he did so with consummate skill.

The ambivalence is the more striking in its treatment of truth and politics. An older conservative temperament that "fears change, distrusts abstract notions, reveres the here and now, and is obsessed by historical continuity," we are told, long ago gave way to the current conservative movement that "had to argue for propositions that had previously been unquestioned." Conservatives now, writes Brooks, "needed to put into words things that had been accepted as given, and they needed to apply abstract ideals to political debate. Some secular conservatives took the ideals of the free market and applied them to politics. Some religious conservatives brought their religious beliefs more closely to bear on political issues" (130).

Then Brooks swings to the other side, worrying that conservatism may "abandon reasoned argument" and "console itself with the glories of transcendence and hope these could compensate for its abandonment of the here and now" (132). Abstract ideals are fine in their place but religious conservatives in particular, we are invited to believe, may take them too far, leading to extremism or escapism, and thus giving conservatism a bad odor. (Instead of "abstract ideals," some of us speak of constituting principles, such as government deriving its authority from the consent of the governed.) Then Brooks swings again. "But the *First Things* symposium, while still an outlier, may also be a harbinger. . . . The Republican party proudly calls itself the party of ideas. Well, Republicans had better learn to take the good with the bad." And here Brooks swings yet again: "Idea-driven people are quick to abandon political parties. They have been known to fly off the handle. And intellectuals sometimes blithely engage in discussion of civil disobedience and revolution, as if talk of these horrendous subjects had no real-world consequences" (133).

Brooks concludes with the suggestion that maybe it would be better if we didn't talk out loud about these dangerous abstract

ideals, citing my statement in favor of public reticence in connection with the Herrnstein-Murray book, *The Bell Curve*. I had
written back then, "America is not an academic seminar limited
to a few utterly dispassionate and socially disengaged intellectuals
interested only in 'the truth'" (133). My point then was that, even
if we accept *The Bell Curve* claim that there is a significant gap in
cognitive skills between blacks and others, there are no acceptable
policy implications that follow, and a great deal of damage can be
done by the public dissemination of the putative scientific finding
that blacks are cognitively inferior. I may have been wrong and
am open to being instructed, but my view was and is that no
good comes from the very public discussion of *The Bell Curve*.
The judicial usurpation of politics is an entirely different matter.
The more the truth about it is publicly disseminated, the more
people who know and care about it, the more likely it is that a
way can be found to set it right. I may be wrong about that, too,
but I think not.

Some neoconservatives are very strong on America as "the
first universal nation," meaning that it is a nation constituted by
ideas rather than by ethnicity, culture, morality, or shared historical
experience. Some of the same people, however, want those ideas
to be kept on a very short leash, lest they bring under judgment
what America has become. And they panic when those ideas are
joined to transcendent truth, as in "the laws of nature and of
nature's God." This begins to look very dangerously like religion.
And we all know that religion is the wild card in the deck,
threatening to break up the political game by fanaticism unloosed.
Moreover, the threat is most alarming when the card is played by
"The Other America" (to employ Michael Harrington's title to a
different purpose) of evangelical Christians.

Of course, this panic is not limited to neoconservatives. Jacob
Heilbrunn of *The New Republic* is, putting it gently, no neocon
(143-54; B53). But Michael Novak gets it right in his extensive
response to Heilbrunn, also in *The New Republic* (B139). Novak
writes: "I suspect . . . that what he really is afraid of is evangelical

Protestants. It is they whom he most patronizes, speaking of them as if, if they are to amount to anything, they need to be tutored either by Jews or by Catholics. It is not attractive that Heilbrunn thinks of them as the hand of the devil. His cover, that he is merely one Jew accusing other Jews of political cynicism, isn't persuasive to those in the line of fire. Demonizing others is illiberal, and so is sowing religious animosity."

In ways both overt and subtle, the assuming and sowing of religious animosities reappears regularly in this controversy. In his journalistically deft discussion in the *New York Times* (B37), Peter Steinfels picks up on Heilbrunn's claim that "at least some of the neocons"—whom he does not name—think the exertions of Catholic and evangelical conservatives "directly threatens Jews" (135). Steinfels writes, "It is the article's most ominous, and of course politically and religiously explosive, sentence. To back it up, Heilbrunn weaves a far-flung theory, transforming the dispute into a war between followers of the political theorist Leo Strauss and followers of Thomas Aquinas. . . . It is an account that will not impress readers who know much about the topic . . . or those who know that [*First Things*] is a leading place for serious discussion by Christians and Jews of their complicated relationships."

Steinfels notes that Heilbrunn swears innocence of any intention to sow religious animosity. "His objective, he said in a phone conversation, was to show up the [Jewish] neoconservatives as being 'hypocrites' for cynically allying themselves with people he thinks should be their natural enemies." The last phrase is employed by Norman Podhoretz when he writes that he and others are accused of "the heinous crime of associating with Christians" who are presumably the "natural enemies" of Jews (100). In a letter to the *Times*, Jacob Heilbrunn strongly protests Steinfels's analysis. "Far from denigrating [the mostly Catholic intellectuals], I sought to treat them respectfully, by recognizing their belief in a transcendent divine law that carries universal obligations, even for nonbelievers. I take their absolutism seriously.

Indeed, the criticism in my essay was directed at the mostly Jewish neoconservatives, who cynically leagued themselves, for reasons of politics, with a theocratic disposition that they do not share" (B45).

Yes, let us by all means preserve the protocols of civility by treating with great respect those of "a theocratic disposition" who would impose their "absolutism" on the rest of us.

# 2

# SPURS UNTO STRIFE

I TURN NOW to the ways in which various commentators
have tried to explain what is behind the explosions occasioned by the *First Things* argument. Almost everybody
except Jacob Heilbrunn rejects his attempt to construe the dispute
as a fight between Christians and Jews, and yet the Christian-
Jewish factor keeps cropping up in the discussion. More precisely,
commentaries regularly refer to the Jewish factor in explaining
the negative reaction to the symposium. Sanford Pinsker is
professor of humanities at Franklin and Marshall College, and
he suggests in *Midstream* that it is essential to understand the
controversy in the context of the "New York intellectuals." (That
phrase is the title of a book by Irving Howe that chronicles the
mainly intra-Jewish battles of the thirties and forties.) "But unlike
the old battle lines that separated hard-line communists from
democratic socialists or Zionists from anti-Zionists," writes
Pinsker, "this time it is the cultural Right that finds itself embroiled
in controversy" (B194).

"The defection of many Jewish intellectuals from the liberal-
left is now a sturdy fact of American political life," observes

Pinsker. The reason for that defection has to do both with Israel and with political-cultural developments in the U.S. "What happened, of course, is that many former left liberals (among them Irving Kristol, Nathan Glazer, and Norman Podhoretz) began to feel itchy about a growing, and often anti-Semitic, opposition to Israel; the irresponsible, revolutionary rhetoric of the New Left; and perhaps most of all, with a sense that America itself was being denounced—indeed, dismissed—as *Amerika*. Indeed, these Cold War warriors saw a belief in institutions eroding and civilization itself in steady decline."

While "the generation of immigrant Jewish intellectuals may have once offered up sharp critiques of capitalism or felt it essential to maintain an adversarial role with regard to much that passed for mainstream culture, they were also unabashed patriots." Pinsker's point is poignantly made also in David Horowitz's recent memoir, *Radical Son*.[1] He describes a childhood in which his parents and their friends, all Jewish and all members of the Communist Party, were actively involved in what can only be described as treasonous activity, and yet were convinced that they were "progressives" patriotically working for the well-being of the country they had so fervently embraced. In Pinsker's view, the neocons who had moved beyond the *Amerika* of the 1960s adversarial culture and were defending what might be called the actual, existing America viewed patriotism in a very different way. "For them, it is high time to retire the word 'experiment' from discussions of what America was, and might yet become."

George Washington and other Founders spoke of America as an experiment, but that was more than two hundred years ago. *First Things* offended by suggesting that the language of experiment is still pertinent and that, as is the nature of experiments, it might succeed or fail—and maybe it is failing. Midge Decter writes in *Commentary*: "What will drive us apart, and has to some extent in very limited quarters already done so, are not differences

1. David Horowitz, *Radical Son* (New York: Free Press, 1997).

over matters of policy but differences in bedrock attitudes toward the United States of America. There are those of us who still have the good sense—the good conservative sense—to regard it, sins and shortcomings and all, as a blessed place in which to live" (BI20). Patriotism cuts in different directions. That fact is captured nicely in a personal exchange on the controversy between William Bennett and Charles Colson. Bennett protested, "But this is *America* we're talking about it!" "That's exactly the point," responded Colson, "this is *America* we're talking about!" [2]

Pinsker, incidentally, is among those who have indicated a quite different reason for what he calls "the firestorm of controversy" sparked by *First Things*. It has to do with a conflict between "now old-line neoconservatives and the new kids on the political block—the 'theocons' as [Jacob Heilbrunn] dubbed them." The idea that there is a neocon establishment may seem implausible to those who view neoconservatism as a small band of insurgents against *the* establishment, but it is true that neoconservatism as a political-intellectual phenomenon has been around for better than twenty years, and its "godfather," Irving Kristol, has on many occasions opined that the term "neoconservatism" can just as well be dropped, since what was called neoconservatism is now, quite simply, conservatism. That does sound like establishment.

The launching of publications was central to the neocon insurgency, and in most of those launchings Irving Kristol had a central role. *The Public Interest*, *The National Interest*, and *The New Criterion* attended to public policy, foreign affairs, and the arts, respectively. Through its predecessor publication, *This World*, Kristol also had a significant role in the beginnings of *First Things*. In the publishing constellation, however, it was understood that *Commentary*, converted to neoconservatism by Norman Podhoretz, was the flagship journal. In the view espoused by some, *First Things*, the relatively "new kid on the political block," was supposed to keep religion in line with neoconservatism's grand

2. Personal conversation with Charles W. Colson, January 1997.

strategy, and "The End of Democracy?" offended by challenging that grand strategy. We broke ranks and thus became a threat. This explanation of the intra-neocon brouhaha will appeal to the conspiracy-minded and those who are not satisfied until every disagreement is reduced to a conflict of interests, but it has little else to recommend it.

While there no doubt is such a creature as "neoconservatism," it is not the tightly organized enterprise that some, mainly critics, imagine. There are no meetings deciding the "neoconservative position" on this or that, never mind orders coming down from Irving Kristol or anyone else. As George Weigel writes in the *Commentary* symposium, "Contemporary American conservatism seems less a 'movement' to me than a complex community of conversation built around certain shared premises" (101; B129). *First Things* offended some neocons not because it presumed to venture beyond its assigned task in the grand strategy but because it pressed those shared premises farther than some were accustomed to. At least that is my reading, knowing full well that others think we violated the premises or introduced new premises on which there was no prior agreement. In any event, the "complex community of conversation," however momentarily shaken, continues. But that is a subject to which we will return when we address the now frequently-heard claim that this controversy has created an irreparable breach in American conservatism.

From within a stream of conservatism that is more self-confident about its place in the American scheme of things, the very Catholic William Buckley sounds downright WASPish in asserting as self-evident truth that "Loyalty always has to be contingent." After all, what was the American revolution about? "We must remember," writes Buckley, "what Burke taught us, that a country to be loved must be lovely" (B14). Richard Brookhiser, who has written brilliantly on the WASP in American culture, takes a similar view of the *First Things* discussion of illegitimacy. Writing in *The New York Observer*, Brookhiser observes:

Such talk has excited liberals, who are eager to whiff a massacre (hopefully, a pogrom) wherever political Christians gather. It has also alarmed some of the supporters of *First Things*, who have resigned from its editorial board in protest .... Many a conservative of a certain age defined him or herself by his resistance to the revolutionary talk of urban rioters, yakking students and *The New York Review of Books*. The return of the repressed among Republicans leaves them depressed. Surely this is an overreaction. It is very American to agonize about whether the system has gone astray; it is almost as American to be paranoid about it. Americans can discuss the question in the 1990s, even as they did in the 1790s, without behaving as crazily as Thomas Jefferson or Alexander Hamilton (B23).

"There is an academic odor to the whole controversy—the odor of tweed and chalk dust," says syndicated columnist William Murchison in an article in *The Human Life Review* (B58). It is as though the academics of *First Things* are just awakening to the fact that the country lacks a moral consensus, without which questions of governmental legitimacy inevitably arise. The critics of *First Things* also seem a touch naïve, Murchison observes: "In fact, some readers appeared to find a trail of gunpowder snaking through the scholarly argumentation: a black thread awaiting only the touch of a match to bring down the roof." Murchison is not surprised that democracy, if not coming to an end, is severely strained. "The composition of differences was easy enough (if never completely easy) in older times when there existed in America what might be called a religious consensus."

That was the case "until a couple of decades ago," but in the current relativistic culture, it is predictable that the courts would overreach their authority. "The Supreme Court, under these new circumstances, operates in an odd but perversely logical way. It substitutes for one kind of prescriptive norm another kind of norm—the norm of normlessness." The American people may not like it, but they don't seem upset enough to do much about it.

"U.S. Grant and the Army of the Potomac appear to have quelled the desire for direct action against perceived oppression. The revolutionary instinct, in which America was born, ain't what it used to be." Maybe judicial usurpation will spark civil disobedience but, without grassroots support, "the chief effect might be an explosion in America's jail population." "And if support *was* compelling, would civil disobedience, or withdrawal from civic life, really be needed?" The fault mainly lies not with the courts or with the government as a whole, says Murchison, but with ourselves, and the only real answer is "conversion," one by one. "Any lasting moral recovery will necessarily reflect a recovery of religion, on which the old consensus rested."

THE MORE GENERALIZED INDICTMENT of the culture has cropped up regularly during the course of the controversy. Richard Cohen of *The Washington Post* implicitly subscribes to it, arguing ("When Morality Begets Violence") that the society is so fragile that any public appeal to a higher morality threatens to set off the crazies among us (B99). Contradicting Cohen in *The New Republic*, Jean Bethke Elshtain of the University of Chicago vigorously defends *First Things'* line of argument (B156). Cohen and others who raise alarums about violence have another purpose in mind, Elshtain suggests. "Why up the ante? Why distort the dangers? I suspect it is to stymie or silence the other side." The same tactic, she notes, was used by opponents of the early civil rights movement under Dr. King:

> A sturdy democratic society accommodates such contesta-
> tions; indeed, given the undeniable moral basis of democracy,
> it virtually guarantees that such conflicts will emerge. The
> urgent call [in *First Things*] for a more decisive church-
> state showdown on constitutional and ethical grounds is
> not, as Cohen insists, a "chilling" prospect. To label it as
> such is to desire political speech itself chilled, so long as
> those put in the political deep freeze are not those whose

views one shares . . . The somewhat misnamed church-state debate has from the beginning involved certain perduring political and ethical questions: Who is one obliged to obey and why? What if the dictates of a government and the dictates of a faith conflict? Indeed, Jean Jacques Rousseau opined that Christianity was a terrible religion because it put people in conflict with themselves. But that is what a religion seriously professed should do: it wouldn't be much of a religion if it didn't.

Elshtain contends, "When we frighten ourselves about the outcomes of tough democratic debate, we lose a sense of balance and proportion." Cohen had raised the specter of the Oklahoma City bombing, to which Elshtain responds: "Blowing up a building and killing men, women and children—one's fellow citizens—is not an act of incivility. It is an act of criminality. It is not an extreme form of political argument. It is an anti-political act that kills argument. . . . The best way to honor the victims of that terrible crime is to cease and desist [from] the facile deployment of 'Oklahoma City' as an all-purpose club to discredit one's opponents as terrorists or the coddlers of terrorists." Elshtain's advocacy of robust political debate about the inescapably moral question that is at the heart of politics—How ought we to order our life together?—does not necessarily assume that the American people are ready for such debate. But it is, she believes, the duty of opinion makers to encourage such debate, rather than to indulge in alarmist and self-serving warnings about morality begetting violence.

Much of this discussion turns on how people perceive the capacity of citizens to act as citizens by engaging fundamental questions about our constitutional order. Distinctions are frequently made between "the people" and "intellectuals," especially intellectuals who view themselves as "philosopher kings" whose task it is to guard the public order against rude populist instincts. This is the reading of the controversy proposed by *Insight* magazine, which very improbably casts me in the role of Socrates, "raising 'regime questions' and incurring accusations of misleading the young and questioning the gods of the state." "Some classically trained conservatives have stopped just short of urging that [Neuhaus] be required to drink the hemlock," *Insight* reports (B142).

Employing different imagery, William Kristol in the *Commentary* symposium makes a similar point, noting that "all sophisticated people" are supposed to wish that the big moral questions swirling around, for instance, abortion "would somehow go away." "But the truth is," writes Kristol, "that abortion is today the bloody crossroads of American politics. . . . It is the focal point for liberalism's simultaneous assault on self-government, morals, and nature. So, challenging the judicially-imposed regime of abortion-on-demand is key to a conservative reformation in politics, in morals, and in beliefs" (94; B125). Ambrose Evans-Pritchard reports on America for *The Sunday Telegraph*, and he tells his British readers that the *First Things* controversy highlights the "rot" that has set into American public life. The fact that the courts have "snatched" from the people the right to decide on moral questions such as abortion is both cause and effect of what has gone wrong. "A war of sorts is being conducted by the elites against cultural and religious outsiders. . . . America is remarkably resilient, however. The fund of Calvinism is not entirely exhausted, and it may be possible to restore the legitimacy of the governing institutions—provided there is a cathartic exposure of sin, starting at the White House. But once a cultural cancer has metastasized, it is exceedingly hard to reverse" (B95).

From the beginning, Scott McConnell of the *New York Post* has been a champion of the *First Things* initiative (he has subsequently been elevated from columnist to editor of the editorial page). In his first intervention, McConnell suggested that the symposium perhaps focused too narrowly on issues such as abortion and gay rights, neglecting the court-supported passion for the elite's "political correctness" in an array of decisions that are "manifestations of American democracy in retreat." The innovations promoted by cultural elites raise the question whether "government responsiveness to the popular will can endure in a society committed to multiculturalism." McConnell cites, as we did in our January editorial, philosopher Michael Walzer's worrying from the left that in recent decades "there is a sense in which the 'left' or some vulgarized version of the left dominated the culture [although] many Americans experienced this left culture as something alien, frightening, or deeply disturbing" (B21).

A very different view of the elites vs. the people is offered by Stanley Hauerwas of Duke University in *Lingua Franca* (B137). Hauerwas is an old friend with whom I have been arguing about these questions for decades. He is very close to Stanley Fish and to Alasdair MacIntyre, who are also at Duke. Fish is the academic bad boy of multiculturalism, while MacIntyre is a distinguished philosopher whose notion of "rival traditions" of moral discourse Hauerwas recruits to the service of his claim that a genuinely public moral discourse is neither possible nor desirable. Nonetheless, Hauerwas is on the editorial board of *First Things* and an ardent supporter of the symposium, which, he says, shows that the journal has "great integrity." At the same time, he challenges our appeal to popular self government. "The problem isn't the courts," Hauerwas says. "The problem is the American people! The conservatives don't want to admit that this is what the American people want! They *want* assisted suicide! They believe in autonomy!"

With Hauerwas and Gertrude Himmelfarb, columnist Garry Wills doubts that the *vox populi* is disposed to side with the argument of *First Things* (B78). The claim that "democracy has been quietly subverted is not based on the facts," he asserts. "The problem is that polls do not indicate that the people are disturbed about their situation. If they are fooled, they do not seem to resent that fact." Wills says he respects those who believe abortion is murder and protest it by various means, including peaceful civil disobedience. Beyond that, however, he sides with Richard Cohen. "But others take the course of violence, committing murder themselves. And a group of people connected with the journal *First Things* is encouraging that attitude by comparing our high abortion rate with the Holocaust and our government with the Nazi regime. Zealots will conclude from this that our regime must be overthrown with force." Wills takes sharp issue with William Bennett's description of our crisis in *First Things*. Bennett, he says, "is simply describing a situation that does not exist." The "desperation" felt by people such as Bennett is the result of their being unable to "entertain the notion that there is no inevitable moral conclusion to be drawn on the issue of abortion—or of assisted suicide, or of gay rights, etc." In sum, to propose that the courts are out of synch with the people is reckless rabbling that can only disturb the peace.

In a comprehensive analysis of the controversy, Scott H. Moore of Notre Dame University connects it with what he believes are similar debates taking place within academic theology and ethics (B235). From the left, says Moore, people such as Stanley Hauerwas and his disciple at Notre Dame, Father Michael Baxter, join *First Things*, on the right, in challenging "the incoherence of En-lightenment Liberalism's status quo." According to Moore, I, along with Hauerwas and Baxter, recognize "the tension between the confessionally particular and the religiously generic and the role this tension plays in the debate over the place of religion in the public square. Indeed, the dispute between the generically religious and the particularly Christian is at the heart of the conflict between [Gertrude] Himmelfarb and Neuhaus. . . ." I, Moore says, see "the inadequacy of purely procedural commitments for ensuring the legitimacy of government." Not so with Himmelfarb. "The strong commitment to 'procedure' is an Enlightenment move, and it is clearly seen in Himmelfarb's assertion that the legitimacy of government should not be discussed under the rubric of religious commitments and that the question of the very nature of government is not up for discussion."

Moore suggests that a deep disagreement between Himmelfarb and me was evident in the papers we each gave at the inauguration of a new president of Baylor University in 1995, both of which were published in the January 1996 issue of *First Things*. While Himmelfarb and I assumed that we were allies at Baylor, defending the idea of a "Christian university" against its various enemies, Moore believes the seeds of the explosion over "The End of Democracy?" were evident enough in those earlier presentations. At Baylor Himmelfarb praised the "dogma" on which the idea of the university rests, which requires a "faith in reason and knowledge, in the rational, dispassionate search for truth, and in the dissemination of knowledge for the sake of knowledge." She juxtaposed postmodernism's "unholy Trinity of race, class, and gender" against the traditional "dogma" of "truth, objectivity, and knowledge." In short, says Moore, "Himmelfarb's 'faith' in the Enlightenment ideal is profoundly religious."

In my "eleven theses" on the Christian university, says Moore, a dramatically different vision is proposed:

> [Neuhaus's] first thesis set Himmelfarb's faith in Enlighten-
> ment neutrality in bold relief: "There is no such thing as a
> university pure and simple." Unequivocally denying the neu-
> trality thesis, Neuhaus continued: "A secular university is
> not a university pure and simple; it is a secular university.
> Secular is not a synonym for neutral." Neuhaus's eighth
> thesis was "In a Christian university there is no 'role' for
> religion. Rather, it is within religion—more accurately, it is
> within the Christian understanding of reality—that every-
> thing finds its role.". . . In her presentation, [Himmelfarb]
> had spoken of religious universities as "respectful of religion
> and of the moral virtues derived from religion." Neuhaus's
> point is the opposite. Within a Christian university, "religion"
> does not occupy a respected "role" precisely because it is
> from within that commitment that all else finds its role
> (B235).

The conflict over the idea of the university applies also to the public order more generally, says Moore. It is essentially a conflict between two religious faiths, the first being faith in Enlightenment liberalism and the second being Christianity. The first faith of liberalism does not easily recognize itself as a religion, and adopts an attitude of tolerance toward self-declared religions so long as they do not interfere with public business. Moore cites the observation of Robert George in *The Chronicle of Higher Education* account of the *First Things* controversy. George said, "Our objection is to the idea that liberalism itself is a kind of neutral playing field, as opposed to a substantive theory about human nature, destiny, and dignity. We dispute the idea that liberalism itself is a neutral view that doesn't compete with others. It certainly has the right to compete in the public square with other philosophies, but it is certainly not given any privileged position by the Constitution" (B145).

While people such as Hauerwas and Baxter exuberantly declare the incompatibility of Christian and Enlightenment religions, "Neuhaus has reluctantly come to articulate [that position]." "Neuhaus wishes that such were not the case," writes Moore, "indeed, he longs to hold the two sides in respectful tension. This is not to suggest that Neuhaus desires an equilibrium, but rather that he thinks that if the state respects the Natural Law, the areas where Christians will find a conflict of conscience will be limited. This is the hope of traditional Natural Law theory, especially as it has been articulated by Thomists like [Jacques] Maritain and Ralph McInerny." There is important truth in Moore's analysis, which has also been proposed by others, and it provides an interesting angle from which to explain why the *First Things* initiative on judicial usurpation occasioned such a strong reaction by critics such as Gertrude Himmelfarb.

Another explanation advanced is that the negative reaction reflects anti-religious and, more specifically, anti-Catholic bigotry. Writing in *The Sunday Times* of London, Christopher Hitchens thinks there may be something to that. "Ever since John F. Kennedy, Roman Catholicism is no longer an issue in American politics. Catholics are now not suspected of taking orders from the Vatican. Yet in their *First Things* manifesto, the Christian fundamentalists appear to be saying that the Pope's teaching on abortion takes precedence over secular courts in the United States" (B52). There are obvious similarities here between Hitchens and Heilbrunn. Not surprisingly, the Catholic League for Religious and Civil Rights responded sharply to the Heilbrunn article in *The New Republic*. The charge "that a few Catholic scholars like Father Richard John Neuhaus and Robert George are threatening Jews, or that their ideas are 'un-American,' is as untrue as it is unethical . . . What *The New Republic* is doing is promoting division among conservative intellectuals, not reporting on it. That it has chosen the club of anti-Catholicism to do so is reprehensible" (B43). *The National Catholic Register* reports that Heilbrunn dismisses such charges as playing "the victimhood game." The *Register* reports: "He emphasized that his article was only referring to a tiny minority of Catholics who believe in the agenda of the authors of the *First Things* symposium. Ironically, he said, his article was intended as an attack on Jewish neoconservatives who have largely left the *First Things* symposium uncriticized" (B84).

The anti-Catholic factor is addressed from a different perspective by Father Toolan in his *America* article:

> Father Neuhaus, having spent most of his adult life as a Lutheran-American, momentarily forgot the history he acquired as a newborn Catholic. Catholics . . . must remember that the church is a newcomer among advocates of religious freedom and democratic polities—and we neglect this *arriviste* status at our peril. . . . In brief, memory of a church that had only lately abandoned its support of an oppressive union of church and state meant that Father Neuhaus, a representative of that church, could not be fully trusted to be the democrat he claimed to be. By my reckoning of his record, such mistrust is both preposterous and unfair. My point is that, given the history he represented, it is sadly understandable (B164).

While I appreciate Father Toolan's friendly intentions, his defensiveness about the Catholic tradition seems to me quite unwarranted. While one need not agree with scholars such as John Courtney Murray and Christopher Dawson that the ideas central to democratic freedom are rooted in medieval Catholic teaching and practice, there is certainly a great deal more to that argument than there is to the claim that democracy is the unique achievement of the secular Enlightenment's struggle against religion in general and Catholicism in particular. Those for whom the very mention of Catholicism triggers alarums about the Crusades and Spanish Inquisition are victims of a historical miseducation that should not be encouraged by Catholic writers. Certainly Catholics in this country, from the seventeenth century Maryland colony onward, need take second place to nobody in their devotion to democratic freedom.

The anti-Catholic factor takes an ominous turn in the position of Irwin Stelzer of the American Enterprise Institute, a position no doubt shared by others. Stelzer writes in the *Commentary* symposium:

> It is even stranger that Jewish neoconservatives should have thought they could pitch an intellectual tent broad enough to attract the protypical former Jewish liberal "mugged by reality" and many Catholics brought up in a tradition that does not welcome dissent from its revealed truths. Jewish intellectuals may be useful exponents of some of the positions of *First Things* Catholics, but they should not expect to be partners in a governing theocracy. Perhaps— and it is only a perhaps—the unraveling of the alliance between the neoconservatives and the *First Things* crowd will liberate the former to seek the support of more natural allies (106; B128).

Whatever else is ill-informed and offensive in such a view, the really curious thing is the implied positioning of Jews, who constitute about 2 percent of the population, against the Christians of the country. While Stelzer refers only to Catholics, were he aware of the views of most Protestants, especially evangelical Protestants, I have no doubt he would think them at least equally guilty of not welcoming dissent from revealed truths and of yearning for a governing theocracy. Heilbrunn of *The New Republic* also speaks of the "natural allies" of Jews but, compared with Stelzer, his position seems like the very model of Jewish-Christian cooperation and trust in the public square. Not to put too fine a point on it, Stelzer's reaction strikes me as both dangerous and bizarre, the danger being tempered by the fact that I suspect it will strike almost everyone else that way as well.

Father Toolan is right to say we must be aware of the negative perception of Catholicism, and of Christianity more generally, in some quarters. He is also right when he says that, for many people, any kind of religion in public "is just plain scary." But I do not think anybody is well served if we are intimidated by the irrational fears and prejudices of dogmatic secularists who would return to the ghetto—albeit an affluent and influential ghetto—in order to defend themselves against the religious and cultural reality of American life. Our natural allies are all who are allied with us— most emphatically including Jews—in the effort to advance what Gertrude Himmelfarb calls the "remoralizing of society."

So WHY THE UPROAR over the *First Things* initiative? We have surveyed a number of answers given to that question, always remembering that we should credit the possibility that people are upset for precisely the reasons that they say they are upset. Of course, taking people at their word does not keep the chattering classes employed. There is also another reason for paying attention to theories and speculations, even outlandish theories and specu- lations, since a controversy such as this tells us important things about the political-intellectual terrain, with its never ending contest to get title to "true conservatism," "the mainstream," "the moral high ground," and other valuable pieces of political real estate.

One explanation of the controversy that we have considered is that *First Things* threatened neoconservatives who, in Arthur

Koestler's phrase, lack self-confidence. In this view, *The New York Times* and *The Washington Post* still define the boundaries of respectable discourse, and neoconservatives fear they may be discredited, being judged guilty-by-association with conservatives who challenge those boundaries. Others, such as Sanford Pinsker, suggest the anxiety has to do with a peculiarly Jewish patriotism, even piety, toward America that cannot abide the "experiment" being called into question. Commentators have also disagreed with *First Things* on the extent to which the American people are aware or approve of what the courts have done and on their ability to function as citizens. We have considered, too, the argument that a quasi-religious belief in the liberal neutrality of the secular Enlightenment is in battle with religious claims that bring Enlightenment neutrality under judgment. Finally, we looked at the evident animus toward religion, more particularly toward religion in public, and most particularly toward Catholicism in public.

Although these analyses and arguments are typically tangled and overlapping, it is possible to sort out discrete lines of contention. One such line is that the entire controversy can be explained in terms of *First Things* having challenged the neoconservative establishment. It is hardly surprising that the left gleefully seizes upon this line, claiming that the challenge has exposed and discredited the entire neocon enterprise. Joe Conason's article in *The New York Observer*, for instance, bears the elegant title, "Hey, We Told You So: Bork's a Raving Loony" (B182). Bork was always an extremist, says Conason. "Recently, however, he has fallen into bad company as a contributor to *First Things*, a radical-right periodical edited in New York by Father Richard John Neuhaus. . . . Here was a bearded right-wing intellectual brooding about the overthrow of the Federal judiciary in a journal of reactionary subversion."

Frank Rich of *The New York Times* writes in a similar vein about "The New New Left" (B183). The *Commentary* symposium, he writes, "was fixated on how some of their own long-standing allies, led by the theologian Richard John Neuhaus, are mimicking

Abbie Hoffman with their calls for resistance to an American 'regime' they liken to Nazi Germany. As Norman Podhoretz accurately puts it, 'the extremist hysteria of the old counterculture of the 1960s is back, this time under a conservative banner.' Right on, indeed." On almost any question one might name, Frank Rich is fiercely and often viciously opposed to the positions of *Commentary* under the editorship of Podhoretz, and perhaps it would be churlish to deny him his pleasure in celebrating what he construes as Podhoretz's rueful admission that those positions end up in extremism.

As I say, it is not surprising that the left attempts to make partisan hay by depicting a neoconservative establishment challenged and thereby exposed. Others write with less evident partisan delight. In the British newspaper, *The Observer*, Martin Walker observes: "They are not yet slamming each other as 'crypto-fascist deviationists' and the disciplines of Lenin's democratic centralism have yet to exact their toll. But in their imprecations against one another's betrayals, the civil war of the American Right is taking on the nastier features of the old Left" (B152). It is at heart, Walker suggests, a battle between "bluebloods and rednecks," with the neocon establishment lining up with the bluebloods. "There is the underlying split between the cultural conservatives whose faith is rooted in God, and the economic conservatives whose devotions are reserved for Mammon. There is the geographical split between the traditional patricians of the country clubs and Wall Street, and the new fervor of the Southern evangelicals, a split shaped by the class difference between the redneck South and the blueblood North. . . . The conservative coalition that Reagan held together is falling viciously apart."

According to A.J. Bacevich of the Paul Nitze School of Advanced International Studies in Washington, the *First Things* affair has shaken neocon assumptions about America's role in the world (B165). Especially for religious conservatives, says Bacevich, the conservative alliance built around the defense of the free world against the Evil Empire is now in tatters. Given a world in which good and evil are no longer sharply defined by ideology, and given the sorry state of American society at home, "the moral terms of reference underwriting U.S. involvement in world affairs for the preceding half century—a crusade pitting freedom against totalitarianism—have expired." Conservatives, and neocons in particular, were once the great champions of American "exceptionalism," but now it is Clinton and liberals who talk about America's global mission, while conservatives have increasing doubts about the presumed moral superiority that underlies that notion.

The liberal elites in charge of the global mission have a simple message for religious conservatives: "In postmodern, multicultural America, your so-called moral issues are sectarian complaints devoid of standing in the public square; when it comes to the world at large, however, universal values exist and the United States has a unique responsibility to ensure that those values will prevail. . . . The role—indeed, the obligation—of the average citizen is to lend support to this mission. To do otherwise, to express reservations about the wisdom, feasibility, or cost of those policies, is to commit the unpardonable sin of isolationism." But, Bacevich suggests, those who are worrying about the end of democracy at home are no longer so easily intimidated by the charge of isolationism.

The United States is far and away the leading arms exporter to the world, Bacevich notes. Put together with our degraded pop culture and dubious innovations such as a universal right to abortion, it is by no means obvious that the U.S. has what the world most needs. Global and domestic anxieties are converging. "Just as in domestic politics the religious Right rejects the model of American society advocated by [liberal] elites, so too will religious conservatives refuse to defer to these elites in foreign policy. Popular defiance in the first instance animates the culture war; in the second instance, it may well destroy the consensus supporting American internationalism as presently configured."

"As with any imperium," Bacevich writes, "the Pax Americana rests ultimately on military power." Many Americans are not convinced that there is a reasonable threat that warrants such a vast military establishment, and wonder about its impact upon our domestic life. "Although unprecedented reliance on military power may not lead straightaway to Prussian-style militarism, it would be absurd to pretend that the United States can sustain its status as the world's only military superpower without incurring significant cultural, social, and political costs." Policies can be justified by appeal to the "cold calculus of *Realpolitik,*" but to do so is to grant the premise that the U.S. exercise of power "is not inherently more virtuous" than the behavior of other nations. Conservative support, and especially the support of religious conservatives, for American foreign policy was inseparably connected with the assumption of virtue. "In short," writes Bacevich,

> examined from the perspective of religious conservatism, the moral content of American foreign policy is not all that moral. Claims, continuously reasserted by President Clinton and members of his administration, that present-day U.S. policies represent a continuation of the defense of moral values that was central to the Cold War are simply not true. Precisely what values are served in expanding U.S. trade with an authoritarian China?. . . . In converting the Persian Gulf into an American military protectorate? In annually peddling billions of dollars of American weapons abroad? The theocon premise may oblige religious conservatives to view such policies in a new light— even if doing so invites conclusions about the uses of American power that bear an uncomfortable resemblance to conclusions once touted by the Left (b165).

Bacevich is usually thought to be a neocon (although of Heilbrunn's "theocon" variety) and is a frequent contributor to *First Things.* He ends the present article by committing the heresy of quoting George Kennan, the noted American diplomat, who wrote in 1950, "We are not yet ready to lead the world to salvation. We have to save ourselves first." In the context of the Cold War, Bacevich says, Kennan's counsel "was singularly ill-advised," but new occasions teach new duties, as the old hymn puts it. Bacevich concludes, "Only by recognizing the extent to which the United States today is poorly equipped for saving others can Americans make a start at the more pressing task of redeeming ourselves." Thus in the view of Bacevich (and he is by no means alone) the "End of Democracy?" debate has ramifications far beyond the judiciary and other domestic discontents. By questioning the "universal nation" and "American exceptionalism" planks of the neoconservative platform, Bacevich puts into question America's place in the world and, not so incidentally, America's presumed protectorate of the Middle East and Israel.

"THE *First Things* CONTRETEMPS suggests that the neoconservative agenda now diverges quite considerably from that of the conservative mainstream," writes Tom Bethell in *The American Spectator* (140; B72). Bethell accuses neocons of thinking they are setting the political and cultural agenda when, in fact, they have lost one battle after another, and, indeed, have lost the war. "[W]e should be realistic enough to see that the Left has utterly triumphed in the cultural war." Neocons take satisfaction from Clinton's use of conservative rhetoric. "It's a tiny triumph," remarks Bethell, "for the sheep to claim that the wolf must wear sheep's clothing." "'Steady as you go,' say the neocons. You're winning already. Don't rock the boat, don't risk being labeled extremist." Arrogating to themselves the task of "policing" conservative opinion, the neocons subscribe to the maxim "No friends to the right," in sharp contrast to liberalism's maxim of "No enemies to the Left." "This asymmetry," says Bethell, "is to be found all over the Western world—the Christian world in particular" (141-42).

In truth, neoconservative voices such as *Commentary* have over the years taken considerable risks to make friends to the Right. One thinks, for instance, of Norman Podhoretz's vigorous defense of Pat Robertson against the charge of anti-Semitism after Robertson published a book in which he uncritically cited anti-Semitic sources. We might go further and say that the very constituting idea of neoconservatism is making friends to the Right. Part of a liberal's being "mugged by reality" is that he wakes up to discover that conservatives were more right than wrong about some very important questions and he decides to make common cause with them, thereby becoming a neoconservative. Which brings us back to the dispute over what Bethell calls "the conservative mainstream."

Tom Bethell's analysis opens the way to our consideration of the phenomenon known as "paleoconservativism." The paleos, as they are called and call themselves, arose as a direct response to neoconservatism, and their view is represented in this volume by Samuel Francis, a Hegel scholar who, in the paleo telling, was fired from his editorial position at the *Washington Times* under pressure from neocons. Much ink has been spilled on the paleocon-neocon wars, almost all of it on the paleo side. Neocons tend to the view that the paleos are beyond the pale, and therefore ignore them, thereby increasing the fury of paleo attacks. In their present form, these unpleasantnesses go back to the beginning of the Reagan administration, and a bright line is drawn at the failure of M.E. Bradford to become chairman of the National Endowment for the Humanities. Bradford, a professor of English at the University of Dallas, and his friends thought he was in line for NEH but, as the story is told, Irving Kristol and William F. Buckley Jr. successfully appealed to President Reagan not to appoint him. The claim was that Bradford had unsavory connections with unreconstructed Southerners whose views on race, states rights, and other questions would turn the confirmation proceedings into a disastrous donnybrook at the very beginning of Reagan's first administration. The NEH position went, of course, to William Bennett.

Bradford has since died, but the incident lives on and is endlessly invoked by paleos who contend that the neocons, with the active collaboration of Buckley and *National Review*, usurped the leadership of the conservative movement, successfully shutting out paleos from positions of influence in the Reagan and Bush administrations. Moreover, it is charged, the neocons cornered the handful of conservative foundations which, while many times outgunned by the large liberal foundations, were all that conservatives had by way of substantial funding. While the neocons were dismissive of the paleos, the paleos declared all-out war on the neocons. Later on, the chief journalistic belligerent in the war would become *Chronicles*, a monthly magazine published by the Rockford Institute in Rockford, Illinois. I suppose a word about the Rockford Institute and my association with it is unavoidable.

In 1984, I had joined with the Rockford Institute in establishing the Center on Religion and Society in New York City. There we published a monthly newsletter, *The Religion and Society Report*, and as mentioned earlier, a quarterly journal called *This World*. In Rockford, Leopold Tyrmand, a Polish-Jewish emigre of considerable charm and eccentricity, edited *Chronicles of Culture*. For a long time everything went swimmingly in this collaboration between New York and "middle America." Until Tyrmand suddenly died of a heart attack and *Chronicles* was taken over by Thomas Fleming, a young man he had hired.

According to the standard paleo account, I accused Fleming and *Chronicles* of anti-Semitism in order to precipitate a break with Rockford and make off with substantial grant moneys from Bradley and other foundations. This is not the place for all the details, but only enough for the reader to understand the paleo reading of the current controversy. I have never accused anyone at Rockford of anti-Semitism. I did say that I was increasingly uneasy about what struck me as their disturbing nonchalance toward the evil of anti-Semitism. This was evident, for instance, in *Chronicle's* championing of novelist Gore Vidal as a model conservative, even though Vidal most certainly is, among other very unattractive things, an anti-Semite.

Since it seemed clear that *Chronicles* was not going to change its editor or its editorial course, by the beginning of 1989 I had proposed an amicable separation between Rockford and the New

York Center. I thought we were both working toward that end when on the morning of May 5, 1989, I arrived at the New York office to find it commandeered by a group of thugs who informed the staff and me that we had forty-five minutes to clear out personal belongings and be gone. So there we were on a rainy Friday morning, plastic garbage bags in hand, trying to hail a cab. In the face of such ludicrous goings on, we had no choice but to treat ourselves to a festive lunch, a rite repeated each year on the anniversary of "The Rockford Raid." Of course the incident was much reported, including a front page story in *The New York Times*, and became, as they say, a defining moment in the saga of contemporary conservatism. The foundations and major publications, such as *National Review* and *Commentary*, rallied to our side, thus deepening the paleo conviction that the perfidious neocons were near-omnipotent in their usurpation of the conservative movement. *Chronicles* and kindred publications were left in the wilderness, muttering about a "real conservatism" that would rise again.

If anyone despises the neocons more than liberals—and especially liberal Jews who think them guilty of treason against their "natural allies"—it is the paleos. They make no effort to disguise their delight at a possible break-up between *First Things* and our neocon friends. Which brings us to Samuel Francis's essay in *Chronicles* (133-38; B161). "Neoconservatism," he says in a statement echoed by other paleos, "is fundamentally a defense of the status quo." The offense of *First Things* was to suggest that "something really is wrong in America," a suggestion that drives toward "something very close to paleoconservatism." In a style undeniably colorful, Francis writes that "the hysterical reaction of the senior neocons to the symposium represents . . . a determination to squelch this tendency before it begins to blossom into a full-blown paleoconservative defection that would leave the neocon sagamores perched on the roofs of their own wigwam while the waters of right-wing dissidence swirl ever higher and ever closer to their noses."

I will say nothing of Francis's confused account of what *First Things* said about conscience, subjectivity, and civil disobedience, since any fair reading of our symposium makes his confusion more than evident. More to the point is his drawing of the line between neocon and paleo with respect to the illegitimacy of the U.S. government. "If it's an 'illegitimate regime' you're looking for, you don't have to wait for court decisions on abortion and euthanasia; we have had nothing but an illegitimate regime in the United States for the last fiifty years, a government dedicated to destroying the Constitution, gutting the restraints on federal power, and subverting the cultural norms and institutions of American society. . . . [*First Things'*] stumbling perception that something is wrong is welcome, but to tell the truth it's just a few decades too late." Thus Francis's title in *Chronicles*, "First Things Last." Francis concludes that "those who insist on standing with Podhoretz and his allies as defenders of a power structure that everyone else has come to reject will find their footholds increasingly slippery and their company increasingly small."

Columnist Charley Reese writes in *Conservative Chronicles* that "poor Richard John Neuhaus" must be regretting that he "broke with the true conservatives to embrace the neoconservatives" (B178). "The neocons turned on his group like a snake on a rat. . . . I expect [they] will get the foundations to cut him off the money teat unless he crawls, repents and does penance for his political heresy." What my colleagues and I failed to understand, says Reese, is that "neoconservatives love big government, not constitutional government." "Their only complaint with liberals is that they (the neocons) want to run the big government."

The neocon resignations from the board of *First Things* were intended "to send a warning about the costs of disobedience," according to Paul Gottfried, a prominent paleo writer (B112). Our symposium had broken the rules. "After all, those who live off the money that neocons collect from brain-dead goyim are expected to observe certain proprieties. They should talk and write about subjects that neocons want to have discussed: e.g., Christian anti-Semitism, the desirability of the Likud government in Israel, and the responsibility of German philosophers for the academic left." Gottfried, a Jew, is a frequent critic of what he views as the illegitimate use of the charge of anti-Semitism to discredit opponents in public debate, and is a friend of Francis's.

"Still, there is no reason to exaggerate the rift that has opened," Gottfried writes:

> The neocons will not likely wage the war against Neuhaus and Bork which they unleashed against the paleos. The new targets of their attacks are not enemies who have to be wiped off the political and social map but wayward followers. It was also easier for the neocons to finish off their already half marginalized opposition on the right than it would be to do the same to Bork or Neuhaus. Unlike, say Mel Bradford or Sam Francis, the last two are celebrities who appear on TV and whose books are respectfully reviewed in the national press. . . . Despite his thuggish, bullying manners, Podhoretz is no fool. This Meyer Lansky of political journalism may scream louder than the rest of his mob, but neither he nor the others will pursue an unwinnable war.[3]

In his own winning manner, Paul Gottfried has more recently been telling friends that *First Things* may be moving toward the paleos, and should therefore, at least provisionally, be exempted from some of the sustained assaults against the neocon gangsters.[9]

Paleos typically do not attempt to disguise the resentment that drives their attack. Joseph Sobran is a frequently brilliant writer who was for years riding high at *National Review* until his repeated attacks on U.S. policy toward Israel and on Israel's supporters in this country put him into disfavor not only with the neocons but also with editor William F. Buckley Jr. (The paleo version, of course, is that Buckley is the obedient servant of the neocons.) Forbidden to write in *National Review* about Israel and Jews, Sobran left the magazine and in recent years has found his voice in a syndicated column in the conservative Catholic

3. Paul Gottfried, private letter circulated to friends.

weekly *The Wanderer* and in his own monthly newsletter. He has also recently published with Free Press a respectably, if skeptically, received book contending that Shakespeare did not write the plays attributed to Shakespeare.

Like other paleos, Sobran has found in the *First Things* dispute another occasion for beating up on the neocons. He has no problem with the thesis that "the abuse of the Constitution endangers the very legitimacy of the federal government . . . since that legitimacy is based on the Constitution itself" (B36). It is the charge of "anti-Americanism" that gets him going, and returns him to a favored subject:

> So Americans who want to reclaim their Constitution are guilty of "anti-Americanism"! Look who's impugning our patriotism. In the December [1996] issue of *Commentary*, Podhoretz complains that everyone is being terribly unfair to Israeli Prime Minister Benjamin Netanyahu. He predicts that the vicious assault on Netanyahu will continue. "What is more," Podhoretz prophesies, "the United States will lead the assault." Sounds anti-American to me. . . . I have never read an article in the neoconservative press that evaluates Israel from an American perspective. The tacit assumption is always—always—that America is to be judged by what it does for Israel, and never vice versa. This may not be "anti-American," but it hardly deserves to be called pro-American. Yet the neocons who resent any suspicion of "dual loyalty" feel free to impeach the patriotism of Americans who worry about the moral health and constitutional integrity of their own country.

Jacob Heilbrunn first publicly introduced "the Jewish factor" into the controversy, but, as he undoubtedly knew, there were passions littering the political landscape and waiting to be ignited. *The Christian News*, a far right publication, observes that "Neuhaus is beginning to learn now what many gentile conservatives in the 1980s found out to their mortification and embarrassment. The neoconservatives, a small cabal of ex-Trotskyite (mainly) Jewish

Manhattan intellectuals took over the conservative movement in the late seventies. . . . They have a paranoid fear that gentile America is bristling with a powerful but well disguised anti-Semitism, and that America outside the safe confines of the Manhattan ghetto is populated with hordes of potential Himmlers, planning to ship them off to concentration camps." The author allows that there are exceptions. "Although hatred of gentiles is a tenet held in common by many Jewish liberals and neocons, there are Jewish intellectuals, such as Paul Gottfried, Jacob Neusner, and the late Murray Rothbard, who are true patriots and determined to live in peace with their Christian neighbors." Now that I am supposedly deprived of "Jewish money," the author wonders, "Will Neuhaus lead a gentile revolt within [neoconservative] ranks?" (B54).

Most paleos have identified with Patrick Buchanan in national politics and, while their opponents deride them as denizens of the political fever swamps, they are adamant in asserting that their day is coming, sooner rather than later. Their strategy, such as it is, involves putting together an unlikely amalgam of discontents. Llewellyn H. Rockwell Jr., a relentless libertarian, publishes *The Rothbard-Rockwell Report* and in "Sic Semper Tyrannis"—recalling John Wilkes Booth—he praises the long and honorable conservative case for tyrannicide (B163). He is only moderately encouraged by the current controversy. "Not that Father Neuhaus and his friends have come full circle. Any principled conservative regards the U.S. government as having been illegitimate since Lincoln's War, or at a minimum since the New Deal. Recent judicial outrages only prove the point."

Rockwell takes his stand with Jefferson, whose "writings provide fodder for such . . . groups as Christian Right radicals and militia members." Those who think that is proof of Jefferson's evil—and he detects a conspiracy among neocons to discredit Jefferson—"merely reveal themselves as un-American." Like other paleos, Rockwell was not at first much impressed with the *First Things* symposium. It seemed to him just another exercise in neocon hand-wringing, providing no frisson of excitement for those with a cultivated taste for tyrannicide. But then other neocons began to attack *First Things*, and he and other paleos were startled into taking another look. Maybe there is more to this than the authors in *First Things* were letting on. If Midge Decter thinks that Neuhaus am strengthening "the devil's hand," Rockwell observes, "he may now deserve some new respect." In sum, the enemy of my enemy. . . . Of course, Midge Decter is a friend, so there goes my new respect.

Theories about a conservative realignment multiply. On a later revisit to the controversy, Scott McConnell of *The New York Post* declares his belief that the *First Things* symposium "was a watershed event." He thinks it was "a neoconservative argument par excellence—and an effective one" (B40). He is puzzled about why some neoconservatives were "so upset." After all, on the substantive issue of judicial usurpation they do not disagree:

> If it is [*First Things'*] tone and rhetoric which concern them—well, it was in many ways a perfect tribute to the neocon style: a marriage of closely reasoned analysis with rhetoric that was both moving and provocative. Go back to the old issues of *Commentary*, the flagship neoconservative journal over the past few decades, in the period when it was seeking to rally Americans to engage a totalitarian menace in a struggle for which many had grown weary, or when it sounded a passionate alarm (as it still does) about develop-ments threatening to Israel. One finds no shortage of highly charged, even alarmist rhetoric—indeed, without such appeals, neoconservatism could not have attained the influence that it did.

McConnell suggests that *First Things* may have opened the possibility of a new political coalition against a liberal judiciary that "undermines democracy, subverts traditional morality, fights to maintain racial preferences, and thwarts efforts to regain control of the nation's borders." If, as he hopes, this happens, "the *First Things* symposium will resonate long after any objections to it are forgotten." Taking a similar view is James Bowman in *The Times Literary Supplement* of London (B171). After saying some very nice things about *First Things*, Bowman deplores "the general tendency of American public discourse to exaggerate fairly narrow differences along the ideological wave-band into polar extremes."

Public intellectuals in America betray a certain skittishness, says Bowman:

> Like so many American political disputes, this one seems reducible to a quirk of the national rhetorical style. Just as, in the 1950s, an intellectually irresponsible right-wing faction rode to a brief period of power by taking the view that all sorts of opinion to its left was tantamount to Communist subversion (not that there was not genuine Communist subversion), so, in the 1990s, an intellectually irresponsible left-wing faction may be tempted to try the same trick by pretending that there is an essential identity of views between Newt Gingrich and the Oklahoma City bombers. . . . And just as we saw a panic on the Left in the 1950s by people trying to dissociate themselves from the Communists, so now there is understandable concern on the right among those who are afraid of being excluded from public debate by the stigma of militias.

His conclusion is that, by exhibiting a greater measure of self-confidence, conservatives can foil the efforts of their opponents "to exaggerate fairly narrow differences along the ideological wave-band into polar extremes."

We have now surveyed, albeit briefly, sundry explanations of why the *First Things* argument turned out to be so very controversial. While I have tried to be mainly reportorial, I trust it is evident that I think some explanations are more persuasive than others. Now we turn to the question of whether, in fact, a "conservative crack-up" has happened or is in the process of happening. Then we come back to the question that started all this, the judicial usurpation of politics, and what might be done about it.

# 3

# DEMOCRACY RESTORED?[1]

C ONSERVATIVE CRACK-UP," a phrase given currency by R. Emmett Tyrrell's book of some years ago, has become something of a cliché in discussions of the *First Things* affair. There are relatively few, however, who seem to believe that a deep and lasting division has occurred. Liberals such as Frank Rich and Garry Wills are having their fun, and we have already discussed the paleoconservatives for whom any time is payback time. Among people who spend a lot of time thinking about "the conservative movement," the house is divided on the question of a significant division. *The Chronicle of Higher Education* says that the *First Things* debate is "so tangled that it could be fodder for a dissertation about divisions on the contemporary right" (B145). Tangled it certainly is, but by the time the dissertation was finished few might remember why the subject once seemed so important.

To be sure, that is not the view of A.J. Bacevich who, as we have seen, sights big realignments on the horizon in both domestic

1. I am grateful to Gerard Bradley of the Notre Dame Law School for his counsel on proposed remedies for judicial usurpation discussed in this chapter.

and foreign policies. That a fundamental reshaping of attitudes is underway seems obvious also to Tom Minnery, head of public policy for Focus on the Family, which probably has the largest daily media audience in the country (B48). He is struck in particular by the radicalizing of Robert Bork, whom he remembers as Solicitor General, arguing before the Supreme Court with an air of great deference and dressed in formal tie and tails. Now Bork suggests in *First Things* that the Court is a band of outlaws. "An outlaw is a person who coerces others without warrant in law," Bork writes. "That is precisely what a majority of the present Supreme Court does" (16; B2). As many have noted, Bork alone of the authors in the original symposium suggested that the tyranny of judicial usurpation may be the result of a flaw in the Constitution itself. These are "radical thoughts," Minnery suggests, and if they are also true, there is no going back to conservative business as usual.

Canadian conservative columnist Lorne Gunter writes, "My family has become dysfunctional, or almost" (B96). He calls *First Things* the "socio-cons" and its critics the "neo-cons," and contends a similar division is evident in Canadian public life. The neocons were riding high when the sociocons disrupted the party. "Most criticism fell just short of accusing the *First Things* writers of sedition. Some went that far. . . . However, what really bothered neo-cons about such talk is that it reminded them, at a time they would prefer to see as their moment of triumph, that there is vastly more wrong with society than public debt and an over-rich social safety net." Gunter ends on the wistful note: "Both sides will also have to remind themselves that their bigger battle is still with liberals and not each other. Once that battle is won, the two clans can resume their internecine warfare." He doesn't sound very hopeful that that will happen.

Peter Stockland, another Canadian, also thinks the divide is all too real (B79). The controversy "is now engulfing conservative intellectuals across the United States [and] odds of the conflict spreading north are significant." The struggle, he says, is over the two "f" words: fiscal and faith. Also in Canada, on the one side are economic conservatives, on the other religious conservatives, and "short of fisticuffs" the struggle in Canada "can't possibly get as uncivil as the bloody rhetorical battles being waged by American conservatives." He notes the formation of a new conservative group in Canada called Civitas, as in civility. Stockland is not optimistic about civility prevailing. "What the war of words represents is the final rupture of the often uneasy 'conservative' alliance that has dominated political ideas in North America for the past fifteen years. . . . Its breakdown opens the ideological field to the foes of conservatism. It will also almost certainly propel many neocons back to where they've belonged all along: among liberals for whom freedom's just another word for someone else having nothing left to lose."

The division over whether there is a great divide is also evident in the *Commentary* symposium. The editorial introduction skewed the discussion by inviting the inference that *Commentary* itself is on the side of the economic conservatives (B115). Norman Podhoretz, among other contributors, attempted to make clear that there are important differences between social conservatives as well (99-100). A minority of contributors seems to agree with Podhoretz about the depth of the difference. Walter Berns speaks of "a breach in conservative ranks that is not likely to be closed" (78; B118). Gertrude Himmelfarb accuses *First Things* of opening "a rift among conservatives that threatens to become a major fault line" (91; B124). And we have considered Irwin Seltzer's dramatic call for Jewish intellectuals to withdraw from fellowship with Catholics and other Americans united for the establishment of a "governing theocracy" (106).

A very different note is struck by Richard E. Morgan, writing in *City Journal*, the publication of the Manhattan Institute (B57). "A potentially harmful family quarrel has broken out among critics of judicial activism," he writes. After discussing the dramatis personae and issues in the quarrel, Morgan suggests, "Surely it is time for deep breaths and reflection all around. . . . If Father

Neuhaus and his authors overstate their point, their critics may underestimate the seriousness of the situation. Unless we find some more effective way to oppose the arrogant elites who work their will on the rest of us through the judiciary, we will eventually have to revisit—more soberly—the serious questions that *First Things* raises." The deep and lasting breach may be delayed, or so it seems.

Many commentators seem to be of the view that the whole affair has clarified what holds conservatives together or has the promise of realigning forces in a positive way. The articles by Tom Bethell (138-42; B72) and John Reilly (163-67; B132) both counsel that the dispute is more about means than ends, and, once older neocons get over the shock of recognizing what was valid in their younger selves, they might see the possibilities in the means of the 1960s serving the conservative ends of the 1990s. In a truly nasty and very personal piece in *The New York Observer* (B104), arch-liberal David Gibson regretfully reports that the affair is a plus for the conservative cause. "If Father Neuhaus went too far, he still managed to push the limits of acceptable debate about the role of the courts further than ever." A host of publications "have all used the symposium not as an occasion to examine their collective conscience but to launch further attacks on the judiciary. Conservatives of every stripe see the issue as a winner, and they're not about to let the Neuhaus tiff get in the way. 'I'd still consider almost everyone involved in this issue an ally,' said *The Weekly Standard*'s William Kristol."

In the *Commentary* symposium, Robert Bartley of the *Wall Street Journal* is insouciant about alleged divisions, urging conservatives to recognize their common enemy in a libertarianism that ignores the cultural and moral rot that is undermining the entire system (B116). David Frum of the Manhattan Institute, an economic conservative who has formerly been very critical of the social agenda in the Republican party, says flatly, "If the social conservatives fail to win their argument, the economic conservatives will not be winning any more elections" (B121). Mark

Helprin—novelist, senior fellow at the Hudson Institute and, somewhat to his embarrassment, speech writer for Bob Dole—is even more forthright:

> The sinews of state are rotten, America's moral life a shambles, its defense neglected almost as much as its children. The notions of right and wrong that have contributed to the slow progress of mankind over 5,000 years have been, as happens now and then, turned on their head. No party can stand in the face of this that is afraid of the wilderness, afraid of defeat, and afraid of rejection. No party can stand in the face of this that does not trust in God, that does not trust in the people to apprehend the presence and justice of God, in precisely the questions that Senator Dole was afraid to face directly in this past election (B123).

As for nervous conservatives who are terrified of being outside the mainstream and economic conservatives who don't want to be associated with the messy moral questions, Helprin is no less forthright: "The sectors of the party that live by the threat to fall away should by all means be encouraged to make good on what they promise. Let them form their own parties or join another."

Arnold Beichman of *The Washington Times* similarly urges conservatives to recognize what binds them together and get on with it (B92). "That there are serious intellectual differences between the neoconservatives and the theological conservatives goes without saying, and there always will be. Only in a movement dominated by something like the Communist doctrine of 'democratic centralism' coupled with purge trials could there be 100 percent accord. . . . Conservatism is more united than its spokesmen think. To break up this unitedness as we approach the twenty-first century would mean the rebirth of a vestigial liberalism, the return of the statists, the central planners with the Big Idea. The American people can't afford such a defeat." After the Cold War it seems there is still a common enemy after all.

Moreover, there appears to be little disagreement among conservatives on the current form of that common enemy. If anyone deserves to style himself a grand old man of conservative politics in America it is William A. Rusher, for many years the publisher of *National Review*. He goes way back, although I do not entirely credit his stories from the Coolidge campaign. In his syndicated column, he cites approvingly the editorial assertion of *First Things*: "What is happening now is the displacement of our constitutional order by a regime [i.e., the judiciary] that does not have, will not obtain, and cannot command the consent of the people." He notes that *The Weekly Standard* "fired a warning shot across *First Things*' bow" but then promptly, without acknowledging any debt to *First Things*, followed that censure with its own rousing editorial, "It's Time to Take on the Judges." Rusher writes: "Republicans and conservatives generally, take note: Here are the makings of a formidable issue in the years ahead. If our judicial legislators don't back off, and fast, an important segment of American opinion is getting ready to come after them" (B42). Regarding *The Weekly Standard*'s not acknowledging its debt, as I faxed William Kristol at the time, there is merit in the maxim that one can get a great deal done if he doesn't worry about who gets the credit.

In this controversy, then, *First Things*' conservative critics have agreed that the Supreme Court's present course threatens democratic self-governance. And most recognize that the Court's decision in *Planned Parenthood v. Casey* has played a most particular role in the judicial usurpation of legislative and executive functions. It was the *Casey* decision that directly raised the question of "legitimacy," and our taking the Court at its word was a crucial factor distinguishing the *First Things* initiative from innumerable other discussions of judicial usurpation. The *Casey* Court said that its legitimacy was "a product of substance and perception that shows itself in the people's acceptance of the judiciary as fit to determine what the Nation's law means and to declare what it demands." In their own words, the justices said their decision must stand or fall upon whether its principles are "sufficiently plausible to be *accepted by the nation*." (emphasis added) This is more than interesting. The implication would seem to be that the Constitution itself could be discarded, so long as "the people" did not object. Surely that is not what the Court meant to say.

What it did say in *Casey* deserves the most careful reading:

> Like the character of an individual, the legitimacy of the Court must be earned over time. So, indeed, must be the character of a Nation of people who aspire to live according to the rule of law. Their belief in themselves as such a people is not readily separable from their understanding of the Court invested with the authority to decide their con-stitutional cases and speak before all others for their constitutional ideals. If the Court's legitimacy should be undermined, then, so would the country be in its very ability to see itself through its constitutional ideals. The Court's concern with legitimacy is not for the sake of the Court but for the sake of the Nation to which it is responsible.

This is very curious indeed. Contra *Casey*, the country has the ability to see itself through its constitutional ideals simply by reading the Constitution. The document is not kept in a sealed vault in the Court's temple precincts. Copies are readily available. The Court's legitimacy is undermined when it is perceived that the Court is not interpreting but is rewriting the Constitution. The Court's logic gets curiouser and curiouser. We are invited to vest authority where we cannot affect the exercise of that authority, and then are told that our approval is necessary to its legitimate exercise. On the one hand, the Court seems not to recognize the authoritative structures of political expression that were negotiated under the old Constitution and, on the other, indicates no way for the people to oppose its decisions under the new dispensation.

We are dealing with something very basic here. Everyone needs to know what is, and what is not, the law. Is the doctrine of *Casey* the law or is it but a proposal—a judicially drafted bill, as it were—awaiting the time when it is "accepted by the nation" and thus becomes law? In that event, opponents of abortion might be viewed as participating in the lawmaking process, or even exercising a constitutional veto, rather than, as the Court implies, undermining "the rule of law." In the *Casey* dispensation of a complex dialogue between the Court and the people, all is politics. There is no nonpolitical measure by which the correctness of the Court's decisions might be judged.

True, the Court says its decision is grounded in the Constitution, but then so much can be, and has been, "grounded" there. The point is that the decision is not required by the text of the Constitution. It is not even required by the Court's construal of the Constitution, it would seem, since only two of the justices presently sitting say they are prepared to defend *Roe v. Wade* as having been rightly decided on the grounds on which it was decided, although the entire point of *Casey* is to reaffirm *Roe*. We are left, then, with the political preferences of a majority of justices as to what abortion law should be. The result is that the *Casey* decision is a political statement hoping to be "accepted by the nation," and accompanied by the warning that its nonacceptance will undermine the country's "ability to see itself through its constitutional ideals."

This is an interesting way of making law, although it is not the way specified in the Constitution of the United States of America. Some might think it a better way of making law, but I expect we will want some details about, *inter alia*, what is meant by a decision being accepted by the nation. Apparently we do not get to vote. In the case of abortion, while most Americans are not sure what the law should be, the survey research of the last two decades suggests that fewer than 20 percent favor abortion on demand as mandated by *Roe*. If acceptance means acceptance by the majority, *Roe, Casey,* and related abortion decisions have failed of ratification and therefore, one may suppose, are not the law. But perhaps majority rule is one of the principles of the old Constitution that are no longer applicable in the new dispensation. Then too, the Court has not indicated the time frame within which its decisions must be accepted or rejected. If the process of determination is open-ended, it would follow that those who resist particular Court decisions, or judicial usurpation in general, are actually working with the Court in fashioning the new constitutional order. Except the Court suggests that those who oppose its decisions are undermining the rule of law. It is all very confusing. A conscientious citizen hardly knows what to do, and may be forgiven at least a twinge of nostalgia for the days of the old Constitution.

Even a brief jaunt through the judicial cuckoo-land of *Casey* moves us to ask what might be done about the judicial usurpation of politics. The already lively debates on this subject are likely to be getting livelier. Few politicians or legal scholars want to challenge the idea of judicial review in its entirety. Courts have long been examining governmental acts—whether statutes, executive orders, or administrative rules—when it is claimed that such acts violate federal or state constitutions. In this way, the courts exercise a kind of veto power. In the past, this has been what might be described as a negative veto. That is, the court simply says to a legislature, for instance, "You can't do this. It violates the constitution by which you are bound. Go back and try to achieve your goal by another means." In recent decades, however, courts increasingly issue what some observers call a positive veto. The courts not only say that a law is unconstitutional, but they go on to say what the law should be and, beyond that, precisely how the law should be implemented. In this way, the courts usurp not only the legislative but also the executive function, as is dramatically evident in instances where courts have taken over the administration of entire school districts in order to implement goals such as racial desegregation. In some cases, the courts have also usurped the power of the purse, imposing new taxes to support their own political schemes.

The mention of schools and desegregation brings to mind, of course, the 1954 decision in *Brown v. Board of Education*. Challenge the contemporary expansion of judicial review and you are likely to be challenged with the question, "So you are opposed to *Brown?*" Some scholars, Robert Bork among them, make a complicated case that *Brown* was rightly decided. Others allow that it was an instance of judicial usurpation, but it was one of those very rare instances in which the normal democratic process had demonstrated its inability to address a widely recognized problem, and in any event, the decision has since been effectively "ratified" by its general acceptance by the people. Yet others frankly say that *Brown* is one of the main sources of our present problem. That decision, more than any other, gave the courts the aura of being the final moral arbitrator in our public life, and emboldened judges to think of themselves as possessing Solomonic wisdom and authority. However worthy the cause of desegregation, with *Brown*, it is believed, our robed servants became our robed masters.

If the end is worthy, the means are a matter of indifference. That is the view that has gained increasing acceptance. This was underscored for me in conversation with a Supreme Court justice. "Imagine how difficult it is," the justice said,

> for a schoolchild today to understand the Nineteenth Amendment that was finally ratified in 1920. He would find it hard to believe that there was ever a time when women could not vote, but if asked how that was changed he would automatically assume that the Supreme Court declared the exclusion unconstitutional. And, if 1920 were 1996, that is exactly what would have happened. There would be no Nineteenth Amendment; there would simply be a Supreme Court decision giving women the vote. The wondrous thing is that most Americans would say, "So what's wrong with that, so long as the goal was achieved?" And maybe there is nothing wrong with that, unless you happen to believe that laws should be made in the ways specified by the Constitution.

Several years ago I was part of a scholarly conference at a distinguished university where a constitutional expert was with considerable vehemence contending that courts are in the process of creating a radically new constitutional order. "The fact is," he declared, "we are no longer living under the Constitution of the United States of America." To which a Supreme Court justice in attendance responded, "Welcome to the second half of the twentieth century." This met with considerable amusement among most of the conferees. But now it seems a growing number of politicians, policy experts, and ordinary citizens are no longer amused.

The courts have established a version of judicial review so comprehensive that it leaves them in firm control of the actual processes of law in America. The Constitution is no longer viewed as the framework or as a background document setting the procedures and limits for the making and enforcing of law, but is seen as the sole controlling positive law of the land. And, of course, the Constitution means whatever a majority of the justices of the Supreme Court says it means. As one friend, a law professor, remarks, "The chief requirement for understanding the Supreme Court's interpretation of the Constitution is the ability to count to five." When a majority of justices the Court decides, those who are on the wrong side of a hotly disputed political issue are put in the position of being virtual enemies of the constitutional order. As several writers in the *First Things* symposium point out, this was what the *Casey* decision most blatantly asserted when the justices called on the American people to follow their direction on abortion or else accept responsibility for throwing into question the very legitimacy of law itself.

CITIZENS WHO PERSIST in believing that disagreement with the politics of the Court majority does not deprive them of their citizenship are pressing a number of measures to check the pretensions of the judiciary. Some of them are more promising than others. Books could be written and, in fact, are being written on these proposals. Here we can only survey sundry proposals for reform, some of them political, some constitutional, and some statutory. Broadly understood, "political" proposals can range from voting for politicians who understand the problem of judicial usurpation to organizing, maybe even arming, citizens for extra-constitutional action. Reforms that are "constitutional" in nature might include anything from an amendment allowing legislative override of court decisions to amendments that substantively redefine the terms of the Constitution itself. Finally, there are "statutory" reforms by which the legislature limits the jurisdiction of the courts in specified areas, or gives clear definition to constitutional terms that legislators believe have been distorted by court decisions (B234).

Recognizing that the Supreme Court sets the pace for the entire judiciary, the most obvious political reform is to elect presidents and senators—those who appoint and those who con-firm—who will put on that tribunal people genuinely committed to the modest role of judges in this constitutional order. But, of course, vacancies on that Court occur rarely. George Bush had just two vacancies to fill, and Jimmy Carter had none. The current Court has only two judges who subscribe quite consistently to an "originalist" reading of the Constitution, Antonin Scalia and Clarence Thomas. Thus real change would require replacing three others with justices of a like philosophy. Hypothetically, this could happen very quickly, if the right justices were accommodating enough to die or retire in the near future. However, given the track record of the appointment and confirmation process, plus the disinclination of justices to die or retire, it could take a generation, and might not happen at all. The reality not to be forgotten is that there is a powerful political, intellectual, and judicial elite that is deeply devoted to the appointment of activist judges who will advance their common purposes in the name of a "living constitution."

Senator Orrin Hatch, chairman of the Senate Judiciary Committee, is key to the confirmation process. Some critics believe he has been excessively protective of his own power in blocking proposals for reform (B174). On the other hand, he has taken an important step in ending the crucial role of the American Bar Association and its screening panel for judges. Since the 1950s, the ABA seal of approval has been an important factor in approving judges, and Senator Hatch recognized that the seal of approval had become increasingly politicized in favor of judicial activists. Even were the confirmation process made much more stringent, however, what a justice will do when once confirmed is notoriously unpredictable. One need only mention President Eisenhower's appointment of Earl Warren or President Reagan's appointment of Anthony Kennedy. The most unpretentious of judges have a famous propensity for "growing" when the legal culture surrounding the Supreme Court convinces them that they have been appointed Platonic Guardians of the public order.

Another route of reform is impeachment, and, as we have seen, some in Congress are pressing that proposal. According to the Constitution, federal judges "hold their office during good behavior." If the House of Representatives impeaches and the Senate convicts by a two-thirds vote, judges can be removed on the grounds of "treason, bribery or other high crimes and misdemeanors." Usurping power that is reserved to the people and their repre-sentatives is certainly more than a misdemeanor and might be viewed as a high crime. As Professor Gerard Bradley writes, "The removal of even a single judge for usurpation of legislative power could be counted upon to send shock waves through the federal judiciary" (b234). "Congress has given up its responsibility to be a check on the court system," says House majority whip Tom DeLay, "and we ought to start exercising it" (b175).

There is enormous resistance to the impeachment option. No Supreme Court justice has ever been convicted by the Senate, even though some were in their final years well known to be senile or more than a little deranged. In the early part of the last century, Samuel Chase was impeached but the Senate failed to convict. In our entire history, only twelve federal judges have been removed, and that includes two who had been convicted of felonies in other courts, plus one secessionist during the Civil War and a couple of public drunks who were on the take. Also against going the impeachment route is the argument that what is sauce for the goose is sauce for the gander, and Republicans do not cherish the prospect of a Democratic Congress removing Republican-appointed judges. Critics of the impeachment proposal add that this is hardly what the Founders meant by an independent judiciary.

Such critics seem to assume, however, that there is no objective standard by which a judge can be measured. In their view, it is all politics. Criticizing the impeachment proposal, Lee Cooper, the president of the American Bar Association, says, "What one person says is making the law, another says is enforcing the law" (B175). The putative defenders of an "independent judiciary" appear to believe that judges should be independent both from political pressures *and* from the Constitution. Those who press the impeachment option, on the other hand, insist that there is a non-partisan standard. Look at a judge's decisions—whether he is a Democrat, Republican, or of unknown affiliation—and see how they measure up against the standard to which he and all public officials are solemnly bound, namely, the Constitution.

But, it is immediately objected, then we would have politicians interpreting the Constitution. Well yes, that is exactly what the representatives of the people are duty-bound to do. That was Lincoln's argument with Stephen Douglas over the notorious *Dred Scott* decision, and his point in his First Inaugural Address when he said that the people had not surrendered their government into the hands of the Supreme Court. The notion that only judges and their colleagues in the elite legal culture can interpret the Constitution is of very recent provenance, and is at the heart of our constitutional crisis.

Another proposal, not entirely new, is that the Congress might increase the number of justices on the Supreme Court in order to get a majority who believe that their job is to judge in accord with the original understanding of the Constitution. That is what

President Roosevelt proposed to do. His radio address of March 9, 1937, has a wondrously contemporary ring:

> The Court, in addition to the proper use of its judicial functions, has improperly set itself up as a third house of Congress—a super legislature, as one of the justices has called it—reading into the Constitution words and implications which are not there, and which were never intended to be there. We have, therefore, reached the point as a nation where we must take action, to save the Constitution from the Court, and the Court from itself. We must find a way to take an appeal from the Supreme Court to the Constitution itself. We want a Supreme Court which will do justice under the Constitution—not over it. In our courts, we want a government of law—not men.

The Constitution says nothing about the Court's size, and it has ranged from five to ten justices at times, although there have been nine members through most of our history. Alternatively, the complexion of the Court could be changed by not filling vacancies. As FDR discovered, however, there is enormous popular resistance to changing the size of the court, and his proposal went down in our civics textbooks as the notorious "court-packing scheme." The sacral status of nine robed oracles in their Greek temple is not of such recent origin.

Or maybe the Congress could hold hearings on Court decisions and subpoena justices to explain their reasons for deciding as they did. This, it is thought, would be playing very high stakes poker indeed, and might well precipitate a great constitutional crisis. What if a justice refused to appear? Would Congress have the nerve to cite him for contempt? And, if it did, how would Congress respond if the Court ruled the citation unconstitutional? The Congress would not be without ways to respond. There is, for instance, the matter of money. While Congress cannot abolish the Court, it could cut back sharply on funding, and it could abolish all the lower federal courts. But such scenarios involve a level of head-on confrontation that defies imagination. While the funding of the courts has sometimes been a partisan issue, it has not been used as a device for disciplining wayward judges, and most people might think that is just as well.

There is the very real possibility of public officials who simply refuse, in the manner of Lincoln, to go along with court decisions. Of course, there are gradations of refusal. And there is the problem that in our recent history it is not men of the stature of Lincoln but Orville Faubus, George Wallace, and Lester Maddox who have threatened resistance, and have done so in the cause of racial segregation. Here again we encounter the legacy of *Brown v. Board of Education*. The cause espoused by the modern resisters discredited, in the eyes of most Americans, the means employed. And the means employed by the Court, however right or wrong constitutionally, is viewed as legitimate because of the cause it served.

As I write, a Superior Court judge in Alabama refuses to take down from his courtroom wall a plaque bearing the Ten Commandments, and the governor supports him by saying that he will resist any effort, including a federal court order, to remove it. Would the governor be supporting the Constitution, or would he be defending it against judges who have substituted their own ideology for the constitutional text? Another question raised is this: Who, besides the parties to the particular suit being decided, is bound by the Court's interpretation? The conventional answer today is that what the Court says is "the law of the land." It was not always so. Those who took a different view are far from being marginal in the history of this constitutional order.

Thomas Jefferson wrote: "The opinion which gives to the judges the right to decide what laws are constitutional, and what not, not only for themselves in their own sphere of action, but for the Legislature and Executive also, in their spheres, would make the judiciary a despotic branch." Andrew Jackson had this to say: "The opinion of the judges has no more authority over Congress than the opinion of Congress has over the judges, and on that point the President is independent of both." The words of Lincoln to similar effect in his First Inaugural Address are familiar to all.

Today there are important stirrings also in state governments. In the state legislature of Washington, for instance, Representative Kathy Lambert is advancing the "Balance of Powers Restoration Act." Under the state constitution, it would limit the effect of a state court finding of unconstitutionality. Upon the written demand of one-sixth of the members of either house of the legislature, the question of constitutionality in the disputed matter would come up for a vote—"the opinion of the judiciary notwithstanding." The proposed Balance of Powers Restoration Act, if approved by the legislature, would be subject to a popular referendum.

THE CONSTITUTION ITSELF has provisions in Article V for its own revision, either by both houses of Congress or by a convention called by two-thirds of the states. While the convention route has never been tried, there have been twenty-seven successful proposals for amendment, including the first ten that we call the Bill of Rights. There is discussion of a constitutional amendment aimed at reining in the judiciary, but nothing specific has been proposed to date. One conceivable limit on a constitutional amendment is the recently suggested idea of unconstitutional constitutional amendments. That sounds strange, but no less a figure than Harvard political philosopher John Rawls asks, "Is it sufficient for the validity of an amendment that it be enacted by the procedure of Article V?" He thinks not, contending that there are "entrenched" provisions in the Constitution that two centuries of "successful practice" put beyond revision. Were that not the case, we are given to understand, the people might get out of hand.

Those less disposed to amending the Constitution by academic diktat suggest a number of possibilities to be explored under Article V. Judge Bork, as noted earlier, has proposed a constitutional amendment that would provide for the legislative override of court decisions by simple majority vote. "If constitutional jurisprudence remained a mess," he has written, "at least it would be a mess arrived at democratically" (B166). One problem with that proposal, some complain, is that, while it might prevent judicial usurpations in the future, it does not remedy the accumulated damage of past usurpations. But, of course, there would be nothing to prevent the Congress, if it had the nerve for it, to override past decisions as well. One might nonetheless doubt the wisdom of giving a bare Congressional majority, rather than three-quarters of the states, authority to ratify "the mess."

Former Attorney General Edwin Meese has another idea, amending Article V itself. His proposal reads: "When two-thirds of state legislatures pass resolutions in support of a proposed amendment to the Constitution, Congress would have to submit it to all the states for ratification" (B102). This would create an additional point of initiative for the amendment process, namely, the states. Three-quarters of the states would still have to ratify, but the change proposed by Meese would free for democratic consideration proposals that might otherwise get bottled up in Washington, which is frequently out of touch with sentiment in the several states.

Then we come to those who claim that judicial review is itself a form of usurpation and should be abolished. Were that to happen, the courts would still be called upon to inquire as to whether a law is valid in the sense of being enacted according to constitutional provisions, but it would seldom, if ever, be in a position of declaring that a law itself is unconstitutional. As every law student knows, this proposal takes us back to the beginnings of judicial review as we know it, *Marbury v. Madison* in 1803. Chief Justice John Marshall invoked Alexander Hamilton in defending judicial review. In the *The Federalist*, Number 78, Hamilton held that the courts must declare all acts void that are contrary to the "manifest tenor" of the Constitution. This, said Hamilton, does not mean that courts are superior to legislatures.

"It only supposes that the power of the people is superior to both."
His argument was that the express will of the people is found in
the Constitution.

This standard is sometimes called the "plain error" or "clear
mistake" rule. Because this very minimalist approach to judicial
review was generally observed, and because John Marshall usually
had a unanimous Court with him, and because the Court did not
presume to make law with respect to social, moral, and religious
questions of great moment, the practice of judicial review did not
throw into question the "legitimacy" of the Court. That situation
unraveled in a very major and finally catastrophic way with the
*Dred Scott* decision of 1857, in which the Court presumed to revise
the constitutional compromise on slavery. Earlier in this century,
the Court was thought to be departing from the "plain error" rule
on economic questions, which prompted President Roosevelt to
attempt expanding its membership.

Critics of current proposals to modify judicial review point
to a Catch-22 in the so-called "supremacy clause" of Article VI.
"This Constitution," it says, "shall be the supreme law of the land;
and the judges in every State shall be bound thereby, anything in
the Constitution or laws of any State to the contrary notwithstanding." No matter how explicit a constitutional amendment
might be in insisting that judges stick to the "plain meaning" of
the Constitution, critics say, almost all judges will treat the
decisions issuing from past acts of judicial review as binding parts
of "this Constitution." Whatever else may be required, it is said,
there must be effective reversals of past acts of judicial usurpation.
That is not achieved by some current proposals. *The Wall Street
Journal*, for instance, editorially urges the passage of any amendment that would reverse a Supreme Court decision, thus letting
the courts know in unmistakable terms that the natives are restless.
Amendment possibilities suggested include school prayer, flag
burning, and term limits for elected officials. Such an amendment
would not prevent the Court from doing dumb things in the
future, but it would give the justices serious pause.

Also being discussed are amendments that might be called "definitional." That is, they would simply but authoritatively define what is meant by a term or institution, and thus cover a wide range of issues that are now in dispute or may be in the future. For example, marriage could be defined by amendment as a legal union of one man and one woman, thus heading off proposals for same-sex marriage or other measures aimed at diluting or abrogating the traditional meaning of that institution. More comprehensively, an amendment could explicitly incorporate the language of the Declaration of Independence with respect to "self-evident truths" and "the law of nature and of nature's God." This might counter the debilitating effect of, for instance, the notorious "mystery passage" of *Casey*, which suggests the only legally cognizable "truths" are the choices of the imperial self.

Harry Jaffa, the constitutional scholar and disciple of Leo Strauss, has long contended that the Declaration is an organic part of our constitutional order, a position also favored, of course, by Abraham Lincoln. There are other ways proposed to bring law back into conversation with moral truth. As of this writing, Representative Ernest Istook of Oklahoma has introduced a religious freedom amendment, backed by 116 cosponsors, that begins with, "To secure the people's right to acknowledge God according to the dictates of conscience," and goes on to allow, *inter alia*, non-governmental prayers in public schools, religious symbols in government space, and government support for religious schools. The above-cited preface to the proposed amendment, some believe, attends to the concern to recognize constitutionally, as does the Declaration, a sovereignty above that of the state. The debate over these questions will almost certainly become more intense now that the Supreme Court has declared unconstitutional the Religious Freedom Restoration Act, enacted only a few years ago by a nearly unanimous Congress.

There are other proposed reforms for reining in the courts, some of which are statutory in nature. They do not require an amendment, but involve the testing of powers that have not been exercised previously. One symbolic—and some think whimsical—idea is to physically lower the judge's bench to the level of the jury, forbid the wearing of robes, and generally eliminate the imperial trappings of the courts. This is part of a broader strategy to "demystify" the judiciary. In the federal judiciary, Congress could reduce the number of judges, eliminate or reduce the number of law clerks, special masters, and other courtiers in the present system. Such proposals have come from the Federalist Society, along with ideas for reducing the number of cases brought in federal courts, with the result of enhancing state tribunals.

Yet other ideas fall into the category that is inelegantly called "jurisdiction-stripping." Article III, Section 2, of the Constitution says, "The Supreme Court shall have appellate jurisdiction, both as to Law and Fact, with such Exceptions and under such Regulations as the Congress shall make." That would appear to provide a very big opening indeed. In its clearest statement on this subject, a unanimous Court wrote (*McCardle*, 1869): "Without jurisdiction the court cannot proceed at all in any cause. Jurisdiction is power to declare the law, and when it ceases to exist, the only function remaining to the court is that of announcing the fact and dismissing the cause."

Efforts to use this "exceptions clause" to counter specific holdings of the Court (on abortion, involuntary school busing, school prayer, and so forth) are filled with problems. One problem is that lawsuits simply end up in lower federal courts or high state courts. People who remember a day when federalism was more vibrant may think that state courts might decide cases quite differently from the federal judiciary, but today that is very doubtful. State judges increasingly follow the precedents of the Supreme Court, which is not surprising in view of, among other things, the elite legal culture reinforced by the all-pervasive influence of the national law schools. Another, and perhaps greater, problem with jurisdiction-stripping is that it is ordinary legislation and would therefore be subject to constitutional review—by the very Supreme Court that the legislature is trying to check. In that event, the Court would likely hold that the Congress must exercise the "exceptions clause" in a manner consistent with the Court's interpretations of the Constitution. Catch-22 again.

Also being explored, as mentioned earlier, is the possibility of term limits for judges, with no prospect of reappointment. Of course, this cuts both ways. If Justice Kennedy must go after five years, so must Justice Scalia. It is complained that this would make the Court "politically dependent," but it is hard to see why that would be the case if a sitting justice knew that there was no chance of reappointment. In the present climate, many other things that have been taken for granted come up for fresh discussion. Why, for instance, should a 5 to 4 majority count as a decision of the Court? In the nineteenth century, the practice was for decisions to be unanimous. The idea of "super majorities" is hardly alien to our constitutional system. For instance, constitutional amendments require super-majorities in Congress and in the number of states ratifying. So maybe the vote of two-thirds of the justices should be required in decisions that even the defenders of judicial activism recognize as effectively amending the Constitution.

Then we come to what some scholars call "the sleeping giant" in this debate over judicial powers, the Fourteenth Amendment, and especially its Section 5. The Fourteenth Amendment was sent to the states in 1866 and ratified in 1868 in the hope that it would settle once and for all the questions that led to the breakup of the Union. The gist of the matter is stated in the Section 1: "All persons born or naturalized in the United States, and subject to the jurisdiction thereof, are citizens of the United States and of the State wherein they reside. No State shall make or enforce any law which shall abridge the privileges or immunities of citizens of the United States; nor shall any State deprive any person of life, liberty, or property, without due process of law; nor deny to any person within its jurisdiction the equal protection of the laws."

Reformers today are looking with most particular interest at the fifth and final stipulation of the Fourteenth Amendment:

"The Congress shall have power to enforce, by appropriate legislation, the provisions of this article." Here, it is thought, is the handle for actually reversing judicial misinterpretations of the Constitution without going through the extraordinary difficulties of the formal amendment process. There is the little matter pointed out by some scholars that the Supreme Court seemed to cut off the Congress at the pass in the 1958 decision, *Cooper v. Aaron*, when the Court declared that its interpretation of the Fourteenth Amendment is the supreme law of the land. Judicial officers are solemnly committed by oath, said the Court, "to support this Constitution," and the decisions of the Court determine what is "this Constitution." In his 1962 book, *The Least Dangerous Branch*, the late Alexander Bickel ruefully observed: "Whatever the Court lays down is right, even if wrong, because the Court and only the Court speaks in the name of the Constitution. Its doctrines are not to be questioned; indeed, they are hardly a fit subject for comment. The Court has spoken. The Court must be obeyed." [2]

Yes, the reformers say, but there is a loophole that invites more careful examination. There is an important distinction between matters of "law" and matters of "fact." After *Cooper*, it seems the Court alone can say what the law is. But the Congress can determine the fact of the matter by which the law will be applied. For example, in 1959 the Court said that literacy tests for voting do not violate the Constitution. Soon afterwards, however, Congress abolished literacy tests and the Court agreed with that "enforcement" exercise on the theory that legislators were in a better position than the Court to determine whether such tests were being used to discriminate against voters on the basis of race. In *South Carolina v. Katzenbach* (1966), Chief Justice Earl Warren said, "We reject South Carolina's argument that Congress may appropriately do no more than to forbid violations." He went on to reject the claim "that the task of fashioning specific remedies

2. Alexander Bickel, *The Least Dangerous Branch* (New York: Bobbs-Merrill, Inc., 1986): 264.

or of applying them to particular localities must necessarily be left to the courts."

Can determining the "fact" determine the "law"? In effect, yes, said lawmakers who supported a Human Life Statute in 1981. Although the measure was never acted upon by the whole Congress, it would have answered a question of "fact" critical to the abortion license established by *Roe v. Wade.* In that decision, the Court declared its inability to determine when human life begins. Assuming this is a factual question, the Human Life Statute would have had Congress find that "the life of each human being begins at conception." The implications for the "due process" and "equal protection" guarantees of the Fourteenth Amendment are obvious.

The Fourteenth Amendment has long been a sore point with people who believe that in our federal system the states and their constitutions should not simply be taken over by the national government. However, anything that appeared to be an assault on the Fourteenth Amendment, as such, would likely be politically suicidal. The civil rights (real and imagined) of Americans have come to depend on that amendment. The goal should be, rather, to restore the balance of power between the coordinate branches of the U.S. government. One way to do that, it is argued, is for Congress to resume responsibility for the rules that govern the Fourteenth Amendment, precisely as the Constitution says Congress should exercise that responsibility. After all, the Fourteenth Amendment is the creature of Congress, and its clear language indicates that it is intended to give Congress, not the Court, wide powers over the polity. As historians have noted, from 1865 to 1868 Congress worked a revolution in constitutional law, and then it grew weary and left the job to the Court, with the result that the Court now declares its decisions to have the effect of rewriting "this Constitution."

For political reasons, if no other, the federal courts tend to defer to Congress. Federalists who want the federal courts to defer to the several states must face the hard fact that the case law of the past provides the federal courts with no principled way of doing that. Restoring a more federal system of government, therefore, begins with restoring the balance between the coordinate branches of the national government. Here again, we are cautioned that a resumption of responsibility by Congress, under Section 5 of the Fourteenth Amendment, does not guarantee outcomes that we would want. As with all the other proposals for reform, this one cuts both ways, depending upon who is in power. An assertive Congress could federalize "liberal" ideas of civil rights to almost anything under the sun. One answer to this concern is that it would almost certainly not be worse than what we have suffered under the Court in recent decades. Another answer is that stupid enactments by Congress can be much more easily undone than decisions of the Court that "constitutionalize" its political preferences. The final consideration, as in this entire discussion, is that Congress' setting the rules is a much closer approximation of the principle that "just government is derived from the consent of the governed."

WE HAVE NOW surveyed a wide range of proposals to remedy the judicial usurpation of politics. All of them are under intense discussion, some are being actively promoted in various political and judicial forums, and a few are being prepared for possible legislative action. The forceful raising of the issue of judicial usurpation appears to have had a significant political effect. Michael Kelly, editor of *The New Republic*, complains, "The right has once again fingered judicial activism as the cause of its woes" (B184). He notes that everyone from Pat Buchanan to William Kristol to House Majority Whip Tom DeLay is issuing full-throated calls for remedies to check the judiciary, including the impeachment of judges. Washington think tanks, such as the Ethics and Public Policy Center, are launching new programs to strengthen checks in the nomination and confirmation procedures for judges. Kelly protests: "Congressional Democrats and Republicans have already corrupted the confirmation process, turning it into an endless round of Borking and counter-Borking. But the damage that has done to the rule of the Constitution is as nothing compared to what DeLay's bright idea [i.e., impeachment] would unleash." The suggested symmetry between Democrats and Republicans, between Borking and counter-Borking, may leave some readers wondering what recent history Kelly has in mind.

Reflecting on recent and outrageous court decisions, an editorial in the *Wall Street Journal* declares: "These rulings land at the very moment that some of our friends are worrying aggressively about an approaching 'end to democracy,' the result of judicial usurpation. Of course, one might equally argue that judicial liberalism, as with liberalism generally, is finally reducing to its inherent absurdities—for example the recent imperative to defend even partial-birth abortion. Perhaps this reflects weakness, not triumph, and offers an opportune time to fight back" (B44).

That this discussion has created an opportune time to fight back also against abuses of power by the executive branch is seconded by conservative stalwart Paul Craig Roberts. Taking off from the *First Things* symposium, he writes in *Business Week*, "Only Congress has the power to restore accountability to the judicial and administrative branches of government. . . . It will take impeachment of judges and assistant secretaries to get the message out that usurpation of the legislative function will not be tolerated." Congress has the power to do it and, if it has the will, "it would find itself leading the most popular revolution since 1776" (B89).

*Legal Times* observes that the judiciary is a long-standing worry of conservatives. The story quotes Charles Cooper, a top Justice Department official under Reagan: "This is a problem that at least since the late 1930s has never been far from the conservative mind. . . . But it comes in peaks and valleys, and I think we are heading toward a peak." The reporter notes that Speaker Newt Gingrich announced before the full House that he has asked Judiciary Committee Chairman Henry Hyde "to look at the issue of judicial activism." Others have noted that, in the January 8, 1997, oral argument on doctor-assisted suicide, justices of the Supreme Court who had never spoken that way before were making cautionary pronouncements about the danger of over-extending the Court's authority and the wisdom of leaving such sensitive questions to the legislative branch. The justices not only follow the election returns but also, as I am reliably informed, arguments about the judiciary in what Richard Cohen of *The Washington Post* calls "obscure" journals such as *First Things*. *Legal Times* reports, "The growing drumbeat on the right is also being heard on the left," and quotes Elliot Mincberg, legal director of the very liberal People for the American Way, "This has moved beyond the intellectual far right. . . . They do have more people willing to listen to them than ever before," Mincberg says. He adds what is, for him, a cheerless thought: "These things are on the cusp of getting into actual policy" (B97).

Although some people today seem to think a public discussion on judicial reform a dangerously radical activity, we should not forget the preamble to the Constitution: "We the people . . . do ordain and establish this Constitution for the United States of America." Popularly debating the Constitution is a very American thing to do and should not be left to professional politicians and the elite legal culture of constitutional scholarship. Any serious effort at reform will, in some circles, meet with outraged cries about compromising the "independence of the judiciary." In the sense that opponents use the term, an "independent" judiciary means the continuation of an imperial judiciary. Those who cannot democratically persuade the people to support their policy preferences have a deep stake in the continuation of judicial tyranny. Any fair reading of the Constitution makes it manifest that the judiciary was never intended to be independent of the people and their representatives, and certainly not independent of the Constitution agreed to by the founders. To deny this is, as Lincoln rightly claimed, to surrender our government into the hands of judges.

All this having been said, the doleful thought cannot be entirely suppressed that the constitutional decline has gone too far, that the damage is now beyond effective remedy. We must hope that is not the case, and work as though that is not the case. But, at the end of the day, it may become evident that judicial usurpation is a permanent fact of life. It may be subject to degrees, and the continuing demystification of the courts may keep them, as political institutions, from overstepping their bounds so often and so egregiously. Popular concern about judicial usurpation will, in that case, likely rise or fall in tandem with specific court decisions.

At the end of June 1997, the Supreme Court came down with several decisions directly pertinent to our discussion. The decision receiving most attention overruled circuit courts that had discovered a new constitutional right to doctor-assisted suicide. In writing for a unanimous Court, Chief Justice Rehnquist noted that the discovery of such a right would abolish centuries of custom and law, as well as the laws of almost all the states. In other words, in the case of assisted suicide such a discovery would do what *Roe v. Wade* did in the case of abortion. Although the reasoning applied against assisted suicide applies with equal force against the abortion license, the Court explicitly maintained its position that the abortion license is a liberty right guaranteed by the Constitution. In the 9-0 decision against assisted suicide, the Court demonstrated its political astuteness in stepping back from an action that would likely have ignited a political firestorm comparable to the continuing storm over abortion.

In its *Agostini* decision of 1997, the Court corrected what was generally recognized as one of its most extreme decisions promoting "strict separation" between church and state. The earlier *Aguilar* decision forbade public school teachers to enter religious schools in order to provide remedial education to disadvantaged children. In the view of many observers, the logic of *Agostini* at leasts opens the way for education vouchers that can be used also in religious schools, a question that the Court will explicitly consider in its next term. Finally, in the *Boerne* decision the Court struck down the Religious Freedom Restoration Act (RFRA), which had been almost unanimously passed by Congress in response to what had been perceived as judicial indifference to the free exercise of religion. As in other recent decisions, *Boerne* was driven by a concern for federalism, as this Court increasingly insists that national laws must not compromise the jurisdiction of the states. Not incidentally, *Boerne* struck a direct blow against the idea discussed earlier in this essay, namely, that the Congress retains a measure of interpretive authority over the Fourteenth Amendment.

In sum, the 1997 work of the Court underscores the ways in which concern about judicial usurpation rises or falls in tandem with specific decisions. In a historically unprecedented Fourth of July statement, "We Hold These Truths: A Statement of Christian Conscience and Citizenship," a wide array of Christian leaders declared that "our constitutional order is in crisis." Among the more than forty signatories were John Cardinal O'Connor of New York and twelve other bishops and archbishops of the Catholic Church, along with Theodosius, Primate of the Orthodox Church in America, and the heads of evangelical churches and para-church organizations such as James Dobson of Focus on the Family, Charles Colson of Prison Fellowship, Bill Bright of Campus Crusade, Richard Mouw of Fuller Seminary, and televangelist D. James Kennedy of Coral Ridge Presbyterian Church.

Generally tracking the arguments of the November, 1996, *First Things* symposium, "We Hold These Truths" criticizes a judicial usurpation that undermines the fundamental principle of democracy that just government is derived from the consent of the governed. With respect to the great moral questions of public life, the courts have created a crisis in which "it seems that people who are motivated by religion or religiously-inspired morality are relegated to a category of second-class citizenship." The Christian leaders warn that, if the present crisis is not effectively addressed, "Increasingly, law and public policy will be pitted against the social and moral convictions of the people, with the result that millions of Americans will be alienated from a government that they no longer recognize as their own. We cannot, we must not, let this happen."

It is far from evident that the courts or the political culture more generally appreciate the gravity of the concern that inspires a statement such as "We Hold These Truths." If reform measures fail or are abandoned, the judiciary will be the entrenched political player that it has been in recent decades, and will go on rewriting "this Constitution"—sometimes cautiously, sometimes recklessly —and, as a nation, we may somehow muddle through with that. But if that is the case, more and more Americans will come to recognize that they are living under a new order to which neither they nor their forebears agreed. Depending upon the ebb and flow of political passions, more and more Americans will begin to talk about the illegitimacy of this judicial regime, and if there is no remedy in sight, they will begin to talk about the illegitimacy of a government that, as the statement says, they no longer recognize as their own. We can only speculate as to what conclusions they may draw from that, but none that I can imagine is very reassuring.

THIS ANATOMY of a controversy would not be complete without noting that the deepest questions engaged by the *First Things* initiative were generally ignored by critics and admirers alike. The argument at the heart of the matter does not most importantly have to do with constitutional interpretation, and certainly not with the gyrations within "the conservative movement." At the heart of the matter is the proposition that we are not God, that God is God. The present controversy reveals once again how our public discourse is disinclined to engage seriously the implications of such a proposition. To speak, as we do in the Pledge of Allegiance, of America as a nation "under God" is treated as a pious rhetorical embellishment. A nation under God, however, means a nation under judgment. The political, cultural, moral, and spiritual crisis of our country is that those who dominate our public discourse, whether on the left or on the right, are unwilling, and perhaps incapable, of acknowledging a higher authority than procedural rules and partisan agendas. This circumstance is what I have elsewhere called "the naked public square," and it is not sustainable. That is why our social and cultural order, along with our constitutional order, is unraveling.

The question of legitimacy has everything to do with the question of authority. By what authority does the government govern? Those who wrote and ratified the Constitution said they governed by the authority of the people. They then guaranteed as the first freedom of the First Amendment the "free exercise of religion," to make sure that a self-governing people would be able to name the transcendent authority by which they, the people, would themselves be governed. Religious freedom was the greatest single innovation of the American experiment. The genius of this order is that the people are free to name the transcendent authority by which they and their government are held accountable. So said James Madison, and so said John Adams, and so said George Washington, and yes, so said Thomas Jefferson as well.

The Founders knew and said that this constitutional order is not a machine that can run of itself, that it must constantly be justified—that is to say, legitimated—by appeal to moral truth and, ultimately, to "the laws of nature and of nature's God." For several decades now, in textbooks from grade school through graduate school, Americans have been miseducated to accept a bowdlerized and secularized version of the founding that omits or declares irrelevant what the Founders insistently declared to be indispensable. The result is that intellectuals, on the left and the right, can no longer give a convincing moral argument for the constituting truths of the experiment. And that, most importantly, is why the experiment may be failing.

In the original symposium, these questions were addressed very specifically by Robert George and Russell Hittinger. It is noteworthy that what they had to say on these matters has been almost totally ignored in the debate. At the end of the January editorial we spoke of authentic religion as a subversive force in any political order. Many of us have been saying that, in a thousand different ways, for many years. Our largely secularized elites, however, hear such language as empty flourishes, until religiously-informed moral judgment does in fact appear to subvert the institutions and habits to which they are attached. Then they react with surprised alarm, and begin to talk about the need to contain religion in public, which is another way of talking about the need to contain the propensity of the American people to express their deepest convictions about how we ought to order our life together.

We are not God. God is God. That sounds awfully simple-minded, embarrassingly naive, at best a truism. Until one hears second-rate lawyers playing philosopher—as in *Casey*—and adum-brating for the nation the meaning of the mystery of life and of the deepest truths by which we are bound. Until one recognizes that the jurisprudence of the courts as it touches upon morality—and it does so more and more—is inexplicable apart from the assumption that God is dead, at least for all public purposes. At least for all public purposes, we are God. More precisely, judges are the oracles of the Unknown God whose statue St. Paul encountered in Athens and who is venerated today in courtrooms across the country. This is called the rule of law, but it is in fact the rule of lawyers. The American experiment began with the declaration of self-evident truths, and it may well be ending with the exclusion of those truths from the public square under the iron rule of "the separation of church and state."

No social order can be sustained without God or, in the absence of God, its gods. Politics, like nature, abhors a vacuum. When the public square is swept clean of normative (and even decorative) reference to the God of Abraham, Isaac, Jacob, and

Jesus, it will be filled with other gods. If we accept the jurisprudence of recent decades, the public square is filled with the god of the Leviathan State, whose laws are definitively framed by the courts, and by the little gods of the autonomous, imperial Self, for whom liberty is indistinguishable from license. A *polis* composed only of the state, on the one hand, and the atomized individual, on the other, is the exact formula for totalitarianism. It is little comfort that it may present itself as democratic totalitarianism. The procedural rules of democracy, when untethered from the substantive truths of democracy, result in the end of democracy.

The measure of our present distance from the founding moment is that substantive truths are today declared inadmissible in our public discourse, our lawmaking, and our jurisprudence. In our elite culture, of which our legal culture is part, it is deemed a conversation stopper to ask, "Whose truths?" Among the best and brightest, "moral truth" is taken to be an oxymoron. You have your morality and I have mine, and who is to say who, if anyone, is right? This evidences an assumption that not only is God dead but so also is our capacity as rational creatures to deliberate the moral truth of anything of consequence. There may be at times convergences of prejudices and counter-prejudices ("your" truth and "my" truth), but such convergences are increasingly scarce and fragile. They are not scarce and fragile among most of the American people, thank God, where they are adhered to not as prejudices but as moral truths. But that is despite the influence of the courts and elite discourse that contemptuously dismiss the truth claims of any morality that transcends human invention, which is to say any morality attuned to the way things really are, to the laws of nature, or, the gods forbid, the laws of God.

In time, pressed relentlessly and beguilingly enough by the mandarins of culture both high and low, enough Americans may come to believe that their moral convictions are but mere prejudices. When that happens, what the Founders called this experiment in ordered liberty will come to an end, either with a bang or a whimper, and everything will be permitted, except for what is forbidden by whatever sovereign will have replaced the sovereignty of the people in a nation under God.

As we said when all this began in November 1996:

> What is happening now is the displacement of a consti-
> tutional order by a regime that does not have, will not obtain,
> and cannot command the consent of the people. If enough
> people do not care or do not know, that can be construed as
> a kind of negative consent, but it is not what the American
> people were taught to call government by the consent of
> the governed. We hope that more people know and more
> people care than is commonly supposed, and that it is not
> too late for effective recourse to whatever remedies may be
> available. It is in the service of that hope that we publish
> this symposium (8; B1).

And it is in the service of that hope that we publish this book.

# BIBLIOGRAPHY

## I. CHRONOLOGICAL LIST OF PUBLICATIONS

*† 1. Editorial. "The End of Democracy? The Judicial Usurpation of Politics." *First Things*, November 1996, 18-20.

*† 2. Bork, Robert H. "Our Judicial Oligarchy." *First Things*, November 1996, 21-24.

*† 3. Hittinger, Russell. "A Crisis of Legitimacy." *First Things*, November 1996, 25-29.

*† 4. Arkes, Hadley. "A Culture Corrupted." *First Things*, November 1996, 30-33.

*† 5. Colson, Charles W. "Kingdoms in Conflict." *First Things*, November 1996, 34-38.

*† 6. George, Robert P. "The Tyrant State." *First Things*, November 1996, 39-42.

---

EDITOR'S NOTE: This bibliography contains three sections. The first is a numbered, chronological list of items that appeared before July 1997; the second is a list of authors cited in the bibliography; and the third is a list of publications cited in the bibliography. All numbers refer to items in the chronological list. There are 237 entries, approximately one for each day since the publication of the symposium. Items which appear in this volume are marked with an asterisk (*); items cited in "The Anatomy of a Controversy" are marked with a dagger (†).

7. Calabresi, Steven G. "Out of Order," *Policy Review*, September–October 1996.

8. Casey, Samuel B. "From the Editor." *Christian Legal Society Quarterly*, Fall 1996, 3.

9. Leo, John. "In the Matter of the Court v. Us." *U.S. News & World Report*, 7 October 1996, 28.

† 10. Rich, Frank. "The War in the Wings." *New York Times*, 9 October 1996.

11. McManus, Michael J. "Government by Judges Is Threat to Morality." *Fresno Bee*, 12 October 1996.

12. Strossen, Nadine. "Slouching Towards Gomorrah: The Politicizing of the Judiciary," *IntellectualCapital.com*, 17 October 1996.

† 13. Thomas, Cal. "Religious Conservatives: Look Beyond 1996." *Newsday*, 22 October 1996.

† 14. Buckley, William F., Jr., "Loyalty to Nation Has a Price Tag." *San Antonio Express-News*, 25 October 1996.

15. Omicinski, John. "Supreme Court Will Shape Social Landscape of 21st Century." *Gannett News Service*, 26 October 1996.

16. O'Sullivan, John. "From the Editor." *National Review*, 28 October 1996, 6.

17. Cimino, Richard. "Court Decisions Creating a Resistance Movement?" *Religion Watch*, November 1996, 2–3.

18. Editorial. "Shrill Rhetoric: The Religious Right's Gallows Humor." *Church & State*, November 1996, 13.

19. Belz, Joel. "One Nation, Over God: If the Courts Supplant Liberty, Can We Still Pledge Allegiance?" *World*, 2 November 1996, 5.

20. Lawton, Kim A. "Is It Ethical Not to Vote? Religious Convictions May Lead Some Voters to 'None of the Above'." *Seattle Times*, 2 November 1996.

† 21. McConnell, Scott. "The End of Democracy?" *New York Post*, 6 November 1996.

22. Wills, Garry. "A Mandate to Get Along." *New York Times*, 7 November 1996.

† 23. Brookhiser, Richard. "Courting Disaster by Fiat." *The New York Observer*, 11 November 1996, 1.

*† 24. Brooks, David. "The Right's Anti-American Temptation." *The Weekly Standard*, 11 November 1996, 23–26.

*† 25. Editorial. "First Things First." *National Review*, 11 November 1996, 16, 18.

26. Kmiec, Douglas W. "When the Federal Judiciary Gets in the Way." *Chicago Tribune*, 18 November 1996.

27. Sobran, Joseph. "Distrust of Government Isn't 'Anti-American'." *Conservative Chronicles*, 20 November 1996.

† 28. Mahler, Jonathan. "Neuhaus' Call for Revolution Touches Off Storm." *Forward*, 22 November 1996, 1.

29. "Correspondence." *The Weekly Standard*, 25 November 1997, 7.

30. Berkowitz, Bill. "Judging the 'Imperial Judiciary'." *Culture Watch*, December 1996.

31. "Correspondence." *The Weekly Standard*, 2 December 1997, 7.

† 32. Neuhaus, Richard John. "Letter to the Editor." *Forward*, 6 December 1996, 6.

33. Colson, Charles. "Letter to the Editor." *National Review*, 9 December 1996, 2.

34. Neff, David. "Judging the Justices." *Christianity Today*, 9 December 1996, 14-15.

35. Wattenberg, Ben. "Citing Conservative Successes." *San Diego Union-Tribune*, 11 December 1996.

† 36. Sobran, Joseph. "Washington Watch." *The Wanderer*, 12 December 1996, 5.

† 37. Steinfels, Peter. "Religious Nuances in Debate on 'Government by Judges'." *New York Times*, 14 December 1996.

† 38. Editorial. "It's Time to Take on the Judges." *The Weekly Standard*, 16 December 1996, 9-10.

39. Feder, Don. "A Conservative Says Who's Not." *Boston Herald*, 18 December 1996.

† 40. McConnell, Scott. "The Neoconservative Revolt." *New York Post*, 18 December 1996.

41. Francis, Samuel. "Courts' Claims to Power Undermine Self-Government." *The Wanderer*, 19 December 1996, 8.

† 42. Rusher, William A. "It's Time to Rein in the Courts." *Viewpoint, United Media*, 19 December 1996, 1.

† 43. Donohue, William. "News Release." *Catholic League for Religious and Civil Rights*, 20 December 1996.

† 44. Editorial. "Who's Boss?" *Wall Street Journal*, 20 December 1996.

† 45. Heilbrunn, Jacob. "Letter to the Editor." *New York Times*, 21 December 1996.

46. Futrelle, David. "Better Luck after the Revolution, Bobby." *In These Times*, 22 December 1996, 7.

47. Williams, Armstrong. "Retipping the Scales: We Must Back Judges Who Put Constitution First." *Rocky Mountain News*, 22 December 1996.

† 48. Minnery, Tom. "Between Respect and Rebuke," *Citizen*, 23 December 1996, 5.

49. Wagner, David. "Who's Who in America's Conservative Revolution." *Washington Times*, 23 December 1996.

50. Cembalest, Robin. "The Featherman File." *Forward*, 27 December 1996.

51. Evans-Pritchard, Ambrose. "Race Ruling 'Threatens Democracy'." *Sunday Telegraph*, 29 December 1996.

† 52. Hitchens, Christopher. "By the Right, Fall in for a Civil War." *The Sunday Times*, 29 December 1996.

*† 53. Heilbrunn, Jacob. "Neocon v. Theocon." *The New Republic*, 30 December 1996, 20-24.

† 54. Schmidt, Kenneth J. "The Neo-Conservative Crack-up." *The Christian News*, 30 December 1996, 20.

*† 55. Editorial. "The War of the Roses." *National Review*, 31 December 1996, 24.

56. Witham, Larry. "Common Ground in the Culture Wars." *Washington Times*, 31 December 1996.

† 57. Morgan, Richard E. "First Things First." *City Journal*, Winter 1997, 11-12.

† 58. Murchison, William. "The 'First Things' Debate: 'Consensus' or Bust?" *Human Life Review*, Winter 1997, 7-14.

* 59. Bork, Robert H. "Letter to the Editor." *First Things*, January 1997, 2.

60. Editorial. "The Imperial Judiciary: As More Liberal Activists Become Federal Judges, Family Advocates Have Serious Cause for Concern." *Christian America, www.cc.org.publications/ca.html*, January 1997.

*† 61. Himmelfarb, Gertrude. "Letter of Resignation." *First Things*, January 1997, 2.

*† 62. Berns, Walter. "Letter of Resignation." *First Things*, January 1997, 2.

63. "Correspondence." *First Things*, January 1997, 2-7.

64. Levenson, Jon D. "Letter to the Editor." *First Things*, January 1997, 3.

65. McInerny, Ralph. "Letter to the Editor." *First Things*, January 1997, 3

\* 66. Bennett, William J. "The End of Democracy? A Discussion Continued." *First Things*, January 1997, 19-21.

\* 67. Decter, Midge. "The End of Democracy? A Discussion Continued." *First Things*, January 1997, 21.

\* 68. Dobson, James C. "The End of Democracy? A Discussion Continued." *First Things*, January 1997, 21-23.

\* 69. Glendon, Mary Ann. "The End of Democracy? A Discussion Continued." *First Things*, January 1997, 23-24.

70. Leo, John. "The End of Democracy? A Discussion Continued." *First Things*, January 1997, 24.

\*† 71. Editorial. "To Reclaim Our Democratic Heritage." *First Things*, January 1997, 25-28.

\*† 72. Bethell, Tom. "First Things First: Is It Right to Entertain Subversive Thoughts?" *The American Spectator*, January 1997, 18-19.

73. "Neoconservatives Battling Over Religion and the Law." *Religion Watch*, January 1997, 4.

74. Shaw, Russell. "Euthanatizing Democracy?" *Our Sunday Visitor*, 1 January 1997.

75. Bruckbauer, David. "What Unites Us?" *The Wanderer*, 2 January 1997, 7.

76. Editorial. "Fighting Judicial Tyranny." *Boston Herald*, 6 January 1997.

77. Jasper, William F. "How Congress Can Save America: Judicial Usurpation." *The New American*, 6 January 1997.

† 78. Wills, Garry. "Religious Right's Imagined Dilemma." *Chicago Sun-Times*, 6 Jaunry 1997.

† 79. Stockland, Peter. "Conservative Alliance Breaks Down." *Calgary Herald*, 8 January 1997.

80. "Letters to the Editor: Judging the Judiciary's Performance." *Detroit News*, 9 January 1997.

81. Neal, Andrea. "Pondering the End of Democracy." *Indianapolis Star*, 9 January 1997.

82. Sterling, Dana. "Professor, Legal Scholar Challenges Religious Views." *Tulsa World*, 11 January 1997.

83. Eckman, Jim. "Perspective Number Two: The End of Democracy? The Judicial Usurpation of Politics." *Issues in Perspective*, 11-12 January 1997.

84. Feuerherd, Petyer. "Indictment of Courts Has Conservatives Divided." *National Catholic Register*, 12 January 1997.

85. Hittinger, Russell. "On Civil Disobedience, or Giving the Temporal Order a Helping Hand." *National Catholic Register*, 12 January 1997.

86. Shaw, Russell. "Would the Pope Call the United States a 'Regime'?" *Our Sunday Visitor*, 12 January 1997.

87. "Correspondence: No Term Limits for Judges." *The Weekly Standard*, 13 January 1997, 9.

88. Kristol, William. "An Agenda for the 105th Congress." *The Weekly Standard*, 13 January 1997, 17-21.

† 89. Roberts, Paul Craig. "Newt Should Keep His Eye on the Enemy: Big Government." *Business Week*, 13 January 1997, 25.

90. Schlafly, Phyllis. "Let's Slam Brake on Imperial Judges." *Chattanooga Free Press*, 14 January 1997.

91. Young, Cathy. "Have the Courts Undermined Culture?" *Detroit News*, 14 January 1997.

† 92. Beichman, Arnold. "The Unity of Being Right." *Washington Times*, 17 January 1997.

93. Taylor, Stuart. "Guarding Against a Duty to Die; Court Can Stay Off Slippery Slope by Keeping Assisted Suicide Bans." *Fulton County Daily Report*, 17 January 1997.

94. "The Further Adventures of Jacob Heilbrunn." *Washington Bulletin*, 18 January 1997.

† 95. Evans-Pritchard, Ambrose. "The Rot Has Reached the Point Where Society Is Failing. Can the Great Republic Survive Cultural Cancer? Ambrose Evans-Pritchard Diagnoses the U.S. Sickness on the Eve of Clinton's Inauguration." *London Sunday Telegraph*, 19 January 1997.

† 96. Gunter, Lorne. "Neo-Cons Battle the Socio-Cons." *The Edmonton Journal*, 19 January 1997.

† 97. Brown, Bruce D. "Right Refocuses Aim at Judiciary." *Legal Times*, 20 January 1997.

98. DeHart, Rhett & Meese, Edwin. "Reining in the Nation's Judiciary." *Washington Times*, 21 January 1997.

† 99. Cohen, Richard. "When Morality Begets Violence." *Washington Post*, 23 January 1997.

100. Judicial Selection Monitoring Project. "Largest Coalition in History to Oppose Judicial Activism." *Judges@cref.org*, 23 January 1997.

101. Mauro, Robert L. "More on High Court's Reticence on Assisted Suicide." *The Wanderer*, 23 January 1997, 10.

† 102. Meese, Edwin. "In Search of Judicial Restraint; Congress Must Take Action to Trim Activism by Federal Judges." *Fulton County Daily Report*, 23 January 1997.

103. Carney, Dan. "High Court Shows Inclination to Rein in Congress: Recent Decisions and Current Cases Indicate Justices Are Re-evaluating Legislative Authority." *Congressional Quarterly*, 25 January 1997, 241-44.

† 104. Gibson, David. "Father Doom: Richard John Neuhaus Calls for Right-Wing Revolution." *New York Observer*, 27 January 1997.

105. Judicial Selection Monitoring Project. "Letter on Judicial Activism, to Hon. Trent Lott, Majority Leader, U.S. Senate." *www.fcref.org*, 27 January 1997.

*† 106. Ponnuru, Ramesh. "Con Job: Theocons v. Neocons? Strauss v. Aquinas? Catholics v. Jews? Or The New Republic v. Reality?" *National Review*, 27 January 1997, 36-39.

107. Jipping, Thomas. "Extraordinary Judicial Activism." *Dateline Washington, www.frc.org/townhall/columnists*, 28 January 1997.

† 108. Hayward, Steven. "'First Things' and Second Thoughts." *Capital Ideas*, 29 January 1997, 1

109. "Letter to the Editor: Disobedience Is Not 'Violence'." *Washington Post*, 30 January 1997.

110. Cembalest, Robin. "The Featherman File." *Forward*, 31 January 1997.

111. "Letter to the Editor: Columnist Appealed to Bigotry." *The Morning Call*, 31 January 1997.

† 112. Gottfried, Paul. "Conservative Wars." *Rothbard-Rockwell Report*, January-February 1997, 11-12.

113. Meese, Edwin and DeHart, Rhett. "The Imperial Judiciary . . . and What Congress Can Do About It." *Policy Review*, January–February 1997

114. Himmelfarb, Gertrude. "Letter to the Editor." *The American Spectator*, February 1997, 10.

† 115. Editors, *Commentary*. "On the Future of Conservatism: A Symposium." *Commentary*, February 1997, 14-15.

† 116. Bartley, Robert L. "On the Future of Conservatism: A Symposium." *Commentary*, February 1997, 15-17.

*† 117. Berger, Peter L. "On the Future of Conservatism: A Symposium." *Commentary*, February 1997, 17-19.

*† 118. Berns, Walter. "On the Future of Conservatism: A Symposium." *Commentary*, February 1997, 19-21.

† 119. Buckley, William F., Jr. "On the Future of Conservatism: A Symposium." *Commentary*, February 1997, 21-23.
† 120. Decter, Midge. "On the Future of Conservatism: A Symposium." *Commentary*, February 1997, 23-24.
† 121. Frum, David. "On the Future of Conservatism: A Symposium." *Commentary*, February 1997, 24-25.
122. Fukuyama, Francis. "On the Future of Conservatism: A Symposium." *Commentary*, February 1997, 26-27.
† 123. Helprin, Mark. "On the Future of Conservatism: A Symposium." *Commentary*, February 1997, 27-29.
*† 124. Himmelfarb, Gertrude. "On the Future of Conservatism: A Symposium." *Commentary*, February 1997, 29-32.
*† 125. Kristol, William. "On the Future of Conservatism: A Symposium." *Commentary*, February 1997, 32-33.
126. Novak, Michael. "On the Future of Conservatism: A Symposium." *Commentary*, February 1997, 33-35.
*† 127. Podhoretz, Norman. "On the Future of Conservatism: A Symposium." *Commentary*, February 1997, 35-37.
*† 128. Stelzer, Irwin M. "On the Future of Conservatism: A Symposium." *Commentary*, February 1997, 37-39.
*† 129. Weigel, George. "On the Future of Conservatism: A Symposium." *Commentary*, February 1997, 39-41.
130. Wisse, Ruth R. "On the Future of Conservatism: A Symposium." *Commentary*, February 1997, 41-43.
* 131. Arkes, Hadley. "From the Camp of the Incendiaries." *Crisis*, February 1997, 14-15.
*† 132. Reilly, John J. "Neocons, Theocons and the Cycles of American History." *Culture Wars*, February 1997, 12-13, 31.
133. "Correspondence." *First Things*, February 1997, 2-7.
134. McKenna, George. "Correspondence." *First Things*, February 1997, 3.
135. Groeschel, Benedict, C.F.R. "Correspondence." *First Things*, February 1997, 3-4.
136. George, Francis E., O.M.I. "Correspondence." *First Things*, February 1997, 6.
† 137. Glenn, David. "The Schism." *Lingua Franca*, February 1997, 24-26.
† 138. Bole, William. "Is This Amerika? Has America Been Seized by Judges Who Think They Rule by 'Divine Right'? Cooling Down the Rhetoric." *Our Sunday Visitor*, 2 February 1997, 6-7.

† 139. Novak, Michael. "Neocon v. Thecon: An Exchange." *The New Republic*, 3 February 1997, 28-29.

140. George, Robert. "Neocon v. Thecon: An Exchange." *The New Republic*, 3 February 1997, 29.

141. Heilbrunn, Jacob. "Neocon v. Theocon: An Exchange." *The New Republic*, 3 February 1997, 29.

142. Wagner, David & Rust, Michael. "GOP Philosopher-Kings Battle for Soul of the Party." *Insight*, 3 February 1997, 12-15.

143. Marx, Claude R. "Are the Courts Too Imperial?" *Investor's Business Daily*, 4 February 1997.

144. Jipping, Thomas. "Clinton Admits Judiciary Out of Control." *Dateline Washington*, *www.frc.org/townhall/columnists*, 7 February 1997.

† 145. Shea, Christopher. "'Natural Law' Theory Is at the Crux of a Nasty Intellectual Debate: Conservative Thinkers Split over View that Some Moral Imperatives Supersede Court Rulings." *The Chronicle of Higher Education*, 7 February 1997, A14-15.

146. Gottfried, Paul. "Managerial State Haunts Welfare of Democracy." *Insight*, 10 February 1997.

147. Kutz, Lawrence A. "The Natural Law and Its Relation to the *First Things* Symposium Issues." Paper presented at the Natural Law Seminar, Washington, D.C., 10 February 1997.

148. Scalia, Antonin. "The Dying Constitution: Vigilante Justices." *National Review*, 10 February 1997, 32-35.

149. Varnell, Paul. "Can the Christian Coalition Survive?" *OutNow!*, 10 February 1997.

150. Williams, Armstrong. "Court Jesters." *National Review*, 10 February 1997, 34-35.

151. Beichman, Arnold. "Undercurrents in the Conservative Tide." *Washington Times*, 11 February 1997.

† 152. Walker, Martin. "Bluebloods and Rednecks at War." *The Observer*, 16 February 1997, 1.

153. Letters. *IntellectualCapital.com*, 20 February 1997.

154. Strossen, Nadine. "A New Kind of Judicial Activism." *IntellectualCapital.com*, 20 February 1997.

155. Charbonneau, "Federal Judges or Federal Rulers?" *Christian Broadcast Network News*, *www.the700club.org*, 24 February 1997.

156. Elshtain, Jean Bethke. "The Hard Questions: Civil Rites." *The New Republic*, 24 February 1997.

157. Varnell, Paul. "The Conservative Attack on Liberty." *OutNow! Gay News* (San Jose, Calif.), 25 February 1997, 2.

158. Varnell, Paul. "Conservatives Continue to Attack Judiciary." *Windy City Times* (Chicago), 27 February 1997, 7.

159. Eastland, Terry. "Deactivate the Courts." *The American Spectator*, March 1997, 60-61.

160. Rabkin, Jeremy. "No Quick Fixes: An Indifferent Public Is No Match for Activist Courts." *The American Spectator*, March 1997.

*† 161. Francis, Samuel. "Principalities & Powers: First Things Last." *Chronicles*, March 1997, 32-34.

162. Futrelle, David. "Uncivil Disobedience: Has the Religious Right Taken Leave of America—or Just its Senses?" *Media Circus*, March 1997.

† 163. Rockwell, Llewellyn H. "Sic Semper Tyrannis." *The Rothbard-Rockwell Report*, March 1997, 1, 7-12.

† 164. Toolan, David. "The 'Catholic Moment' under Seige." *America*, 1 March 1997, 3-9.

† 165. Bacevich, A.J. "Exporting the Culture Wars." *Crisis*, March 1997, 23-26.

† 166. Bork, Robert H. "The Conservative Case for Amending the Constitution." *The Weekly Standard*, 3 March 1997, 21-24.

167. Editorial. "Strict Constructionism: Original Intent or Right Wing Ruse?" *The Liberal Constitutionalist*, 3 March 1997.

168. Rees, Matthew. "Judging the Judges." *The Weekly Standard*, 3 March 1997, 14-15.

169. Callahan, Peter. "Bill Would Let Legislature Override Courts." *News Tribune*, 3 March 1997.

170. Rothberg, Donald M. "Conservatives Divide Over How to Combat Activist Judges." *Chicago Tribune*, 5 March 1997.

† 171. Bowman, James. "First Things." *Times Literary Supplement*, 7 March 1997.

172. Gigot, Paul. "Potomac Watch: GOP Mulls Fighting Bill's Dread Judges." *Wall Street Journal*, 7 March 1997.

173. Davenport, Dale. "Insurrection, Right or Left, Is Dangerous." *Sunday Patriot-News*, 9 March 1997.

174. Ponnuru, Ramesh. "Latter-Day Liberal? The Senior Senator from Utah Is Not All He's Hatched Up to Be, But He Could Yet Become a Conservative Hero." *National Review*, 10 March 1997, 41-43.

† 175. Seelye, Katherine Q., "Conservatives in House Are Preparing an Impeachment List of Federal Judges." *New York Times*, 14 March 1997.

176. Biskupic, Joan. "Bork Uncorked." *Washington Post*, 16 March 1997.

177. Editorial. "What's An Activist?" *National Law Journal*, 17 March 1997, A18.

† 178. Reese, Charley. "Federal Judges Act Like Dictators." *Conservative Chronicle*, 19 March 1997, 3.

179. "Letter to the Editor: From the Defense." *America*, 22 March 1997, 34.

† 180. Weigel, George. "Letter to the Editor: A Correction." *America*, 22 March 1997, 34.

181. Bork, Robert. "Letter to the Editor." *Washington Post*, 24 March 1997.

† 182. Conason, Joe. "Hey, We Told You So: Bork's a Raving Loony." *New York Observer*, 24 March 1997.

† 183. Rich, Frank. "The New New Left." *New York Times*, 27 March 1997, 29

† 184. Kelly, Michael. "Judge Dread." *The New Republic* 31 March 1997, 6

185. Sproul, R.C. "You Say You Want a Revolution?" *Covenant Syndicate*, 1:13 (Spring 1997), 1.

186. Dunn, Thomas and Norton, Anne. "Introduction." *Theory and Event*, Spring 1997.

187. Barber, Sotirios. "Father Neuhaus and the Constitution." *Theory and Event*, Spring 1997.

188. Connolly, William E. "The Desanctification of Subjectivity." *Theory and Event*, Spring 1997.

189. Rogin, Michael. "Dear *Theory and Event*." *Theory and Event*, Spring 1997.

190. "Conservatives on the Edge." *Wilson Quarterly*, Spring 1997, 120-21.

191. Arkes, Hadley. "Summoned to Respect." *Crisis*, April 1997, 10-11.

192. Olson, Walter. "Judge Dread: Robert Bork." *Reason*, April 1997, 41-45.

193. "Correspondence." *First Things*, April 1997, 2-4.

† 194. Pinsker, Sanford. "The Neoconservative Culture Wars." *Midstream*, April 1997, 17-18.

195. Editorial. "DeLay and the Courts." *Fort Worth Star-Telegram*, 7 April 1997.
196. Editorial. "Polling Place Results: Voters vs. Courts." *IntellectualCapital.com*, 17 April 1997.
197. Kolasky, Bob. "Judging the Judiciary." *IntellectualCapital.com*, 17 April 1997.
198. "Letters." *IntellectualCapital.com*, 17 April 1997.
199. Meese, Edwin. "The Judiciary v. the Constitution?" *IntellectualCapital.com*, 17 April 1997.
200. Strossen, Nadine. "Just Cause: Why We Need an Independent Judiciary," *IntellectualCapital.com*, 17 April 1997.
201. Hittinger, Russell & Colson, Charles. "Private Liberty . . . Public Chaos." *Washington Times*, 22 April 1997.
202. Colson, Charles. "Can We Still Pledge Allegiance?" *Christianity Today*, 28 April 1997, 96.
203. "Letters to the Editor." *Commentary*, May 1997, 3-11.
204. Oakes, Edward T., S.J. "Letters to the Editor." *Commentary*, May 1997, 4-6.
205. Finn, James. "Letters to the Editor." *Commentary*, May 1997, 6-7.
206. Bottum, J. "Letters to the Editor." *Commentary*, May 1997, 10.
207. Brown, Harold O.J. "Mixed Messages." *Religion & Society Report*, May 1997, 1-2.
208. Gottfried, Paul. "Picking Friends in the Conservative Wars." *Rothbard-Rockwell Report*, May 1997, 9-11.
209. Troy, Daniel. "Can Cameras in the Court Bring Justice?" *Washington Times*, 2 May 1997.
210. Rosen, Jeffrey. "Judicial Bashing." *Dallas Morning News*, 4 May 1997.
211. Cantor, George. "A Struggle for the Conservative Soul: Battle on Government's Legitimacy Erupts after U.S. Compared with Early Nazi Years." *Detroit News*, 11 May 1997.
212. Benne, Robert. "Today's Refuge." *The Cresset*, Pentecost 1997, 36-39.
213. Leo, John. "Creations of the Elite Legal Culture." *Washington Times*, 15 May 1997.
214. People for the American Way. "Right Wing Watch Online." *www.pfaw.org*, 15 May 1997.
215. Pettifer, Anne. "The Grand Inquisitors." *The Humanist*, 15 May 1997, 30-33.

216. Lewis, Neil A. "Impeach Those Liberal Judges! Where Are They?" *New York Times*, 18 May 1997.

217. American Civil Liberties Union. "'Court Stripping': Congress Undermines the Power of the Judiciary—An ACLU Special Report." June 1996.

218. Francis, Samuel. "Letters to the Editor." *Chronicles*, June 1997, 5.

219. Hittinger, Russell. "Letters to the Editor." *Chronicles*, June 1997, 4-5.

220. "Letters to the Editor." *Commentary*, June 1997, 5-10.

221. Donohue, William A. "Letters to the Editor." *Commentary*, June 1997.

222. Stelzer, Irwin M. "Letters to the Editor." *Commentary*, June 1997.

223. Gottfried, Paul. "Letters to the Editor." *Commentary*, June 1997.

224. Berns, Walter. "Letters to the Editor." *Commentary*, June 1997.

225. People for the American Way. "Right Wing Watch Online." *www.pfaw.org*, 6 June 1997.

226. Editorial. "GOP's 'Judge Not' Strategy." *San Francisco Examiner*, 8 June 1997.

227. Marx, Claude R. "Hyde on Judging Judges—and Presidents." *Investor's Business Daily*, 16 June 1997.

228. Cooper, N. Lee. "Preserve and Protect Our Delicate Balance." *American Bar Association, www.abanet.org*.

229. Editorial. "Judicial Activism: 'Judicial Tyranny'? or Just Doing Their Jobs?" *The Liberal Constitutionalist*.

230. Ethics and Public Policy Center. "The Project on the Judiciary." *www.eppc.org*.

231. Family Research Council. "Court Jester Awards," *www.frc.org*.

232. Judicial Selection Monitoring Project. "The 'Hatch Pledge'." *www.fcref.org*.

233. People for the American Way. "Republicans and the Religious Right." *www.pfaw.org*.

† 234. Bradley, Gerard. "Reining in the Judges." Unpublished manuscript.

† 235. Moore, Scott H. "The End of Convenient Stereotypes: How the *First Things* and Baxter Controversies Inaugurate Extraordinary Politics." Unpublished manuscript.

236. Stackhouse, Max. *Christian Century*. Forthcoming.

237. Robertson, Brian. "What Is Conservatism Coming To?" Regeneration Quarterly 3:2 (Spring 1997), 35-38.

## II. List of Authors Cited

## III. List of Periodicals Cited

# CONTRIBUTORS

HADLEY ARKES is the Edward Ney Professor of Jurisprudence and American Institutions at Amherst College and the author of *The Return of George Sutherland: Restoring a Jurisprudence of Natural Rights*.

WILLIAM J. BENNETT was President Reagan's Secretary of Education. He is currently codirector of Empower America and a John M. Olin Fellow at the Heritage Foundation.

PETER L. BERGER, University Professor at Boston University, is the author of, among other books, *Pyramids of Sacrifice*, *The Capitalist Revolution*, and most recently, *A Far Glory*.

WALTER BERNS is a resident scholar at the American Enterprise Institute and professor emeritus of government at Georgetown University.

TOM BETHELL is the Washington correspondent of *The American Spectator*.

ROBERT H. BORK is the John M. Olin Scholar in Legal Studies at the American Enterprise Institute and author of *Slouching Towards Gomorrah: Modern Liberalism and American Decline.*

DAVID BROOKS is a senior editor of *The Weekly Standard.*

CHARLES W. COLSON is the chairman of Prison Fellowship and the 1993 recipient of the Templeton Prize for Progress in Religion.

MIDGE DECTER was, until her retirement in 1995, the Distinguished Fellow of the Institute on Religion and Public Life. She is the author of *Liberal Parents, Radical Children.*

JAMES C. DOBSON is the founder and president of Focus on the Family, a religious advocacy group based in Colorado Springs, Colorado.

SAMUEL FRANCIS is a contributing editor of *Chronicles: A Magazine of American Culture.*

ROBERT P. GEORGE is an associate professor of politics at Princeton University and the author, most recently, of *Making Men Moral: Civil Liberties and Public Morality.* He wishes to thank William L. Saunders for his extensive help in preparing his essay.

MARY ANN GLENDON is the Learned Hand Professor of Law at Harvard University.

JACOB HEILBRUNN is the associate editor of The New Republic.

GERTRUDE HIMMELFARB, whose most recent book is *The De-Moralization of Society: From Victorian Virtues to Modern Values,* is a professor emeritus of history at the City University of New York.

RUSSELL HITTINGER is the Warren Professor of Catholic Studies and Research Professor of Law at the University of Tulsa.

WILLIAM KRISTOL is the editor and publisher of *The Weely Standard.*

MITCHELL MUNCY is the editor in chief of Spence Publishing Company.

RICHARD JOHN NEUHAUS is the editor in chief of *First Things.*

NORMAN PODHORETZ, a senior fellow at the Hudson Institute, was the editor in chief of *Commentary* for thirty-five years and is now its editor at large.

RAMESH PONNURU is the national reporter of *National Review.*

JOHN J. REILLY is the book review editor of *Culture Wars.*

IRWIN M. STELZER is the director of regulatory policy studies at the American Enterprise Institute.

GEORGE WEIGEL is a senior fellow at the Ethics and Public Policy Center. His books include *Soul of the World: Notes on the Future of Public Catholicism* and *The Final Revolution: The Resistance Church and the Collapse of Communism.*

## Colophon

This book was designed and set into type by Mitchell S. Muncy,

with cover art by Richard Rossiter, Double R Design,

and printed and bound by Quebecor Printing, Kingsport, Tennessee.

❦

The text face is Adobe Caslon,

designed by Carol Twombly,

based on faces cut by William Caslon, London, in the 1730s,

and issued in digital form by Adobe Systems,

Mountain View, California, in 1989.

❦

The paper is acid-free and is of archival quality.